IDENTITY CRISIS

IDENTITY CRISIS

Israel and the Church

DON SCHWARZ

A Division of WINEPRESS PUBLISHING

ISBN 1-4141-0183-X
Library of Congress Catalog Card Number: 2004092655

Acknowledgments

A special thanks goes to my mother Yehudit who has been kneeling before the Lord on my behalf for many years. I am thankful for her intercession.

Special thanks goes to John McTernan for his counsel and support in prayer and encouragement.

I am greatly thankful to Bob Francis for his counsel and prayer support as well.

Special thanks to Ron and Sheila Garner for their encouragement and help with the beautiful graphics for the cover.

I am also thankful to Doug Horne for his help in pre-editing.

A very special thanks goes to my wife, Suzanne, who has had to live with me during these intense last three years. She has stood where many would not.

Special thanks to Ryan Holland for his help with the bibliography.

Table of Contents

Introduction

"This is a Jewish book written to the Jews, by the Jews, for the Jews, and for any Gentile that has been grafted into the promises given to them by God." Those were the words of the Gentile pastor holding a Bible up at a nondenominational church in Houston, Texas. I am a Jew who heard these words at a time in my life when the God of Israel was teaching me for the first time what it meant to be a Jew.

My Jewish mother told me about Jesus the Jewish Messiah when I was five years old. Soon thereafter I prayed "the prayer" and was baptized. My Jewish mother and Gentile father had been divorced years earlier. He was a cool, good-looking, criminal law attorney, and I idolized and followed after him instead of Jesus. I observed the broad easy road my father was on and desired that path much more than the narrow difficult one my mother was traveling. So I decided to be uncontrollable until my mother would let me move in with my dad. She finally gave in when I was ten years old. From the age of fourteen until the age of thirty-two, I went not only the way of the world, but also the way of extreme destruction and depravity.

At the age of thirty-two however, I began remembering much that my mother had shared with me regarding Israel, the times in which we are living, and my calling to tell people about Jesus. God mercifully raised up laborers to bring His gospel to me again. Sickened by sin, worldliness, and years of death and destruction, I raised my hands in the air on a Saturday night with tears streaming down my face, and I was changed. I wasn't sure what had happened to me except that for the first time in my life, I really felt clean.

One of my identities had been that of a drug addict. Since the time I was fourteen years old, I had been hooked on one type of illicit drug or another. From the age of nineteen until Jesus saved me, I had been severely chained to cocaine. Satan used cocaine as his instrument to shackle me for years, and then the Lord Jesus completely delivered me. The extreme sins that had a firm grasp on my soul were no match for the fear of the Lord. I was fearfully trembling before Jesus. He absolutely consumed my thoughts. I was married to a Gentile woman who had stood by me through the worst times a woman could endure. She too had experienced the love of Jesus. We truly are walking, talking miracles.

We started attending a nondenominational church where I began to learn what it means to be a Jew. Contrary to what most believe, I began learning that believing in Jesus is a very Jewish thing to do. This is also where the God of the universe began to teach me about the special relationship between His church and Israel.

Over time the Lord began revealing to me, in clear terms, that the church in the West is in critical condition and faces a serious crossroad. The bride of Messiah has important decisions to make regarding her relationship to the Bridegroom Jesus, which will be clearly observed in the decisions the church makes regarding her relationship (or lack thereof) with Israel.

The purpose of this book is to help bring to light what has been kept in the dark for too long. May King Jesus and His people be blessed by this effort.

CHAPTER 1

My Identity Revealed

Therefore, if anyone is in Christ, he is a new creation . . .

(2 Corinthians 5:17)

Imagine if you will, a thirty-two-year-old Jewish man from Ohio that moves to Houston, and learns what it means to be Jewish in a Gentile church in Texas! Of course we know that God has a sense of humor. Shalom y'all! I understood little what being Jewish meant.

That is the plight of most of my people. We just don't know who we are and what we are doing here. As I was introduced to people who loved me because I am Jewish, I was amazed! These people really were strange, as they believed that by blessing the Jewish people, they too would be blessed. God raised up many faithful and godly people who taught me the Jewish Scriptures. I was beginning to learn who Jesus Christ wanted me to be, as all things truly had become new.

I took my first trip to Israel a year after being saved by Jesus Christ. It was with this same group of strange people who, as a result of their love for Jesus, love the land of Israel and the Jewish people. When I was in line to get on the plane, the Israeli security person asked me if I was Jewish. I answered her in the affirmative, and she asked me what I was doing with this church group. I told her something to the effect that they had believed in our Messiah. She then asked me if I was carrying a Bible, and I again answered her in the affirmative. When she asked me if she could see it, my first thought was that this was a security measure. Then I quickly realized that her request was an appointment from our Messiah! She listened as I shared Messiah Yeshua (Jesus) with her through the prophets. She accepted a small New Testament Bible from us and pocketed it discreetly. This was not some chance encounter. No, the God of Israel was teaching me who I am so that I could then share with others who the Lord wants them to be!

There were some pitfalls and distractions that became especially difficult; one specifically pertains more to a Jewish person: How should I apply the Law of Moses to my life? I then learned that this is a common problem, especially in the Jewish believing congregations, or the Messianic movement. I should add that there are problems everywhere there are people.

God's Word says in Philippians 2:12–13: *Therefore, my beloved, as you have always obeyed, not as in my presence only, but now much more in my absence, work out your own salvation with fear and trembling; for it is God who works in you both to will and to do for His good pleasure.* This doesn't mean that we can earn our salvation, but commands us to seek after God's ways and plans. Then we are to do whatever it takes to live out this life for Him, which takes faith, effort, and sacrifice. He and I together worked out this crisis in my life regarding the understanding of adherence to the law, which I will later explain in detail. There is a Scripture that may give you a hint as to what the Lord showed me: 1 Timothy 1:8: *But we know that the law is good if one uses it lawfully.* . . . The Lord gave me the answer and delivered me from this dilemma.

I also hit another pitfall, which taught me about dead religion that is alive and prospering in the church. I know, because I went through a time of miserable stagnation. You see, when initially saved, I had received Jesus, yet I got something later that is dreadful and deadly. I caught a bad virus called religion. I became one of those hard-hearted religious people that everyone has a right to dislike. Thankfully, the Lord chastened me and softened my heart to the Father once again. The time then came when we knew God was moving us to a new congregation. The only way to explain it is that we knew it was His time to take us into a new season.

CHAPTER 2

Sojourning

. . . for you have not passed this way before.

(Joshua 3:4)

I was sitting outside on Sunday morning before church. We had a house in the country outside of southwest Houston. I had an unusual sense that day of the presence of the Lord and special fellowship with Him by the Holy Spirit. It was something out of a movie, as the dewdrops were slowly falling from the leaves of the majestic oak trees and the sun was burning off the moisture on the grass, the Lord was speaking to my heart. I was seeking the Lord for our next move as He was leading us to a new church on the other side of town. What would be next? Would we stay here in the country; would we move? In what type of ministries would we be involved?

I was reading my Bible in Hebrews eleven and meditating on the sojourning of Abraham. As I was thinking about the fact that we are pilgrims and aliens on this earth, the words "You have not passed this way before" from the book of Joshua kept going through my mind. I just knew that God was speaking to me, and that I (with my family) was going to need King Jesus more than ever.

17

The reason for this intense reliance was that we didn't know where we were going! Just like Abraham and Joshua it would be necessary to trust God, even though I didn't know where He was leading us. Oh, what a feeling to not know where you are going, and for that to be a good thing! You see, we really don't know even when we think we do.

So my family and I went to this new church in Houston. My goodness, it was a small city. It had fourteen thousand members! The praise and worship was alive and spoke clearly of Jesus Christ. The preaching was clear, exciting, and challenging. Yet as we met and talked with people, we soon noticed that there was something terribly wrong.

Remember, we had left a church that preached about our identity in Jesus as being Jewish. Not that Gentiles who believe in Jesus are supposed to try to be Jewish, but our faith is Jewish. We didn't do Jewish things or even celebrate the Jewish feasts, but we were taught to some degree to love the Jewish people and that we will be blessed by God as we bless Israel. We will look at what God's Word says in the Old and New Covenant about this in the next chapter. What God was going to reveal to me over the next few years about our faith changed my life forever. If you will seek Jesus with your whole heart, I believe He will change yours also.

We had not been at this church long before I was introduced to a man with a large ministry that operated outside the church. He would travel the world with the gospel and was well known in this congregation. As we began to speak I asked him what he thought about Israel and the Jewish people.

When he answered I couldn't even respond because of the startling things he said. He shared with me how the Jews had their chance and blew it, so God raised up the church to carry on the work the Jews had neglected. He went on to tell me that God is through with the Jews. I was so angry with myself for not first defending God's word, and then His covenant people. I just didn't know what to say. The attitude behind the words is what was most shocking. There was bitterness, a sense of disgust with even the mention of those *Jews*. I had experienced this in the world, but never had I imagined that it was in the hearts of followers of the Jewish Messiah. Remember, I had only been exposed to those strange people that I spoke about earlier.

Sadly, this was just to be the beginning of my little Christian world abruptly being made much larger. I had one encounter at lunch with a man involved with this ministry, and he too informed me of such horrible information. He, knowing I am Jewish, told me how stupid the Jews were for rejecting Jesus. This time I was more prepared and shared with him the danger of walking under the curse spoken of in Genesis 12:1–3. He didn't seem to understand, and I was beginning to see a pattern that was very disturbing.

I began to ask people who professed Christ what they thought of the Jewish people. The responses ranged from anger, mere tolerance, professed love with not much *umph* behind it, to "they are God's people and we are to love and support them." I must share a story of a pastor who truly is a man of God. I know this because I spent time with him in prayer and counsel. He didn't talk about his love for us but demonstrated it. That is why the story I am going to share is so surprising.

We were leaving church, and the pastor asked me to come over so that he could introduce me to someone. I walked up to him with great expectancy, as I always enjoyed speaking with this dear man. As he introduced me to someone, I thought I was in a dream, or more accurately a nightmare. He introduced me as someone who used to be a Jew, but now was a Christian. How could this be? How could this dear, loving, godly man say something so wrong?

Did Matthew, Mark, John, and James not go to their graves Jewish? Was John the Baptist a Baptist? Is Jesus going to reign from the Vatican, while the nations go to Rome to celebrate the "Christ Mass?" No, we see in Zechariah 14 the Gentiles (nations) going up to Jerusalem to celebrate the Feast of Tabernacles in obedience to and worship of the Root of David, Jesus (Revelation 22:16).

I again was shocked beyond the ability to respond with anything but a handshake and pleasantries that were appropriate with a first meeting. What could I say; what could I do? I sensed frustration, but what if anything does Jesus want me to do with it. Should I just say, "Oh well, that's just the way it is," or should I tell these people about our identity. And if so, where would I start? Little did I know that this was just the beginning of a call from God on my life.

I had already answered Jesus' call to the degree that I understood it. I have markers that I can look back to, "standing stones" if you will, that help me remember what God has done. We formally had started a ministry that was birthed out of what the Lord was already doing in our lives. I had a burning desire to see the lost saved, and to challenge the church of our day to be whom God has called us to be. Those two things were the primary goals, or missions, of our ministry. Yet, I had never considered the things God was beginning to reveal to me. I thought I had this "Jewish Christian thing" down pretty well and sensed no real need of continuing education. However, the Lord God had other plans.

In the midst of these other things, listen to what else God did. I went to a local gymnasium, as I do much less than I should. I was wearing a shirt that reads "Jesus Made Me Kosher," which was designed by a large Jewish ministry. A girl who worked at the gym asked me if I was Jewish and believed in Jesus. I answered her yes on both counts, and she told me of a Jewish teacher named David Stein. She asked if I would come and listen to him. I, as I earlier said, felt no need because I had this Jewish thing down as well as I needed.

Every time I would go into this place she would tell me of this man's ministry and that he was now spending much time in Israel. I had been to Israel many times by now, and as I mentioned, really felt that I had no need for this type of ministry. I was very pleasant to this nice lady, yet I wasn't getting what God was doing. I finally thought to myself, "Maybe God is doing something here," so I listened to a tape series he taught on Israel.

Oh, my great God and Savior Jesus! I was humbled, and broken by the anointed words this man spoke about the Lord's chosen people. I was driving up the road crying like a baby. My mother had just returned to Jerusalem from a two-year visit in the States. I e-mailed her to tell her of these wonderful tapes I was listening to, and you could never guess what her response was. She e-mailed me back saying, "Never mind that, I just left a Bible study in Jerusalem and met a man from Texas named David Stein."

God was doing a great work in me, and confirming it with this man. Imagine the timing and logistics of what I just shared with you. Could this be coincidence? I don't have blind enough faith to believe that this was a chance encounter. No, this was the sovereign work of a holy God, and He was getting my attention. I began praying and seeking God's face to see what this all meant. I was truly hearing from Him in my spirit, and through His word in ways that were refreshing and new. I received Holy Spirit truth, "hot off the press" of God's will for my life. I met with David Stein and his wife in Jerusalem soon thereafter, and the Father began revealing to me glorious things that I will be sharing in this book from here on out.

This all began to take place with a series of breakings and hum-blings, as I like to call them. Things were taking place, and still do, to enable me to hear from God without becoming arrogant, so that I can be useful. I naturally have the inclination to feel pretty special when I hear from God. This makes me puffed up instead of thankful that I have been shown mercy enough to be used as an instrument of God's grace. God renewed my sensitivity to the call of His Spirit that had been drowned out by noisy religion. The dry stale religion was breaking like the bricks of the walls of Jericho!

I began having a relationship with Jesus again! Why? So I can have this wonderful knowledge that I have received? No, so that I can share with you in fear and trembling what God is showing me. Our great God is sanctifying me while preparing me to do His will. What a great Father we have in heaven! Be confident that He is doing this in you too, wherever you are, that whatever is going on in your life is to change you to be more like Jesus, and to challenge you to do His will (Philippians 1:6; 2:12–13).

One of these humbling situations took place a week before I was going to Jerusalem. I was preaching at a three-night outdoor revival and was only scheduled to preach one or two nights. Though the pastor had planned on preaching the last night, he decided that the Lord was leading him to have me speak again. As I was preaching on judgment, holiness, and other great truths of God, something was very wrong. Instead of sensing the power of the Lord, I felt very alone. I almost sensed that I was not supposed to be up there preaching at all. I didn't sense God's authority to be speaking about these holy issues. As the pastor gave a call to repentance, he said, "There is someone out there who is a pretender, and you need to stop pretending tonight." Guess to whom I am sure he was speaking. It was me!

The Lord showed me over the next few weeks, as I was in a whirlwind of confusion, chastening and humbling, that I didn't know what I thought I knew. Among other things, Jesus was revealing to me that though my faith was sincere, in some ways it wasn't authentic. I was sincerely wrong in many ways, including how to walk with the Lord. Again, He was revealing the iniquity in my heart, some of which was a result of modern Western religion.

I was in the woodshed of the Lord, but I needed it. This was necessary to bring me to a place where I would seek after Him for the truth in terms of walking with Jesus by His Spirit. I had been indoctrinated with false teaching in many ways, which I will explain in great detail in this book. At the same time I was missing so much of the truth of the real Jesus Christ, and how we are to believe in Him. Why must we believe rightly in Him? It is so that we can live out His plans and purposes for our lives.

One of the things that came from this is a greater understanding of the desperate need for a pure faith that is not based on the traditions of men, but on the word and person of God. Through this humbling process God began revealing to me how tainted my faith was by man's philosophies and traditions.

Another one of those challenges came to me at a Sunday morning Bible study. I had just returned from my second trip of the year to Israel. During that trip I was able to share Jesus with many Jewish people, speak at a church in Jerusalem, and was on quite a spiritual mountaintop! Experience has shown me that this is a place to be very prayed up and wary. I was asked to preach at a church that a friend pastors, and then give a testimony of my trip to a Bible study class. The pastor and I had initially come from the same church in which I began, and I felt confident about sharing things about Israel in his church.

I told the class that to not be a Zionist at this time was to set oneself against God. One in the class angrily spoke out, saying, "Define your terms" with regard to the word *Zionist*. Minus the spirit (and I mean this in the biblical sense) in which the demand was made, this would have been appropriate, as the word *Zionist* has many meanings. As I went on to explain in brief terms, so that I could continue from the interruption, I responded that Zionism is the gathering by God of the Jewish people back to their land, to be later ruled by the Jewish Messiah Jesus. This was not a satisfactory definition, and another began speaking up as well. One blurted out that I was telling them lies, another blamed the Jews for killing Christ. I was amazed and quickly became angry.

I, not expecting this and not spiritually prepared for it, began rebuking them; the whole thing was very unpleasant. What James said in his first chapter is true: . . . *the wrath of man does not produce the righteousness of God.* The whole thing became rather ugly, and I found myself calling these people to ask their forgiveness. I wasn't asking forgiveness for my words but for my motive, which was anger. My pastor friend was completely dumbfounded by the matter, and admitted that this challenged him, as it did me, to discover from God exactly where He stands, and what His will is regarding handling this type of deception. This truly was a difficult time of humbling and breaking.

Proverbs 24:16 reads, *For a righteous man may fall seven times and rise again, but the wicked shall fall by calamity.* Discouraging as this was, the Lord used it in challenging me to study His word and humble myself before Him. The Lord challenged me to learn what His word says and to know how to answer this unbiblical *stuff* that I soon discovered has been infecting His body (the church) for some 1700 years. He was also teaching me how to do it in love and humility.

Like one of the guys at that church said: "If you push me I will just push back." I won't go into the theological accuracy of his comment, but I will take instruction for myself and ask Jesus for lowliness and humility. It has taken me years to learn something else: Some people aren't ready to hear some things. I must pray for some, and wait until God says, "Speak." When you discover the contents of this book about Israel and the church, maybe you will need to learn this in new ways as well. You see, God used what had taken place to drive me to His word and my knees for the truth. Funny thing about the truth: If you want it, it is out there, but when you get it, what will you do with it? *Ask, and it will be given to you; seek, and you will find; knock, and it will be opened to you* (Matthew 7:7).

During the last century in the 90s there was a popular movie called *A Few Good Men.* Jack Nicholson played a military base commander who ended up being caught in some unseemly activities. Don't worry, I am going somewhere with this. Tom Cruise's character was a military attorney trying to get to the bottom of Nicholson's transgressions. The attorney says to the commander on the witness stand, "All we want is the truth!" The reply from the stand is the point that I am trying to make, and will result in a question in a moment. The reply was "You can't handle the truth!"

As the Lord Jesus began to show me about much of what we call Christianity in America and in modern Western churches, I was brought to a crisis of faith that I could have never imagined. I will tell you things from the Scriptures that show us that our faith has been changed, and we have been robbed of much of the genuine, and in many ways given a counterfeit. We mustn't forget that we as followers of Jesus have an enemy!

Many in leadership know about these changes to our faith and choose to let well enough alone. However, we have been called to run a race, and by God's grace that is what I am going to do! Many have been handed this changed faith down through the ages and don't know any better. However, does not knowing something give us an excuse before God? His word says in Hosea 4:6: *My people are destroyed for lack of knowledge. Because you have rejected knowledge, I also will reject you from being priest for Me; because you have forgotten the law of your God, I also will forget your children.* As we discuss this verse later in the book, it may have a deeper personal impact on you. If the heart of man is really seeking after truth, the Lord will reveal it. Ignorance isn't bliss, because the Lord Jesus wants to reveal Himself and will hold us accountable if we won't seek after Him.

Remember, I wrote a moment ago about a question I would ask you. Here it is: *Can you handle the truth?* Will you seek for the truth from the Lord Jesus Christ and let the theological chips fall where they may? Will you let our heavenly Father reveal His Son to you? Can He show you who He wants you to be, even if that means forsaking false traditions and beliefs that you have been taught that are embedded in our religion?

Is following Him that important to you? Remember what Jesus said in Matthew's fifteenth chapter as He was rebuking the religious leaders of that time? For what was He scolding them? What was the iniquity that led them so far from God? It was their traditions and false worship of the God of Israel. They knew the Scriptures, and were highly educated. Yet Jesus said, *"These people draw near to Me with their mouth, and honor me with their lips, but their heart is far from Me, and in vain they worship Me, teaching as doctrines the commandments of men"* (Matthew 15:8–9).

Like them, have we become religious and hard-hearted, worshiping Jesus our way, and not His? Are we using the name of God to carry out our agenda? Have we accepted false, man-made beliefs and rituals, in which we are too entrenched to repent?

Before reading any further, will you ask King Jesus to fill your heart with a renewed desire to worship Him in spirit and truth? May He grant us the humility and repentance necessary to do so. Amen.

CHAPTER 3

Covenant as It Relates to Israel and the Church

"God is not a man, that He should lie, . . ."

(Numbers 23:19)

As believers in Jesus Christ, our primary goal should be to worship the Father in spirit and in truth (John 4:23–24). Many people when questioned regarding any given issue would tell you what they believe God thinks. One hotly contested example would be the Middle East conflict. For example ten different people that identify themselves as Christians—let's forego the other religions—may give ten different answers to the question of who the disputed land belongs to. Should the land be divided? Is it Israel or Palestine?

The truth regarding this controversial issue is clear, and this dilemma, like many others that have the world in an uproar, can be understood through God's word. It is not surprising that unbelievers are having so much trouble knowing God's will regarding this or any other problem. However, we in Christ are expected to understand God's will to some degree. *Be diligent to present yourself approved to God, a worker who does not need to be ashamed, rightly dividing the word of truth* (2 Timothy 2:15). You see, this issue is not controversial to the Lord Jesus Christ. That is what makes it so simple.

The problem is that God's thoughts and ways are higher than ours (Isaiah 55:8–9). The Lord gives us solutions to this problem. He has given us His word and the ability to discern by God the Holy Spirit. The Bible is the final word of God, yet people have a tendency to try to impose upon God what they think He should do. We attempt in our own feeble efforts to force our agenda upon God Almighty. There is something we should know that will clear things up and revolutionize our walk with the Lord. Understanding this principle is not only necessary to worship the Father in Spirit and truth, but will also help us know our true identity in Christ, and our biblical relationship to Israel. This important gold nugget of truth is *covenant.*

God operates by covenant. While the world is striving and fighting to accomplish its goals and aspirations, the Lord is simply and methodically keeping His age-old promises. If you don't understand covenant, you will have unnecessary difficulty understanding God's ways. If you don't understand God's ways, you will most likely place yourself on the wrong side of the Lord in some of life's most important matters. I would like to share some important basics of covenant that pertain to the goal of restoring the biblical relationship between Jesus Christ, His church, and the nation of Israel.

God makes conditional and unconditional covenants. The following is an explanation of these covenants by a man named Dr. Arnold Fruchtenbaum:

> The covenants of the Bible are of two types: A **conditional** covenant is a proposal of God to man conditioned by the formula *if you will* whereby He promises to grant special blessings to man providing he fulfills certain conditions contained in the covenant. Man's failure to do so often results in punishment. An **unconditional** covenant is a sovereign act of God whereby He unconditionally obligates Himself to bring to pass definite blessings and conditions for the covenanted people. This

covenant is characterized by the formula *I will* which declares God's determination to do as He promises.

He goes on to say:

Only one of the five covenants made with Israel is conditional: the Mosaic Covenant. The other four covenants with Israel are all unconditional: the Abrahamic, the Land, the Davidic, and the New Covenants. Four things should be noted concerning the nature of the unconditional covenants made with Israel. First, they are literal covenants and their contents must be interpreted literally as well. Secondly, the covenants that God has made with Israel are eternal and are not in any way restricted or altered by time. Thirdly, it is necessary to reemphasize that these are **unconditional** covenants, which were not abrogated because of Israel's disobedience.

I must end quote here for a moment to say, shouldn't we be glad that we aren't kicked out of the covenant with Jesus for our disobedience?

Because the covenants are unconditional and totally dependent upon God for fulfillment, their ultimate fulfillment can be ex-pected. The fourth thing to note is that the covenants were made with a specific people: Israel.[1]

We see this unconditional covenant in Genesis (interesting that so much goes back to Genesis) as God speaks to a man named Abram. God tells him in Genesis 12:1–3, 7 that He will do some very specific things for Abram.

---

[1] Arnold Fruchtenbaum, http://www.ariel.org/ff00021f.html. This site also contains further study of Fruchtenbaum's teaching on covenant.

Now the Lord *had said to Abram: "Get out of your country, from your family and from your father's house, to a land that I will show you. I will make you a great nation; I will bless you and make your name great; and you shall be a blessing. I will bless those who bless you, and I will curse him who curses you; and in you all the families of the earth shall be blessed."*

Verse 7: Then the Lord *appeared to Abram and said, "To your descendants I will give this land." And there he built an altar to the* Lord, *who had appeared to him.*

Before we clarify the meaning of these Scriptures, let's look at a few more in Genesis 15.

In Genesis 15:6 God does something that is extremely important. He declares Abram righteous. Why? What does he do to be declared righteous by God? *And he believed in the* Lord, *and He accounted it to him for righteousness.* Abram became righteous by believing in the Lord just like you and me! He didn't keep any laws or complete any acts of righteousness. He simply left his gods in Ur of the Chaldeans as a result of his believing in the true and living God. Many today say that you don't have to repent to be saved. I like the analogy a pastor in Houston, Texas, gave when he said, "For me to go to Cleveland I have to leave Houston. To go to Jesus I have to leave my sin." Abram left Ur of the Chaldeans to go to the Lord.

In Genesis 15:8 Abram asks God for confirmation of the promises that He had made. *And he said, "Lord God, how shall I know that I will inherit it?"* God's response is very significant, and must be understood to discern God's plans and purposes as they relate to our relationship to Israel. In Genesis 15:9–11 God commanded Abram to bring five types of animals: heifer, goat, ram, turtledove, and pigeon. He was told to cut the animals in half, except the birds, and line them up so there would be space to walk between the bloody carcasses. Why? The reason is that in those days men would walk between pieces of cut flesh to make a covenant. They would say such things as, "May what has happened to these animals happen to me if I break this covenant." In Abram's time this would have been considered an agreement that only death could break. I imagine it would have been a bloody mess!

Genesis 15:18 states: *The Lord made a covenant with Abram, . . .* In the Hebrew text the word for *made* is *karat* which means *to cut.* The word for covenant is *beriyth.* The definition is (don't miss this) an immutable, unbreakable, agreement made by passing between pieces of cut flesh. Have you ever heard the term "to cut a deal"? Do you remember in the old Western movies how the American Indians would cut their wrists and make a blood-brother pact? This concept came from the type of covenant that is in our Bible. On this day the Lord cut a deal with Abram.

Something else that we see in Genesis 15:12, 17–18 is that God knocked out Abram, and there appeared a smoking oven and a flaming torch, which passed between the pieces of cut flesh.

Now when the sun was going down, a deep sleep fell upon Abram; and behold, horror and great darkness fell upon him. . . . And it came to pass, when the sun went down and it was dark, that behold, there appeared a smoking oven and a burning torch that passed between those pieces. On the same day the Lord made a covenant with Abram, saying: "To your descendants I have given this land, from the river of Egypt to the great river, the River Euphrates."

God put Abram to sleep and used a smoking pot and a flaming torch to represent Himself walking between the pieces of cut flesh. This is the Lord obligating Himself to bring to pass the promises in this covenant without any conditions on Abram. It is unconditional. My hope is that after reading this book you will see why it is so very important to understand covenant. God makes a blood covenant with Abram (later named Abraham by God) and his descendants.

The actual word for descendants is *seed*. God then clarifies what He means by descendants.

In fact, for us today, this is one of the most clarifying places of Scripture in the Bible in terms of understanding the major part of the Middle East conflict. It is a conflict between the seed of God's plan and the seed of man's. In Genesis 16 Sarai, who is Abram's wife, in an effort to help God keep His promise, comes up with a plan that is seriously impacting our world today. She was growing very old, had been barren all her life, and they were still anticipating a son who would bring forth these promises given to them by God. She suggested that Abram have relations with her Egyptian servant Hagar to bring forth a son who would be used of God to carry out the terms of the covenant. Hagar then brought forth Ishmael.

The Angel of the LORD spoke to Hagar and said, ". . . *Behold, you are with child, and you shall bear a son. You shall call his name Ishmael, because the LORD has heard your affliction. He shall be a wild man; his hand shall be against every man, and every man's hand against him. And he shall dwell in the presence of all his brethren*" (Genesis 16:11–12). Let's see how God weighs in on this cooked-up plan to help Him along with His promise.

The Lord Himself tells us who the descendants of the covenant are. Genesis 17:19–21: *Then God said: "No, Sarah your wife shall bear you a son, and you shall call his name Isaac; I will establish My covenant with him for an everlasting covenant, and with his descendants after him. And as for Ishmael, I have heard you. Behold, I have blessed him, and will make him fruitful, and will multiply him exceedingly. He shall beget twelve princes, and I will make him a great nation. But My covenant I will establish with Isaac, whom Sarah shall bear to you at this set time next year."*

Here we see that Abraham and Sarah took matters into their own hands instead of waiting on God. I am glad that I never do that! Of course we all have, and there is a wonderful principle here of the need for waiting on the Lord. In the Bible we learn the origin of part of the Middle East crisis. It is the war between Ishmael and Isaac.

We saw earlier that Ishmael would be wild and against everyone. Does that not describe his descendants in this conflict today? You see, Ishmael's descendants for the most part have bought into Islam, which we will discuss later in this book. Authentic Islam demands *jihad* or holy war against those who don't believe in Allah. It also demands that the covenant land be in the hands of believers in Allah.

In Genesis 28:13–15 God establishes the next descendant of the covenant. Here God comes to Jacob in a dream and we find the story of Jacob's ladder.

> *And behold, the* LORD *stood above it and said: "I am the* LORD *God of Abraham your father and the God of Isaac; the land on which you lie I will give to you and your descendants. Also your descendants shall be as the dust of the earth; you shall spread abroad to the west and the east, to the north and the south; and in you and in your seed all the families of the earth shall be blessed. Behold, I am with you and will keep you wherever you go, and will bring you back to this land; for I will not leave you until I have done what I have spoken to you."*

The same covenant that God made with Abraham, then confirmed to Isaac, is being established through Jacob.

We then see Jacob given a new name by God. *And He said, "Your name shall no longer be called Jacob, but Israel; for you have struggled with God and with men, and have prevailed"* (Genesis 32:28). God Almighty changed Jacob's name to Israel. He and his descendants are the rightful owners of that land in dispute today. There, isn't it simple?

Let's continue to look at the roots of this controversial, though very simple-to-understand, conflict. Now we know from the Bible that Isaac had a half brother named Ishmael and he would be a wild man that would be against everyone (Genesis 16:12). We also know that the covenant was confirmed through Isaac not Ishmael. We see in Scripture that Jacob had a brother. Let's look at the beginning of this relationship.

> *Now Isaac pleaded with the LORD for his wife, because she was barren; and the LORD granted his plea, and Rebekah his wife conceived. But the children struggled together within her; and she said, "If all is well, why am I like this?" So she went to inquire of the LORD. And the LORD said to her: "Two nations are in your womb, two peoples shall be separated from your body; one people shall be stronger than the other, and the older shall serve the younger."*
>
> (Genesis 25:21–23)

This is the origin of the other part of the Middle East conflict. The brother of Jacob is Esau, the father of the nation of Edom. Through much of the Old Testament we see the struggle between Esau and Israel. God confirmed the covenant to go to Israel from Isaac. God chose Israel not Esau (Romans 9:7, 13). The descendants of Ishmael and Esau are fighting today for the land of Israel. The promise that God made with His friend Abraham (the Abrahamic covenant) is a reality that will be imposed upon us by the Lord Jesus Christ whether we believe it or not. Quite frankly, God isn't concerned about the challenges to His covenant that are made by arrogant little man. How do I know?

The second chapter of the Book of Psalms gives me the answer.

> *Why do the nations rage, and the people plot a vain thing? The kings of the earth set themselves, and the rulers take counsel together, against the LORD and against His Anointed, saying, "Let us break*

Their bonds in pieces and cast away Their cords from us." He who sits in the heavens shall laugh; the LORD shall hold them in derision. Then He shall speak to them in His wrath, and distress them in His deep displeasure: "Yet I have set My King on My holy hill of Zion."

(Psalm 2:1–6)

The Lord has a plan that is going to come to pass and the conflict will be over.

There are other very clear, yet seldom taught, passages regarding covenant of which I am hopeful we take notice. Isaiah 24:5–6: *The earth is also defiled under its inhabitants, because they have transgressed the laws, changed the ordinance, broken the everlasting covenant. Therefore the curse has devoured the earth, and those who dwell in it are desolate. Therefore the inhabitants of the earth are burned, and few men are left.* Since God is so serious in this passage about the everlasting covenant, it would be wise to find out what that covenant is.

1 Chronicles 16:14–19: *He is the LORD our God; His judgments are in all the earth. Remember His covenant forever, the word which He commanded, for a thousand generations, the covenant which He made with Abraham, and His oath to Isaac, and confirmed it to Jacob for a statute, to Israel for **an everlasting covenant, saying, "To you I will give the land of Canaan as the allotment of your inheritance,"** when you were few in number, indeed very few, and strangers in it.*

This removes all of the controversy! God is serious about this covenant land that He gave to Israel. We will see in greater detail how God is going to deal with those that break His covenant.

The terms that God sets in His promises are vital to know. In this covenant God promises to Abraham land and a great nation (physical people). He also promises that through Abraham's seed

35

all the nations of the world will be blessed. He goes on to promise that He will bless those who bless Abraham's descendants and curse the ones that curse him. The word *curse* that refers to those who curse Abram actually means *to esteem lightly*. Listen to Pastor John MacArthur: "Those who curse Abram and his descendants are those who treat him lightly, despise him, or treat him with contempt. God's curse for such a lack of respect and disdain was to involve the most harsh of divine judgments. The opposite was to be true for those who bless him and his people."[2] Why are these terms of covenant not taught as basic foundational truths in so many churches today? Why don't we have a clear understanding of these promises of God?

There are those who believe that the church has replaced Israel. Many would say that we in the church are now the descendants of the promise and that the Jewish people are not. In their estimation it is because of the Jewish disobedience to the law, or the rejection of Jesus that they are no longer in this covenant. If the Abrahamic covenant is based on obedience to God, we had all better get ready for a hot eternity! The Jews have not been excluded from this covenant. If the Lord doesn't keep His covenant with them, what makes you think that He will keep it with you? You might say, "But I am in a different covenant." Let's see what the Bible says and go with God's word.

Everything about this covenant is based on a promise to Abraham from God. The promise of land, physical descendants, blessings, protection, and spiritual descendants from the nations are all fulfilled in one Person. Galatians 3:8: *And the Scripture, foreseeing that God would justify the Gentiles by faith, preached the **gospel** to Abraham beforehand, saying, "In you all the nations shall be blessed."* Here we see that the Gentiles receiving Jesus as their Messiah are the nations being blessed in the Abrahamic covenant. Don't you see? The new covenant, which includes the mostly Gentile church at this

---

[2] *The MacArthur Study Bible* (Nashville: Word Publishing, 1997), 32.

time, is the fulfillment of the Abrahamic covenant! The Gentiles called out to follow Jesus are part of the kept promises of the Jewish covenants. The very root of our faith is Jewish!

We also see God keeping His promise to the Jews in Matthew 1:21: *And she will bring forth a Son, and you shall call His name Jesus, for He will save His people from their sins.* Who are His people? To whom was the angel talking? He was speaking to Joseph, a descendant of King David, a Jew. Jesus came to fulfill the promises of the covenants that He made to the Jews! Thankfully, the Abrahamic covenant also contains a promise to the Gentiles! The Abrahamic covenant is fulfilled in the New Covenant.

Remember the dialogue that Jesus had with the Pharisees in Matthew 22:41–46?

> *While the Pharisees were gathered together, Jesus asked them, saying, "What do you think about the Christ? Whose Son is He?" They said to Him, "The Son of David." He said to them, "How then does David in the Spirit call Him 'Lord,' saying: 'The Lord said to my Lord, "Sit at My right hand, till I make Your enemies Your footstool"'? If David then calls Him 'Lord, how is He his Son?'" And no one was able to answer Him a word, nor from that day on did anyone dare question Him anymore.*

We know the answer is that Jesus Christ the Lord, the physical descendant of King David, is God the Creator who is also a Jewish man!

He has saved the Jews that believed in Him in the past and will continue to save those who believe in Him in the future. His name in Hebrew means *Jehovah is salvation,* so that in Matthew 1:21 the translation would go something like this: You shall call His name *God is salvation* for He will save *His people* from their sins.

37

For those who believe that the Abrahamic covenant applies only to the church, while the rest of the covenant somehow has been made obsolete, I would like to mention something that may help. You cannot separate the land from the Jewish people, the blessings and cursing, or the spiritual global descendants. He keeps His promise *for* all or how can we know that He keeps His promise *at* all?

This is all about His name and His word. What did Satan say to Eve in the garden in Genesis 3:1? *"Has God indeed said, . . ."*? He is doing the same thing today. We see this in Ephesians 6:10–11: *Finally, my brethren, be strong in the Lord and in the power of His might. Put on the armor of God, that you might be able to stand against the wiles of the devil.* Don't buy the devil's lie and miss out on the truth regarding God's covenants.

There are other reasons people give to assert that the Abrahamic covenant doesn't apply to modern Israel, therefore our relationship to them as believers in Jesus is not important. One such assertion is that the Old Testament is law and the New is grace. In their minds this nullifies the writings of the Old Testament or greatly reduces their importance. To them I must say that I humbly disagree.

You see, it has been grace through faith in the Messiah all the way. We see in Habakkuk 2:4: *"Behold the proud, his soul is not upright in him; but the just shall live by his faith . . ."* It was grace in the Garden of Eden that God didn't execute final judgment on Adam and Eve, so that we could have life in Jesus. It was grace through faith when the Lord instructed Noah to build an ark. It was grace as He raised up judges for Israel after they had broken God's laws so terribly. It was God's grace that David was talking about in Psalm 51:12–13 after He had miserably broken God's commands: *Restore to me the joy of Your salvation, and uphold me by Your generous Spirit. Then I will teach transgressors Your ways, and sinners shall be converted to You.* This is the same grace that saves you and me when we sin.

If the covenant the Lord made with Abraham still applies to the Jews, why then have so many Jewish people not been in the land? Why have they been scattered and butchered for almost two thousand years? The Mosaic covenant is conditional. It is an "If you will, I will" covenant. In Deuteronomy 28:1 God says, "*Now it shall come to pass, if you diligently obey the voice of the L*ORD *your God, to observe carefully all His commandments which I command you today, that the L*ORD *your God will set you high above all nations of the earth . . ."* Blessings and abundance were promised as long as they kept the laws that God gave through Moses.

However, we see in Deuteronomy 28:15–16, 62–66 that disobedience to the law would result in cursing and dispersion to the nations.

> *"But it shall come to pass, if you do not obey the voice of the L*ORD *your God, to observe carefully all His commandments and His statutes which I command you today, that all these curses will come upon you and overtake you: Cursed shall you be in the city, and cursed shall you be in the country."* Then in verses 62–66: *You shall be left few in number, whereas you were as the stars of heaven in multitude, because you would not obey the voice of the L*ORD *your God. And it shall be, that just as the L*ORD *rejoiced over you to do you good and multiply you, so the L*ORD *will rejoice over you to destroy you and bring you to nothing; and you shall be plucked from off the land which you go to possess. Then the L*ORD *will scatter you among all peoples, from one end of the earth to the other, and there you shall serve other gods, which neither you nor your fathers have known—wood and stone. And among those nations you shall find no rest, nor shall the sole of your foot have a resting place; but there the L*ORD *will give you a trembling heart, failing eyes, and anguish of soul. Your life shall hang in doubt before you; you shall fear day and night, and have no assurance of life.*

This is exactly what God has done, yet the story isn't over.

Does the breaking of the Mosaic law nullify the covenant that the Lord made with Abraham, Isaac, and Israel? Does their disobedience kick them out of the covenant? Paul, speaking about the Abrahamic covenant, answers that question in Galatians 3:17: *And this I say, that the law, which was four hundred and thirty years later, cannot annul* (or nullify) *the covenant that was confirmed before by God in Christ, that it should make the promise of no effect.* God's word says that the Mosaic law in no way changes the Abrahamic covenant.

Is God still blessing those who bless the descendants of Abraham, Isaac, and Israel? Is He cursing the one who esteems the Jews lightly, despises them, or holds them in contempt? Please seek after King Jesus the Jewish Messiah for the answer, as there is so much to gain and so very much to lose. God has His ways, plans, and purposes. Before you continue reading will you pray and seek God's face for the truth?

Does the Mosiac law nullify the Abrahamic covenant?

CHAPTER 4

Identity Crisis

Remember that you do not support the root, but the root supports you.

(Romans 11:18)

Many people think that believing in Jesus Christ is a Gentile concept and not a Jewish one. They don't associate any Jewish identity with believing in Jesus. Sadly, a great percentage of born-again Christians don't see a relationship linking themselves, Israel as a people, the land, and their Lord. The fact that God used Jews to write the whole Bible with the possible exception of Luke and Acts, is something that has "come in under the radar" to many. The reality that the first church was in Jerusalem, and was made up of Jews, is a mystery to a surprising number in the modern church.

In the second chapter of Acts as the Diaspora Jews (those scattered to the other nations) had gathered to celebrate the Feast of Shavuot (Pentecost), the Holy Spirit fell and the church of Jesus Christ was birthed. On that day Peter preached what the Jewish prophets had said about the Jewish Messiah Jesus. What then happened? Acts 2:41: *Then those who gladly received his word were baptized; and that day about three thousand souls were added to them.* A Jewish apostle was preaching to a Jewish audience from the Jewish prophets, and three thousand Jews received Jesus as the Jewish Messiah.

Most Bible scholars believe that the book of James (more accurately Jacob) was written by the half brother of Jesus as he led the church in Jerusalem. How did the deceptive notion, that to believe in Jesus is an inherently Gentile idea, become so widely believed in the church of Jesus Christ? There are Jews and Gentiles who are guilty of promoting this lie in many ways and at many levels. Ultimately, the father of lies is Satan. Let's see what the Bible says. Then in later chapters we will look at the who, why, where, and how questions that caused this identity crisis.

The terms *Jew* and *Jewish* are derived from the name of the tribe of Judah. Judah is one of the twelve tribes of Israel. The terms have come to mean the descendants of Jacob or Israel. When you see the word "Jew" used in the New Testament gospels, it is talking about the physical children of Jacob. Abraham, Isaac, and Jacob were the first Hebrews or Jews.

We see in Galatians 3:7–9 that Abraham believed *something* that God shared with him so that he could be saved. What do you think that *something* was? *Therefore know that only those who are of faith are sons of Abraham. And the Scripture, foreseeing that God would justify the Gentiles by faith, preached the* **gospel** *to Abraham beforehand, saying, "In you all the nations shall be blessed." So then those who are of faith are blessed with believing Abraham.* What did Abraham believe to be righteous? He, like you and I, believed the gospel of Jesus Christ. He may not have had the revelation we have been blessed with, but at the least he believed that through Isaac would come the Jewish nation and the blessed Gentiles, which would be established by God.

There is a song that we learn in church as little children that would be beneficial to revisit. "Father Abraham had" many what? That's right, sons: "Many sons had father Abraham. I am one of them and so are you, so let's just praise the Lord." But some professing Christians won't praise the Lord about their own identities if they recognize what it is. Why? It is because their faith, their Messiah, and their spiritual heritage is Jewish. We were just informed in Galatians 3:7 that we are sons of the first Jew! What does that make us who believe in the gospel of Jesus Christ? Gentile believers in Jesus are spiritual descendants of Abraham, and then Isaac, and Jacob through which God confirmed the Abrahamic covenant. Gentiles who believe in Jesus are spiritually adopted members of a Jewish family!

The Jewish people who believe in Jesus are physical and spiritual descendants of Abraham, Isaac, and Jacob. Romans 9:1–5 shows us the physical relationship:

> *I tell the truth in Christ, I am not lying, my conscience also bearing me witness in the Holy Spirit, that I have great sorrow and continual grief in my heart. For I could wish that I myself were accursed from Christ for my brethren, my countrymen according to the flesh, who are Israelites, to whom pertain the adoption, the glory, the covenants, the giving of the law, the service of God, and the promises; of whom are the fathers and from whom, according to the flesh, Christ came, who is over all, the eternally blessed God. Amen.*

We see the Jews who are spiritual children of Abraham in Romans 9:27. *Isaiah also cries out concerning Israel: "Though the number of the children of Israel be as the sand of the sea, the remnant will be saved. . . ."* In the end God will only consider the Jews who believe in Jesus to be children of Abraham (John 14:6).

Author Edith Schaeffer, wife of philosopher, author, and teacher Francis Schaeffer, wrote a book titled *Christianity IS Jewish*. In it she writes much about our spiritual father Abraham. Speaking of the New Jerusalem she says:

> We see that the foundations are filled with the beauty of precious stones which are named, all twelve of them, stones like emerald, topaz, amethyst. Twelve? Yes, there are twelve stones, different for each foundation, and in the foundations are the names of the twelve Apostles. So the Old Testament is represented by the twelve tribes of Israel named on the gates and the New Testament is represented by the twelve Apostles named in the foundations. Do you want to know something amazing? Every one of those people named is a Jew. How can anyone say Christianity is anything but Jewish? What about the Gentiles? Don't you remember that every single person coming to live in this city has been "born again"—and that the second birth makes each one a spiritual child of Abraham, as well as a child of the living God?[3]

We must see that the entrance (gateways) and foundations of our faith are Jewish as we are sons of Abraham.

Are the roots holding up the New Covenant (New Testament) Jewish? There are more than a few verses to help us answer that question. However, we will just cover a few. The Father makes it perfectly clear so, as with anything else, those who seek for the truth will find it.

In Jeremiah 31:31–33 we can read about the New Covenant:

Behold, the days are coming, says the LORD, *when I will make a new covenant with the house of Israel and with the house of Judah—not according to the covenant that I made with their fathers in the day that I took them by the hand to lead them out of the land of Egypt,*

---

[3] Edith Schaeffer, *Christianity IS Jewish* (Wheaton: Tyndale House, 1975) 218.

My covenant which they broke, though I was a husband to them, says the LORD. But this is the covenant that I will make with the house of Israel after those days, says the LORD: I will put My law in their minds, and write it on their hearts; and I will be their God, and they shall be My people.

Is this not the New Covenant that we in the church have been rebirthed into with Jesus? It involves God writing His laws on our hearts, and it is called a New Covenant. We easily accept that part of the equation, but with whom is the covenant made? Is it the Gentiles of a Roman or Greek religion? No, it is a Jewish covenant made by the God of Israel with the Jews.

We see the same covenant in Ezekiel 36:24–27:

For I will take you from among the nations, gather you out of all countries, and bring you into your own land. Then I will sprinkle clean water on you, and you shall be clean; I will cleanse you from all your filthiness and from all your idols. I will give you a new heart and put a new spirit within you; I will take the heart of stone out of your flesh and give you a heart of flesh. I will put My Spirit within you and cause you to walk in My statutes, and you will keep My judgments and do them.

God puts His Spirit in the Jews in this covenant much like He does with us today. This is very interesting!

Maybe this covenant is to the Gentiles first and then the Jews will be saved later. Maybe the Gentile church has been found worthy to take up where the Jews disobeyed and rejected Jesus. He then, in mercy, will call the Jews when the church is done with its work. There are big problems with that line of thinking. It is out there, and I have encountered it more than once. Romans 1:16: *For I am not ashamed of the gospel of Christ, for it is the power of God to salvation for everyone who believes, for the Jew first and also for the Greek.* Some say this means that the Jews rejected Jesus, to whom He first came, and now God is through with the Jews, and the gospel is for the Gentiles not the Jewish people. I will deal with the source of that doctrine in a bit, yet look further with me at the identity of this life-saving gospel.

As we read Luke's account of what has been called the Last Supper in the twenty-second chapter, what type of ceremony do we see?

> When the hour had come, He sat down, and the twelve **apostles** with Him. Then He said to them, "With fervent desire I have desired to eat this **Passover** with you before I suffer; for I say to you, I will no longer eat of it until it is fulfilled in the kingdom of God."
>
> (Luke 22:14–16)

And when the hour was come, He sat down, and the twelve **apostles** *with Him.* This is the Jewish Messiah (Christ) celebrating the Jewish Passover.

> Then He took the cup, and gave thanks, and said, "Take this and divide it among yourselves; for I say to you, I will not drink of the fruit of the vine until the kingdom of God comes." And He took bread, gave thanks and broke it, and gave it to them, saying, "This is My body which is given for you; do this in remembrance of Me." Likewise He also took the cup after supper, saying, "This cup is the **new covenant in My blood**, which is shed for you."
>
> (Luke 22:17–20)

Do you notice a theme here?

Who is this Jewish Messiah talking to at this Jewish feast, and what is He demonstrating to them? He is explaining to Jews the fulfillment of the *new covenant in His blood* that was promised to them in Jeremiah 31:31. Is Jesus picturing His broken body with

"Wonder Bread?" No, it is Jewish unleavened bread with holes and stripes much like the Jews use today to celebrate Passover. Many believe these holes and stripes picture the Lamb's slaughter, which was about to take place to save us from our sin. So we have a Jewish Messiah, at a Jewish celebration, talking to Jewish apostles about His and their Jewish New Covenant. Does that tell you anything? Might there be something Jewish to the identity and faith in Jesus Christ?

As we continue to look at the foundation of our faith to establish a sense of genuine identity, let's ask some questions. Where was the first church? Of whom was it comprised? Was it Rome with all of its power and prestige? Was it made up of Greeks and Romans and full of the great thinkers of the day? Were they those lettered men that the world looked to because of their superior philosophy and accolades from the highest institutions that man had to offer?

Were the leaders Jesus chose rabbis or trained theologians? No, we can see in Acts and James that the first church was in Jerusalem. The three thousand born again in Acts chapter two were God-fearing Jews, many of which had come to celebrate the Jewish Feast of Shavuot (Pentecost). The very first church was led by Jewish fishermen, and those with other nonreligious or mundane occupations.

In Revelation 22:16 we see that Jesus not only came the first time as a Jew, but He will return as one in all His glory!

*"I, Jesus, have sent My angel to testify to you these things in the churches. I am the **Root and the Offspring of David**, the Bright and Morning Star."*

There, judging the nations will be the glorified Jewish Messiah! He will be as Jewish as the beard of Moses, and I wouldn't want to be one who doesn't like the Jews on that day! His name is Yeshua, and He is coming to rule and reign from Jerusalem, not any other city. He was, is, and will be Jewish! That's why the angel tells Joseph in Matthew 1:26 that He will save *His people* from their sins. Know that during the millennial reign of Christ on earth after this age, the nations will be required to come up to Jerusalem to celebrate the Feast of Tabernacles. This is found in Zechariah's fourteenth chapter.

In the book of Ephesians the apostle Paul is speaking about the relationship between Gentiles and Jews. He compares their former condition to their new life in Messiah Jesus.

> *That at that time you were without Christ, being aliens from the commonwealth of Israel and strangers from the covenants of promise, having no hope and without God in the world. But now in Christ Jesus you who once were far off have been brought near by the blood of Christ.*
>
> (Ephesians 2:12–13)

We see that before the Gentiles come to Jesus Christ they are aliens and strangers from what? They are aliens of the commonwealth of Israel, which refers to citizenship and the benefits thereof. They are strangers to the Jewish covenants without hope and without God. Why are they without hope or God? The only way to forgiveness of sin and a relationship with the God of Israel is by entering into the New Covenant, which fulfills the Abrahamic covenant, both of which God made with Israel. Gentiles, who were outside the Jewish covenants in the time of Jesus' earthly ministry, were called "far off," and the Jews were "those who were near" to God.

Of course, we know that many Gentiles drew much nearer to God than most of the Jews as a result of God's mercy on the nations and His plan for the ages, which will include Jew and Gentile (Romans 11:28–36). Nevertheless, we see that the Gentiles were far off and were brought near, thus fulfilling the Abrahamic promise, and entering into the New Covenant God made with the Jews.

We can see where, or better to whom, the promises of covenant point in Acts 3:25–26:

> . . . *You are sons of the prophets, and of the covenant which God made with our fathers, saying to Abraham, "And in your seed all the families of the earth shall be blessed." **To you first, God, having raised up His Servant Jesus**, sent Him to bless you, in turning away every one of you from your iniquities.*

The promise God made to Abraham was fulfilled in our Lord. Jesus is the promise!

In Romans chapters nine through eleven, the Lord has Paul go into great detail to emphasize right thinking toward the Jewish people. As we look at Romans 11:11–25, we see Paul's concern for a great identity crisis and terribly wrong ideas in the church resulting from distorted thinking about the Jews. Romans 11:11:

> *I say then, have they stumbled that they should fall? Certainly not! But through their fall, to provoke them to jealousy, salvation has come to the Gentiles.*

Paul spends the next few verses explaining the responsibility of the Gentile church to make Israel jealous of them. Why? The Gentile church is receiving the grace and mercy from the Messiah that the Jews rejected. He also continues to emphasize the great revival of Israel. The Scriptures he uses help us identify the identity crisis in the church. The realization of this identity crisis could revolutionize the body of Christ in a glorious way!

In Romans 11:16–24 the Holy Spirit uses the analogy of two olive trees. One of the olive trees is Jewish and has a Jewish root that consists of the authentic church fathers Abraham, Isaac, and Jacob. There is another olive tree, which is the Gentiles, that has an interesting relationship to the Jewish tree.

49

Romans 11:16–24:

For if the first fruit is holy, the lump is also holy; and if the root is holy, so are the branches. And if some of the branches were broken off, and you, being a wild olive tree, were grafted in among them, and with them became a partaker of the root and fatness of the olive tree, do not boast against the branches. But if you do boast, remember that you do not support the root, but the root supports you. You will say then, "Branches were broken off that I might be grafted in." Well said. Because of unbelief they were broken off, and you stand by faith. Do not be haughty, but fear. For if God did not spare the natural branches, He may not spare you either. Therefore consider the goodness and severity of God: on those who fell, severity; but toward you, goodness, if you continue in His goodness. Otherwise you also will be cut off. And they also, if they do not continue in unbelief, will be grafted in, for God is able to graft them in again. For if you were cut out of the olive tree which is wild by nature, and were grafted contrary to nature into a cultivated olive tree, how much more will these, who are natural branches, be grafted into their own olive tree?

These verses instruct us that the ancient Jewish faith holds up our modern belief system in Jesus. We also see that some of the branches from the wild olive tree are *grafted into the Jewish tree.* If you are a Gentile believing in Jesus, you have been grafted into the faith of the Jews. I have spoken to so many Christians that boast against the Jews for not believing in Jesus, while in their great wisdom they do believe. They say things like, "The Jews had their chance and rejected Christ, so He raised up the church to do what the Jews wouldn't." What are those doing who say such things? They are disobeying God's word!

We just saw that God tells us specifically not to boast against the broken-off branches, which are the Jews who have disbelieved. He tells us instead to remember that their original holy faith holds up our faith, and that we, instead of being haughty, should fear. We are to realize that our faith is Jewish! It has Jewish roots that will give us sustenance and life if we will just seek after the truth and receive this life-giving sap. Isn't it an understatement to say that the root of a tree is very necessary?

To get around this many teach that the root spoken of here is Jesus. The problem is that Paul isn't talking about the Lord in these verses. He is explaining the relationship between the Jews and the Gentile church. He is doing all that he can to make sure we think appropriately about the Jews. Why? Remember the blessing and cursing from Genesis involving right and wrong thinking toward the descendants of Abraham, Isaac, and Jacob? In Romans he tells us not to be haughty but to fear; he tells us to not boast against them. We are instructed to realize how important their faith is to us. Paul goes as far as saying that it is their faith that keeps our faith alive. Isn't that what a root does for a tree?

In Romans 11:28 we see the root specifically mentioned:

Concerning the gospel they are enemies for your sake, but concerning the election they are beloved for the sake of the fathers.

It is the faith of our true church fathers Abraham, Isaac, and Jacob that is the root. Some don't see this because of how they have been taught or because at first glance they remember Jesus is the root in some other places in Scripture.

One of the most basic Bible interpretation principles is that context is king. That means the context that a word is used in helps us to define and then accurately interpret the usage of that word. Sadly, many aren't as interested in the truth as they are in holding on to wrong interpretations that will justify their boastful, haughty, and even cursed ideas about the Jews. I would rather be blessed!

In Romans 11:25–27 we can take instruction from Paul regarding the reality of God's plan for Israel and how we should think.

> *For I do not desire, brethren, that you should be ignorant of this mystery, lest you should be wise in your own opinion, that blindness in part has happened to Israel until the fullness of the Gentiles has come in. And so all Israel will be saved, as it is written: "The Deliverer will come out of Zion, and He will turn away ungodliness from Jacob; for this is My covenant with them, when I take away their sins."*

God tells us not to be wise in our own estimation and to get wisdom from Him since He has plans and timing for the Jewish people, which includes saving all of Israel. Israel in this passage, are the righteous Jews who will accept Jesus Christ (see Romans 9).

Illustration of Two Trees of Romans 11

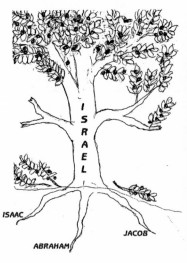 

Pictures, Types, Shadows

One of the most powerful displays of God's power and sovereignty is His ability to use the lives of other people, and the things here on earth, to give us understanding of heavenly realities. We find this repeatedly in the Old Testament, especially in the lives of the Jewish people and their faith in the God of Israel. These artistic acts of the Lord are called pictures, types, and shadows. I will give a few examples. The Lord told the Jewish people in Leviticus, with specific instruction, to build a tabernacle and to perform ceremonies and rituals therein. Later they built a temple with much of the same concepts and rituals. The temple and the rituals point to, among other things, Jesus, salvation, and a tabernacle in heaven. Hebrews 9:24:

> *For Christ has not entered the holy places made with hands, which are copies of the true, but into heaven itself, now to appear in the presence of God for us.*

We see more physical pictures of spiritual truth in Hebrews 11:17–19:

> *By faith Abraham, when he was tested, offered up Isaac, and he who had received the promises offered up his only begotten son, of whom it was said, "In Isaac your seed shall be called," concluding that God was able to raise him up, even from the dead, from which he also received him in a figurative sense.*

Here we see God orchestrating the life of Abraham and Isaac to picture Himself giving up His only begotten Son and then resurrecting Him. Isaac was, in a figurative sense, a picture of Christ.

In Hebrews 10:1 God shows us that the Law of Moses was only a shadow, not the end but the beginning, as the blood sacrifices in the Old Testament were a shadow of the perfect future sacrifice.

*For the law, having a **shadow** of the good things to come, and not the very image of the things, can never with these same sacrifices, which they offer continually year by year, make those who approach perfect.*

Isaac, Moses, and Joseph were all pictures of Christ. In the Old Testament book of Exodus, Moses, who was the deliverer of the Jews in bondage to Pharaoh in Egypt, is a type of He who was to come and say, "Let my people go" from the clutches of Satan and sin's slavery. His name is Jesus!

Joseph was rejected by his brothers, sold into servanthood, and thrown into prison in Egypt. Then, as there was a famine in the land, God raised him up from the prison to second in command over the most powerful country on the planet. He saved Egypt from the famine and then revealed himself to his brothers, saving them from starvation. In John 1:11 we see that Jesus was rejected by His own. *He came to His own, and His own did not receive Him.* We see in Philippians 2:7 that Jesus, though He is God, took on the form of a bondservant, which is a willing slave. He was held in custody, beaten, and He was put into the prison of a grave. However, death the jailer was unable to hold Him as He was resurrected from the grave and exalted to second-in-command under the Father. He has spread His gospel to the nations in their time of spiritual famine, and is about to reveal Himself to His brothers and save them, as we have seen from the Scriptures in Romans. Isn't this exciting?

God pictured Himself in the lives and faith of the Jews in a way that helps us to understand Him. These examples just scratch the surface of how much our faith can be enriched, as we appreciate and glean from the Jewishness of our faith. These people were giving their very lives to picture spiritual truths from which we can benefit. That is why in Hebrews 11 God lists those in the hall of faith from the Old Testament. Hebrew 11:39–40:

And all these, having obtained a good testimony through faith, did not receive the promise, God having provided something better for us, that they should not be made perfect apart from us.

Most of these were Jews or Gentiles who had become proselyte Jews. Their faith is the spiritual root of our faith. It is Satan's plan to keep the two separated. He doesn't want the Jews to know Jesus, nor does he want the Gentile church to be held up by our healthy strong root.

The Feasts Of The Lord

Another example of the life giving sap from our heritage is an understanding of the Feasts of the Lord. Why? The answer to that question is found not only in the Old Testament but also throughout the New. Did you know that the Passover is a picture of our salvation, among other things? In John 1:29 we hear John the Baptist say, *". . . Behold! The Lamb of God who takes away the sin of the world!"* Notice that he didn't call Jesus the Easter bunny, but that he called Him the Lamb. He was referring to the Jewish Passover Lamb. The Feast of Firstfruits is mentioned approximately eight times in the New Covenant.

Unleavened Bread, Shavuot (Pentecost), Rosh Hashanah, Yom Kippur, Tabernacles, are all fulfilled in Jesus and directly involve, and seriously impact our lives now! Why? Jesus is fulfilling these feasts. Unleavened Bread, Passover, and Firstfruits, have already been fulfilled. In basic terms Rosh Hashanah, Yom Kippur, and Tabernacles are the Rapture, the cleansing of Israel, and the thousand-year reign of Jesus. There are also applications for the feasts in our day-to-day lives, as they contain spiritual principles that God will hold us accountable to live out in this life. All of this God gave and comes to us through the Jews, of which you are spiritually related if you are born again.

Why then don't we desire to understand the Jewish heritage of our faith? Why aren't these things taught in most churches today? We will answer that question in later chapters, but first let's see what the Bible says regarding our responsibility to the Jews.

CHAPTER 5

Our Responsibility to the Jewish People

"Your people shall be my people, and your God, my God."
(Ruth 1:16)

There is something we must first establish before delving into the biblical instruction that God gives His body regarding how we are to think of, and then behave toward, His chosen people. If it weren't for some Christians we wouldn't have to further specify or answer a question for which the world already has a clear understanding. The question is, "What is a Jew today?" Some professing Christians would say that only those who are physical descendants of Jacob who believe in Jesus are Jews. Others would say that since the church is the New Israel, we who believe in Jesus, whether of physical lineage to Isaac or not, are now the true Jews.

I have personally been told that because of verses in the second chapter of Romans, those in the church are now the true Jews.

For he is not a Jew who is one outwardly, nor is circumcision that which is outward in the flesh; but he is a Jew who is one inwardly;

and circumcision is that of the heart, in the Spirit, not in the letter; whose praise is not from men, but from God.

(Romans 2:28–29)

It is true that Paul is telling the religious, proud, unsaved Jews that they are not righteous, and that Gentiles who believe in Jesus are. But does he mean that there are no longer Jews and that the church has become the true Jews?

To understand this we must know certain things about the book of Romans. Romans chapters one, two, and part of three are written to establish the absolute guilt of all mankind. Romans 1:18–32 establishes that the Gentiles are guilty though they were without the revelation of God through the law, as creation and nature itself reveals God to them, which leaves them without excuse and condemns the nations. Romans 1:18–21:

For the wrath of God is revealed from heaven against all ungodliness and unrighteousness of men, who suppress the truth in unrighteousness, because that what may be known of God is manifest in them, for God hath showed it to them. For since the creation of the world His invisible attributes are clearly seen, being understood by the things that are made, even His eternal power and Godhead, so that they are without excuse, because, although they knew God, they did not glorify Him as God, nor were thankful, but became futile in their thoughts, and their foolish hearts were darkened.

In the first chapter of Romans God establishes the guilt of the Gentiles without the law.

In light of this, the natural thing for religious Jews to think is they are off the hook by rite of physical descent from Abraham. "Those pagan Gentiles are in trouble but I am O.K. because I came from Abraham and I am of the Law of Moses." Cleverly, Paul accurately turns things around on the self-righteous Jew and calls the "far off" Gentile "near to God," while indicting the religious Jew and labeling him as the one "far off" from God. He calls the believing, forgiven-by-Jesus-Gentile a better Jew than he, and a legitimate heir of Abraham. Does Paul do this to replace the Jews with the church? Of course not! He uses this play on words to establish that both Jew and Gentile are condemned without the blood of Jesus!

He, like an attorney arguing the most important case in history, makes his closing argument in the third chapter of Romans, which establishes the guilt of humanity and the only way to salvation. Let's listen to a portion of the barrister's closing statements on the Gentiles and Jews in Romans 3:21–26 (KJV):

> But now the righteousness of God without the law is manifested, being witnessed by the Law and the prophets; even the righteousness of God which is by faith of Jesus Christ unto all and upon all them that believe: for there is no difference: For all have sinned, and come short of the glory of God; being justified freely by his grace through the redemption that is in Christ Jesus: Whom God hath set forth to be a propitiation through faith in his blood, to declare his righteousness for the remission of sins that are past, through the forbearance of God; to declare, I say, at this time his righteousness: that he might be just, and the justifier of him which believeth in Jesus.

Do you see the replacement of the Jews with the church in this passage? No, it is a clear-cut case that both Gentiles and Jews have sinned and desperately need the forgiveness that can only be realized in Jesus Christ!

In Romans 3:1–2, one verse after the often misinterpreted "true Jew" Scripture, Paul talks about the blessing of being a physical Jew descended from Abraham.

What advantage then has the Jew, or what is the profit of circumcision? Much in every way! Chiefly because to them were committed the oracles of God.

Here Paul refers to the intact, not replaced by the church, Jewish people as those who were entrusted with the oracles of God such as those found in Romans 9:1–5.

The reality is that the Jews are the physical descendants of Israel just as much as your national blood lineage makes you Italian, German, Greek, and so on. This is difficult for many to accept because they lightly esteem Israel as an illegitimate nation, so they don't recognize the Jews as a nationality. After reading this, if you are still having difficulty figuring out who the Jews are, just refer to Pharaoh, Haman, Hitler, Yasser Arafat, and the many Muslim terrorist organizations. They have identified them without any confusion.

This established, we are going to look at a book of the Bible that illustrates New Testament truths regarding Israel, the church, and Jesus our Redeemer in breathtaking fashion! I have personally taught this book to pastors and laypeople of different denominations. I have also watched God reveal Himself to them as they listened to this wonderful story. This is one of many places in Scripture that I will give, which instructs how God expects us to think of the Jewish people.

In the book of Ruth we see God's plan for the ages. This may be difficult for many Christians to see due to a lack of teaching on covenant and the prophets. However, if we keep the things we have spoken of in mind, a whole new world opens up to us. God is working history, current events, and the future around the Jews, the land of Israel, and His church. Now, let's look at the story of Ruth.

In Ruth 1:1–2 we see Elimelech, Naomi, Mahlon, and Chilion leave Bethlehem to go to Moab as a result of a famine in the land. This seems uneventful and of little significance on the surface. However let's look deeper. Bethlehem means *House of Bread*. Jesus is the Bread of Life and was born in Bethlehem. They left the House of Bread in time of famine.

> *Now it came to pass, in the days when the judges ruled, that there was a famine in the land. And a certain man of Bethlehem, Judah, went to dwell in the country of Moab, he and his wife and his two sons. The name of the man was Elimelech, the name of his wife was Naomi, and the name of his two sons were Mahlon and Chilion—Ephrathites of Bethlehem, Judah. And they went to the country of Moab and remained there.*
>
> (Ruth 1:1,2)

The Jewish people rejected the Bread of Life and were dispersed to the nations as a result of a spiritual famine. (Remember, the Old Testament contains pictures, types, and shadows of the New.) Their two sons, Mahlon and Chilion, have names in Hebrew that reflect this as they mean *Sick* and *Pining*. This is a picture of the dispersion of the Jews to the nations, which is commonly called the Diaspora. Yet, God has a plan for the ones who left the House of Bread.

The father Elimelech dies, and afterward his and Naomi's sons marry two Moabite women and then the sons die. Oh, but wait, this is a glorious story! In Ruth 1:6 we see the Lord begin to restore Israel:

> *Then she [Naomi] arose with her daughters-in-law that she might return from the country of Moab, for she had heard in the country of Moab that the LORD had visited His people by giving them bread.*

---

[4] *MacArthur Study Bible*, 368.

The blessing of bread from the Lord, which brings Naomi back to the land, is a picture of the Jews coming back from the dispersion as the nation of Israel is reborn physically, and then like us spiritually!

Listen again to Pastor John MacArthur: "The return of physical prosperity only shadowed the reality of a coming spiritual prosperity through the line of David in the person of Christ."[4] Who is bringing them back? We see in Ezekiel 36:24–29:

> For I will take you from among the nations, gather you out of all the countries, and bring you into your own land. Then I will sprinkle clean water on you, and you shall be clean; I will cleanse you from all your filthiness and from all your idols. I will give you a new heart and put a new spirit within you; I will take the heart of stone out of your flesh and give you a heart of flesh. I will put My Spirit within you and cause you to walk in My statutes, and you will keep My judgments and do them. Then you shall dwell in the land that I gave to your fathers; you shall be My people, and I will be your God. I will deliver you from all your uncleannesses. I will call for the grain and multiply it, and bring no famine upon you.

This is just the beginning as the story beautifully unfolds. As the first chapter of Ruth continues, Naomi, the Jewish mother-in-law, is exhorting her widowed daughters-in-law not to return with her to the land of Israel. Let's pick up in Ruth 1:14–18:

> Then they lifted up their voices and wept again; and Orpah kissed her mother-in-law, but Ruth clung to her. And she said, "Look, your sister-in-law has gone back to her people and to her gods; return after your sister-in-law." But Ruth said: "Entreat me not to leave you, or to turn back from following after you; for wherever you go, I will go; and wherever you lodge, I will lodge; your people shall be my people, and your God, my God. Where you die, I will die, and there will I be buried. The LORD do so to me, and more also, if anything

*but death parts you and me." When she saw that she was determined
to go with her, she stopped speaking to her.*

Many Bible commentators say that Orpah is a picture of false
conversion. I tend to agree. In Ruth 1:10 she commits to sojourn
with Ruth toward the House of Bread:

*And they said to her, "Surely we will return with you to your
people."*

Orpah then turned back, returning to her people and their
false gods. I am reminded of the parable of the soils in which four
types of people profess salvation, yet only one is truly saved. The
one that bears fruit, or has faith that works, as James would say, is
truly saved from the wrath to come. Orpah's life reveals that her
commitment is not genuine.

Ruth is a picture of the Gentile church. She recognizes the
importance of clinging to Naomi (the Jew) as she is sojourning
back to the land of her people. Ruth also desires to follow Naomi's
God. Notice the relationship between the people and their God.
"Your people will be my people and your God my God." How someone
can believe in Jesus Christ, have the Holy Spirit within them, and
not love the Jews is a question I just can't answer with certainty.
I think many are simply one of the three unfruitful soils. Others
who are truly saved have been indoctrinated with things we will
later identify.

In Ruth 1:19 the women in Bethlehem express their excitement
at seeing Naomi. *"Is this Naomi?"* Then in the next two verses
Naomi answers:

*"Do not call me Naomi; call me Mara, for the Almighty has dealt
very bitterly with me. I went out full, and the Lord has brought me*

63

*home again empty. Why do you call me Naomi, since the L*ORD *has testified against me, and the Almighty has afflicted me?"*

(Ruth 1:20–21)

Naomi means *full* and Mara means *bitter*.

The Jews went out in great number as God kept His promise of judgment and scattered the Jewish people throughout the nations from Israel. This was a result of their not keeping the conditional covenant made with Moses. However, God is bringing a remnant back to the land. The modern Jewish people sense their heavy affliction from the Lord like Naomi did. Isaiah 10:22:

For though your people, O Israel, be as the sand of the sea, a remnant of them will return; the destruction decreed shall overflow with righteousness.

So we see that Elimelech, Chilion, Mahlon, and Naomi are a picture of the Jewish people who left the House of Bread in famine. Naomi is a picture of the afflicted remnant returning to Israel.

As we move into the second chapter we see Ruth the Gentile benefiting from a Jewish law pertaining to the needy. Israeli landowners were required to leave the outskirts of the harvest for the poor and the stranger from which to *glean* food.

There was a relative of Naomi's husband, a man of great wealth, of the family of Elimelech. His name was Boaz. So Ruth the Moabitess said to Naomi, "Please let me go to the field, and glean heads of grain after him in whose sight I may find favor."

(Ruth 2:1–2)

In the new covenant a Gentile woman came to Jesus and asked if she could glean crumbs from Jesus. Matthew 15:21–27:

Then Jesus went out from there and departed to the region of Tyre and Sidon. And behold, a woman of Canaan came from that region and cried out to Him, saying, "Have mercy on me, O Lord, Son of David! My daughter is severely demon-possessed." But He answered her not a word. And His disciples came and urged Him, saying, "Send her away, for she cries out after us." But He answered and said, "I was not sent except to the lost sheep of the house of Israel." Then she came and worshiped Him, saying, "Lord, help me!" But He answered and said, "It is not good to take the children's bread and throw it to the little dogs." And she said, "Yes, Lord, yet even the little dogs eat the crumbs which fall from their masters' table."

Don't forget this story as it ties in marvelously with the end of Ruth's story.

Ruth is gleaning in a field owned by a wealthy man named Boaz, a close relative of Naomi. There is another Jewish law found in Deuteronomy 25:5–10 which involves a close relative marrying the widowed woman in the family for the purpose of keeping the family name alive. This was a near relative or kinsman *redeeming* the widow from her hardship. The near relative could also redeem his kinsmen from slavery, which is found in Leviticus 25:47–49. Jesus redeems those who believe in Him from the slavery of sin. The term for this person is a *kinsman redeemer*. Boaz is the kinsmen redeemer as we shall see, and is also a picture of the Lord Jesus Christ!

As chapter two continues, Boaz notices Ruth and asks his servant about her. After recognizing her commitment to Naomi, he approaches Ruth. Ruth 2:8–12:

Then Boaz said to Ruth, "You will listen, my daughter, will you not? Do not go to glean in another field, nor go from here, but stay close by my young women. Let your eyes be on the field which they reap, and go after them. Have I not commanded the young men not to touch you? And when you are thirsty, go to the vessels and drink from what the young men have drawn." So she fell on her face, bowed down to the ground, and said to him, "Why have I found favor in your eyes, that you should take notice of me, since I am a foreigner?" And Boaz answered and said to her, "It has been fully reported to me, all that you have done for your mother-in-law since the death of your husband, and how you have left your father and your mother and the land of your birth, and have come to a people whom you did not know before. The Lord repay your work, and a full reward be given you by the Lord God of Israel, under whose wings you have come for refuge."

This is so rich, and we could camp out here for hours! Yet for the sake of staying on track, let's just note two observations. It is the testimony of Ruth's love for Naomi and not her words that got the attention of Boaz. It is our actions of love toward the Jewish people and not our words that will get the attention of Jesus Christ our Kinsmen Redeemer. We hear a great number in the church talk about their love for the Jewish people, but where is the action that leads to a testimony? Second, we see that our love in action is fully reported to the Lord. He will bless us just as He told us in Genesis, as we work in His field of harvest and bless the Jewish people.

As we read Ruth 2:14–19 the glory of this story continues to unfold!

Now Boaz said to her at mealtime, "Come here, and eat of the bread, and dip your piece of bread in the vinegar." So she sat beside the reapers, and he passed parched grain to her; and she ate and was satisfied, and kept some back.

I must stop here to say something. We see the Gentile Ruth being blessed by the Jewish covenants (Abrahamic and Mosaic) and being satisfied by the grace of the kinsman redeemer Boaz. Ruth is blessing Naomi and being blessed by God in return, which is promised in the covenant of Abraham. The Mosaic Law required the landowners to provide a portion of the harvest for gleaning.

I will continue from verse 15:

And when she rose up to glean, Boaz commanded his young men, saying, "Let her glean even among the sheaves, and do not reproach her. Also let grain from the bundles fall purposely for her; leave it that she may glean, and do not rebuke her." So she gleaned in the field until evening, and beat out what she had gleaned, and it was about an ephah of barley. Then she took it up and went into the city, and her mother-in-law saw what she had gleaned. So she brought out and gave to her what she had kept back after she had been satisfied.

I will stop here to remind you of the Gentile woman Jesus was speaking to who asked that she might receive crumbs falling from the master's table. We see Boaz letting the grain bundles fall purposely to Ruth the faithful Gentile.

Back to our story at Ruth 2:19:

And her mother-in-law said to her, "Where have you gleaned today? And where did you work? Blessed be the one who took notice of you."

Folks, as we labor in the fields of the Lord's harvest and love Israel, the Lord will bless us, and Naomi will take notice. So what if the Jews take notice of we Gentiles who believe in Jesus? The answer is found in the book of Romans. As Paul is writing about the Jewish people, look at what God has him say:

I say then, have they stumbled that they should fall? Certainly not! But through their fall, to provoke them to jealousy, salvation has come to the Gentiles. Now if their fall is riches for the world, and their failure riches for the Gentiles, how much more their fullness!

For I speak to you Gentiles; inasmuch as I am an apostle to the Gentiles, I magnify my ministry, if by any means I may provoke to jealousy those who are my flesh and save some of them.

(Romans 11:11–14)

By the command of the King we are to lead them to their Messiah by provoking them to jealousy.

There is a married couple who are my dear friends, and great Christian supporters of Israel. The wife was in Israel and the Lord Jesus anointed her to minister to some Jewish college-age youth. While spending time with them she was able to see these Israelis as God sees them.

You see, she has a love for Naomi. At one point, as she was talking to them, God moved on her spirit. She looked up into the sky and said something like this, "Lord, I don't know what to say to them. I know they are your chosen people, but chosen for what? They are all in sin." Her compassion and love for them overwhelmed some of these Jewish young people to the point of weeping and a desire to know God. One reached out, grabbed her arm and said, "I am so *jealous*! I want to know Him like you do!" Wow! What a Ruth! Oh, that we all would take instruction from this modern day Ruth and have a desire to bless Naomi.

The Lord unfolds His plan even further in Ruth 2:20 and 3:1–4:

Then Naomi said to her daughter-in-law, "Blessed be he of the Lord, who has not forsaken His kindness to the living and the dead!" And Naomi said to her, "This man is a relation of ours, one of our close relatives."

(2:20)

Then Naomi her mother-in-law said to her, "My daughter, shall I not seek security for you, that it may be well with you? Now Boaz, whose young women you were with, is he not our relative? In fact, he is winnowing barley tonight at the threshing floor. **Therefore wash yourself and anoint yourself, put on your best garment and go down to the threshing floor; but do not make yourself known to the man until he has finished eating and drinking. Then it shall be, when he lies down, that you shall notice the place where he lies; and you shall go in, uncover his feet, and lie down; and he will tell you what you should do."**

(3:1–4)

What is happening here? Naomi the Jew is showing Ruth the Gentile how to be accepted by her kinsman redeemer. This custom is assuring Boaz that even though Ruth is younger in years, it is appropriate for them to be wed. Ruth is asking him to be her kinsman redeemer.

What else is taking place? That which has significance for us today is pictured in this beautiful story of redemption. Just to remind us how sovereign God is I would like to share something with you. One night during the time I was studying Ruth and processing the biblical information and revelation from God, I was listening to a Christian radio station in Houston, and an old time preacher was talking about Ruth. He began speaking about the very things God was showing me! It is amazing what he said about Naomi telling Ruth to go to Boaz. This is showing us that the Jews gave us the Kinsman Redeemer Jesus Christ! Naomi tells Ruth to wash herself, anoint herself, put on her best garment, and to lie down at the feet of Boaz until he tells her what to do. The Jewish Scriptures, covenants, and feasts show us the only way to Jesus. We must be washed clean from our sin, anointed by the Holy Spirit, have the stained garments of sin removed and replaced with garments of righteousness, and we must fall down at the feet of Jesus for mercy! Don't you see that this is the story of our redemption and it all comes from the God of Israel through the Jews?

We should be very thankful to God for the Jewish people. We are indebted to them for showing us their God! You might say, "This sounds wonderful, but do we see such a notion in the New Testament?" I am glad you asked. Romans 15:26–27:

> *For it pleased those from Macedonia and Achaia to make a certain contribution for the poor among the saints who are in Jerusalem. It pleased them indeed, and they are their debtors. For if the Gentiles have been partakers of their spiritual things, their duty is also to minister to them in material things.*

In Acts 10:1–5 we see a Roman soldier stationed in Israel who was a believer in the God of Israel. This sense of gratitude provoked him to give alms to the Jewish people. We are indebted to the Jews!

As we move ahead to Ruth 3:10–11, we see Ruth's loyalty and love blesses the kinsman redeemer Boaz:

> *Then he said, "Blessed are you of the LORD, my daughter! For you have shown more kindness at the end than at the beginning, in that you did not go after young men, whether poor or rich. And now, my daughter, do not fear. I will do for you all that you request, for all the people of my town know that you are a virtuous woman."*

Ruth's love for Naomi and Boaz at the end is even stronger than at the beginning. We have an opportunity in the church to love the Jews, and Jesus the Kinsman Redeemer, here at the end more than some did at the beginning. By the end of this book you will understand how unloving so many in the church have been to Naomi. May we take instruction from Ruth and be a loving daughter-in-law. Then the Lord will be pleased to call us His virtuous bride.

As a great number of hearts in the modern church are turning away from the Lord, He is raising up many to shine brightly! The faith of these pure, faithful lovers of Jesus Christ will have a characteristic that will be demonstrated with action. Do you know what that character trait will be? It will be *faith*. Do you remember the Gentile we spoke of earlier? Hear Jesus' words as He healed her daughter after she humbly asked for the crumbs from the Jews' table. Matthew 15:28:

> *Then Jesus answered and said to her, "O woman, great is your faith! Let it be to you as you desire." And her daughter was healed from that very hour.*

Being a Ruth is a humble act of obedience that demonstrates great faith in the Kinsman Redeemer Jesus!

Shall we see how God unfolds the end of the story, which is just the beginning of much of His plan for the ages to come? Ruth 4:13–15:

> *So Boaz took Ruth and she became his wife; and when he went in to her, the LORD gave her conception, and she bore a son. Then the women said to Naomi, "Blessed be the LORD, who has not left you this day without a close relative; and may his name be famous in Israel! And may he be to you a restorer of life and a nourisher of your old age; for your daughter-in-law, who loves you, who is better to you than seven sons, has borne him."*

Please, patiently hang in there with me as, with the Lord's help, I tie this together. As the result of the Jewish influence on Ruth's life, she met Boaz the kinsman redeemer. We see Jesus quoted in John 4:22: *". . . salvation is of the Jews."* The result of this relationship of love between Ruth, Naomi, then Boaz not only brings salvation to Ruth (the church) but also to Naomi (the Jews). She was told that Ruth was better to her than seven sons. Of course, one son would have been a blessing. However, seven sons is a phrase used to illustrate perfection. Yet, Ruth's love surpassed any good daughter in the way she had blessed Naomi her mother-in-law. She was compared to seven sons.

We saw that the Lord didn't leave Naomi without a redeemer or close relative, namely Boaz. The Scriptures we just looked at also show us that the Lord, through Ruth's love, was a restorer of life and a nourisher in Naomi's old age. We also read that the women said a blessing about the close relative, "*. . . and may his name be famous in Israel!*" How does this all tie in? Please follow me and watch the salvation of God! In Ruth 4:18–22 we see part of the genealogy of King David.

Now this is the genealogy of Perez: Perez begot Hezron; Hezron begot Ram, and Ram begot Amminadab; Amminadab begot Nahshon, and Nahshon begot Salmon; Salmon begot Boaz, and Boaz begot Obed; Obed begot Jesse, and Jesse begot David.

Of course we know because of a **covenant** God made with David in 2 Samuel 7:12–13 that a King would reign from David's throne forever. There are two persons in this lineage to note as they pertain to our story. Matthew 1:5–16:

*Salmon begot Boaz by Rahab, **Boaz begot Obed by Ruth**, Obed begot Jesse, and Jesse begot David the king. David the king begot Solomon by her who had been the wife of Uriah. Solomon begot Re-hoboam, Rehoboam begot Abijah, and Abijah begot Asa. Asa begot Jehoshaphat, Jehoshaphat begot Joram, and Joram begot Uzziah. Uzziah begot Jotham, Jotham begot Ahaz, and Ahaz begot Heze-kiah. Hezekiah begot Manasseh, Manasseh begot Amon, and Amon begot Josiah. Josiah begot Jeconiah and his brothers about the time they were carried away to Babylon. And after they were brought to Babylon, Jeconiah begot Shealtiel, and Shealtiel begot Zerubbabel. Zerubbabel begot Abiud, Abiud begot Eliakim, and Eliakim begot Azor. Azor begot Zadok, Zakok begot Achim, and Achim begot Eliud. Eliud begot Eleazar, Eleazar begot Matthan, and Matthan begot Jacob. And Jacob begot Joseph the husband of Mary, of whom was born Jesus who is called Christ.*

The Gentile Ruth is used of God to be in the adoptive legal genealogy of the Messiah Jesus Christ! I say adoptive because God the Father, not Joseph, is Jesus' Father.

The Jew Naomi introduces Ruth, the faithful Gentile, to the God of Israel, and she is redeemed from her hardship. Then when she had all but lost hope, after having been afflicted of the Lord, Ruth is used of God in the plan of salvation for Naomi as He also redeems and nourishes her in her old age. The Jewish covenants, Scriptures, and prophets brought the Gentiles (Ruth) to the Kinsman Redeemer Jesus while, at the same time, a righteous Gentile (Ruth) is used of God to give the Messiah back to the Jews. Some of the early so-called church fathers were horrible to the Jews, which I will clearly demonstrate. Now, the modern followers of Jesus have a chance to be better than seven sons to them!

We can now fulfill the role of a Ruth to the Jewish people and bless them as they return to the House of Bread! The time is soon coming when Jesus will come back and redeem Israel in the years of her old age. Zechariah 12:10:

And I will pour on the house of David and on the inhabitants of Jerusalem the Spirit of grace and supplication; then they will look on Me whom they pierced. Yes, they will mourn for Him as one mourns for his only son, and grieve for Him as one grieves for a firstborn.

The Jews will then be full not empty, and Jesus the Kinsman Redeemer will be famous in Israel forever!

So, we have a responsibility to be a Ruth to the Jewish people. Will we love them unconditionally with a firm commitment to God? Do you remember the vow Ruth made to the Lord?

*". . . Entreat me not to leave you, or to turn back from following after you; for wherever you go, I will go; and wherever you lodge, I will lodge; **your people shall be my people, and your God, my God.***

Where you die, I will die, and there will I be buried. The Lord *do so to me, and more also, if anything but death parts you and me."*
                                                    (Ruth 1:16–17)

The name Orpah means *stubborn* in Hebrew. Ruth means *friendship*. Will you be an Orpah or a Ruth to the Jews? Remember, the Kinsman Redeemer Jesus is watching.

CHAPTER 6

Where Are the Watchmen?

I have set watchmen on your walls, O Jerusalem . . .

(Isaiah 62:6)

We just spent an entire chapter observing how God used the book of Ruth to demonstrate, among other things, that those called out to worship Jesus Christ are to be a friend to the Jewish people. Is there more? Is Ruth just an isolated blip on the screen of God's plans and responsibilities for the church? Some would deem the "Ruth thing" as a less-than-important responsibility when weighed against the other meaningful tasks that Jesus gave us. Not so! As we look at the whole body of Scripture, we will find God's broken heart over wayward Israel, and that He has called us to support the Jews in many ways.

> *How beautiful upon the mountains are the feet of him who brings good news, who proclaims peace, who brings glad tidings of good things, who proclaims salvation, who says to Zion, "Your God reigns!" Your **watchmen** shall lift up their voices, with their voices they shall sing together; for they shall see eye to eye when the LORD brings back Zion.*

(Isaiah 52:7–8)

Typically, the meaning of this verse is taught a little differently than Isaiah had intended. A friend of mine, who is a pastor, was at our home and I shared this Scripture with him. As he looked at it for the first time without the skewed context in which he was originally taught it, I sensed his spiritual eyes being opened up, and then watched his physical countenance leap with joy and amazement! How could he not have seen this before?

He had never seen this as being the good news of the gospel being taken to the Jewish people. Who else but the church could accomplish this? Who has the responsibility to bring the good news? Of course it is the church of the Lord Jesus Christ! What mountains are being spoken of here? Is this a generic reference to mountains to illustrate the importance of taking the gospel to the nations? As much as world evangelism is our responsibility, Isaiah 52:7 is not a good Scripture to teach that principle. These are the hills around Jerusalem, and the good news is to the Jewish people! When Isaiah says, "Who says to Zion, your God reigns!" who is Zion? Whose God is He? In this passage Zion is the Jews and the Creator of the universe is their God! Psalm 125:2:

> As the mountains surround Jerusalem, so the LORD surrounds His people from this time forth and forever.

Paul gives good cross-references in Romans 1:16; 10:15 and Ephesians 6:15.

The necessity to provoke the Jewish people to jealousy and to share the gospel with them has been neglected in great measure as a result of great misunderstanding. Romans 1:16:

> For I am not ashamed of the gospel of Christ, for it is the power of God to salvation for everyone who believes, for the Jew first and also for the Greek.

God has ordered it so that the gospel is to be presented to the Jew first and then the non-Jew (Greek). The way that many have been taught to subvert this order is to believe that since the Jews rejected Jesus, the gospel is no longer to them first. However, hadn't the time when many of the Jews cried out "crucify Him" already passed when the book of Romans was written? Had Paul forgotten this fact?

At a conference in Fort Worth, Texas, Dr. Arnold Fruchtenbaum spoke about the New Testament Greek sentence structure of Romans 1:16. He concluded that since the verb usage references . . . *the gospel of Christ, it is the power of God to salvation* and *to the Jew first and also for the Greek.* Then for today's gospel to not be to the Jew first, it must also not be the power of God for salvation any longer. Folks, believe me, the gospel is still God's power to save and we are still to be getting the gospel to the Jews first!

Was there a greater evangelist ever in the history of the world than the apostle Paul? When Paul went to the Gentiles with the gospel, to whom did he go first? He first went to the synagogues, or while in Roman captivity he first called the Jewish leaders to come to him so he could explain Messiah to them first before going to the Gentiles. Here is a list of places where Paul went to the Jews first: Cyprus, Acts 13:4; Antioch, Acts 13:14; Iconium, Acts 14:1; Thessalonica, Acts 17:1; Berea, Acts 17:10; Corinth, Acts 18:4; Ephesus, Acts 19:8; Rome, Acts 28:17. Why did Paul go to the Jews first among these Gentiles? Because the gospel is to the Jew first and then to the Gentiles.

You might be thinking that you never see any Jewish people in your sphere of relationships, so this is insignificant to you. America has roughly the same number of Jewish people as does Israel! For me, the Lord didn't begin sending them into my life until my heart was predisposed to minister life to them. I have a story, of many, that illustrates the power of God in bringing Naomi together with Ruth.

I took my son to a Little League baseball field to practice with him during the off-season. This field is in a small southeast suburb of Houston, Texas. There was a limited amount of activity because of the time of year. I was standing at the concession stand, which was open as they had some high school sporting practices taking place. I was minding my own business when a young man walked up to me and informed me that he was thankful that another Jew lived in the area. He had noticed my Star of David necklace with a cross in the middle of it. This is when things got interesting.

When he inquired why I had a cross in my Star of David, I told him that I was glad that he had asked. I then shared the gospel of his Jewish Messiah with him for about two hours. In good Jewish tradition we debated back and forth, yet he heard the power of God to salvation and that is what matters. Here is the exciting part of the story. He was an Israeli police officer visiting in the USA! How could this be anything but the Lord Jesus? What are the odds of an Israeli policeman bumping into another Jew with a Star of David with a cross in it, at a ball field in off-season, in a southeast Houston suburb? This is one of a multitude of such encounters that God has engineered in my life. He will do the same for you if you will just line your heart up with God's economy, and prepare yourself to share Jesus with the Jews.

I believe this most vital duty, of sharing the gospel with the Jews, is really a subresponsibility, if you will, of one specific call the Lord gives. This call is inclusive of many tasks for the church toward the Jewish people. This high calling to the born again takes on many faces through Scripture, which should show us how important it is to fulfill. One reason God repeats things in the Bible is to stress the importance for such things to be understood.

What is this ministry to the body of Christ? It is that of a *watchman.*

I have set watchmen on your walls, O Jerusalem; they shall never hold their peace day or night. You who make mention of the LORD, do not keep silent, and give Him no rest till He establishes and till He makes Jerusalem a praise in the earth.

(Isaiah 62:6–7)

What did a watchman do? The term is used to describe someone on the walls around the city keeping watch to protect the citizens inside. A few of the definitions: keep, guard, observe, give heed, night watch.[5] "The basic idea of the root word is 'to exercise great care over.'"[6]

Now do you see why all of the responsibilities the Lord has given His church pertaining to the Jewish people spring from this? We are to be exercising great care over the Jews. This great care takes on many forms as Scripture teaches us. We had better take heed of Isaiah 62:1:

For Zion's sake I will not hold My peace, and for Jerusalem's sake I will not rest, until her righteousness goes forth as brightness, and her salvation as a lamp that burns.

I would like to pose a question to those who wonder if the church is supposed to be the watchman.

Did they ever put a blind person on the wall to watch? Well, of course not, that would be silly you might say. Do you think God is putting blind people on the wall for the Jewish people? Who are the only people in the world who can really see what is going on? The answer: those who belong to Jesus and have the Holy Spirit giving them the mind of Christ (1 Corinthians 2:16).

---

[5] Harris, Gleason L. Archer, and Bruce K. Waltke, *Theological Dictionary of the Old Testament, vol. 2,* (Chicago: Moody Press, 1980) 939.
[6] Ibid.

Here is the question that absolutely broke my heart, and I am confident breaks the heart of our Savior: Where are the watchmen? What are the watchmen doing? While the Jews need a Messiah, where are the watchmen? As Jerusalem is under attack by demonized civilian murderers, where are the watchmen? When a Palestinian gunman broke into a house in Israel and looked right into the eyes of a five-year-old child and intentionally shot her at point-blank range, where was the church of the Jewish Messiah? As the current American administration is attempting to give Judea, Samaria, and half of Jerusalem away to Islam, where is the church? Where is the church while Jerusalem is under siege politically by the nations (including our government), and Israeli men, women, and children are dying?

I think we find the answer in the book of James in chapter 4:4:

Adulterers and adulteresses! Do you not know that friendship with the world is enmity with God? Whoever therefore wants to be a friend of the world makes himself an enemy of God.

Sadly, the answer to the question of the current status of the watchmen is that they, in large numbers, are sleeping with the world. Most professing Christians are indifferent and many are literally standing confidently on the side of the enemy. I will go into greater detail on this phenomenon later.

Why would our Father in heaven give us the responsibility of watchman? We know the Lord doesn't have to explain why because He is God, yet we are also His friends and children. By nature of this relationship at times the Creator of all things does stoop down and share with us His reasons, plans, and purposes. The answer to the above question is one of those merciful cases. You see, the Lord did have the apostle Paul instruct the reason we are to handle the Jews with such care.

Please read Romans 11:11–14 with me:

I say then, have they stumbled that they should fall? Certainly not! But through their fall, to provoke them to jealousy, salvation has come to the Gentiles. Now if their fall is riches for the world, and their failure riches for the Gentiles, how much more their fullness! For I speak to you Gentiles; inasmuch as I am an apostle to the Gentiles, I magnify my ministry, if by any means I may provoke to jealousy those who are my flesh and save some of them.

In case you don't think this is every believer's responsibility, look at the phrase *"For I speak to you Gentiles."* Who do you think that leaves out? It is the predominantly Gentile church's responsibility to make the Jews jealous as we are being loved by their loving, merciful Messiah, whom they have rejected. Generally speaking, it is interesting that Jews respond to Gentile believers better than Jewish ones. There are sociological and religious reasons, but I believe the reality is, this is God's order.

Here we see that God, in His infinite mercy and wisdom, decided to use the stumbling of the Jews to save the Gentiles. He did this not only to demonstrate His mercy and love, but also to use the Gentile church to make the Jews jealous. That is why we are to be watchmen. As the church is a "Ruth" fulfilling all of her God-given tasks, they see their Messiah in us! This makes them jealous of us because we are close to their God and now they are the ones who are far off. Jesus wants us to bring His beloved back to Him!

Remember the lady who was talking to the Jewish college students about Jesus? Remember what their response was? "I am so jealous, I want to know Him like you do."

My, is she not a Ruth? God's magnificent plan is so overwhelming that Paul can't help but stop and give Him all the glory.

Oh, the depth of the riches both of the wisdom and knowledge of God! How unsearchable are His judgments and His ways past finding out!

(Romans 11:33)

It is not until we have God's heart for the land of Israel and the Jewish people that we can accomplish our work. Why? It is because much of our effort will be works of the flesh, not of His Spirit. I was sharing these truths with a friend, and a couple of Scriptures powerfully leaped off the pages into his heart.

> *Oh, that my head were waters, and my eyes a fountain of tears, that I might weep day and night for the slain of the daughter of my people!*
>
> (Jeremiah 9:1)

Not only is the Lord heartbroken over the Jewish people, but you see His servant Jeremiah with the same grief. Are you the Lord Jesus' bondservant? My friend said that he wanted this to be his prayer. He went on to admit that his heart wasn't grieved, like the heart of his Savior, over the Jews. How about you? Is your head *waters*, and your eyes *a fountain of tears* for wayward Israel? Mine weren't until the Lord did that work in me. I can now honestly say that much of the time my heart is burdened for the salvation of the Jews.

Look at the heart of the Lord Jesus through His apostle Paul in Romans 9:1–5:

> *I tell the truth in Christ, I am not lying, my conscience also bearing me witness in the Holy Spirit, that I have great sorrow and continual grief in my heart. For I could wish that I myself were accursed from Christ for my brethren, my countrymen according to the flesh, who are Israelites, to whom pertain the adoption, the glory, the covenants, the giving of the law, the service of God, and the promises; of whom are the fathers and from whom, according to the flesh, Christ came, who is over all, the eternally blessed God. Amen.*

Don't you want your heart to beat with the same rhythm of your Messiah Jesus? Do you want the same thing that He wants?

In Psalm 137:4–6 there is a call to be burdened for Jerusalem from the Lord's perspective.

How shall we sing the LORD's song in a foreign land? If I forget you, O Jerusalem, let my right hand forget its skill! If I do not remember you, let my tongue cling to the roof of my mouth—if I do not exalt Jerusalem above my chief joy.

Here we see the well-known, yet in some Christian circles little-honored, Scripture in Psalm 122:6–9.

Pray for the peace of Jerusalem: "May they prosper who love you. Peace be within your walls, prosperity within your palaces." For the sake of my brethren and companions, I will now say, "Peace be within you." Because of the house of the LORD our God I will seek your good.

Are you praying with a burden from the Lord Jesus about His city as it is being assaulted by the world?

Additionally, we the church of King Jesus are to comfort the Jews. Isaiah 40:1–2:

"Comfort, yes, comfort My people!" says your God. "Speak comfort to Jerusalem, and cry out to her, that her warfare is ended, that her iniquity is pardoned; for she has received from the LORD's hand double for all her sins."

This is another Scripture that is often taken as meaning the church where it reads "My people." Who is God instructing? There are two answers. He is instructing Isaiah to comfort the Jews and prophesying of their future return from Babylon. The church is to also comfort Israel as many of the Jews will be delivered from iniquity by the second coming of Messiah Yeshua! In case there is some doubt, we see in verse 2 that "My people" are in Jerusalem.

To whom does that point? This is an admonition from the Lord to comfort the Jewish people.

As we consider the importance of answering the call to be Israel's watchmen, let's take a look at a Bible passage that may be motivating. It is in the Old Testament book of Esther. Remember, Queen Esther was put in a very difficult position. She was asked not only to risk her position with all of its comfort and prestige, but her very life. Faced with going to the King of Persia without an invitation, which carried a possible death sentence, to tell him that she was Jewish and that his right-hand man had deceived him into issuing a decree to kill all of the Jews, what advice was given to her? Her older cousin Mordecai tells her:

> *"For if you remain completely silent at this time, relief and deliverance will arise for the Jews from another place, but you and your father's house will perish. Yet who knows whether you have come to the kingdom for such a time as this?"*
>
> (Esther 4:14)

You see, God will deliver the Jewish people just as He did from Pharaoh, Haman, and Hitler, just to name a few. The question is: What will we do?

Please also see that, like Esther, we have been raised up as royalty for such a time as this. First Peter 2:9–10:

> *But you are a chosen generation, a royal priesthood, a holy nation, His own special people, that you may proclaim the praises of Him who called you out of darkness into His marvelous light; who once were not a people but are now the people of God, who had not obtained mercy but now have obtained mercy.*

God will raise up those in His body to stand in the gap for the land of Israel and the Jewish people. Those who will not obey Him will suffer loss. We, like Esther, have attained royalty for such a time as this.

Would you like a modern example? There was a family in Holland with the name of ten Boom. The ten Boom family had been praying for the Jewish people and the peace of Jerusalem for a hundred years. This faithful family's ministry was interrupted by the Nazis during World War II. As Hitler's henchmen came through Holland, the ten Booms saved the lives of some eight hundred Jewish people by hiding them. What did it cost them? They were caught and put into German labor camps. The only survivor of this difficult trial was Corrie ten Boom. It cost all of the others their very lives! Do you think the ten Booms would be sitting around with indifference toward the Jewish people at this time? Oh no, these were Jesus' followers who understood their purpose for having attained royalty. These are people who have handed the baton to us. Will we take it and run, or will the Lord set us aside and raise up others who will answer the call?

Therefore we also, since we are surrounded by so great a cloud of witnesses, let us lay aside every weight, and the sin which so easily ensnares us, and let us run with endurance the race that is set before us, looking unto Jesus the author and finisher of our faith, who for the joy that was set before Him endured the cross, despising the shame, and has sat down at the right hand of the throne of God.

(Hebrews 12:1–2)

CHAPTER 7

Identity Crisis: The Source

Put on the whole armor of God, that you may be able to stand against the wiles of the devil.

(Ephesians 6:11)

If there is a special, identifiable relationship between the body of Messiah, the Jewish people, and the land of Israel, why then do we in Christ not understand it? Why is that concept so foreign to so many who are born from above? If our Creator has given us, His followers, extensive responsibilities to the Jewish people, why don't we know it? We certainly cannot fulfill these works from God if we don't sense that they exist.

How would the enemy of the Lord fight most efficiently to keep the people of the Messiah from accomplishing His work? The most effective way would be to make them think incorrectly about their own identity. We know from God's word that the way we think determines our behavior.

For as he thinks in his heart, so is he.

(Proverbs 23:7)

How could the devil confuse us so terribly with regard to our own identity? The best way would be to change the tactic of openly fighting against the church, and to instead join it!

The fact that by the fourth century Jesus' church was mostly Gentile was a glorious, stunning fulfillment of what the Jewish prophets had predicted many years earlier. Isaiah 42:6–7:

"I, the Lord, have called You in righteousness, and will hold Your hand; I will keep You and give You as a covenant to the people, as a light to the Gentiles, to open blind eyes, to bring out prisoners from the prison, those who sit in darkness from the prison house . . ."

Also in Isaiah 65:1:

"I was sought by those who did not ask for Me; I was found by those who did not seek Me. I said, 'Here I am, here I am,' to a nation that was not called by My name."

How glorious that God fulfilled these prophecies by raising up the predominantly Gentile church!

By the fourth century the church had also experienced the changes that are logical and reasonable with regard to culture and thought, as it transitioned from being mostly Jewish to predominantly Gentile. There were cultural influences such as musical styles, food, ways of speaking, and other traditions that on the contrary of subtracting from, added to the body of Christ like the beautiful blended colors of a peacock's tail. Remember, earlier we had seen that the word of God is very clear about the Gentiles being grafted into the Jewish tree. The root of that tree holds up and nurtures the faith of those called out to worship Jesus Christ. Many of its branches were now Gentiles that had been grafted in from the wild olive tree.

Whenever God does something beautiful you can be sure that until Jesus comes to reign on earth, Satan will not be far behind to damage God's work as much as God's people will let him. This happened in the church; the damage that began to take hold in the third century, and then crystallized in the fourth century, has been handed down through the generations, infecting many of Jesus' people like a bad virus.

In the early fourth century Constantine founded the Catholic Church, and Christianity became Rome's state religion. This new brand of Roman Christianity spread through the body of Christ, and the two in many ways became one. I do not deny that many in the Catholic Church at that time were people of God. It was a very confusing time and quite frankly it is very confusing today, and we desperately need Jesus to sort it out. However, we have more information, and I believe a higher accountability today than they did then. Why? We have the benefit of history and can look back to see what terrible things have been done in the name of Jesus. This should help us to avoid those who have a propensity for religious evil. I would also add that we might be surprised when we find out how deceptive Satan has been in our own midst.

Remember earlier when I asked the question, "Can you handle the truth?" This is one of the places you will need to start handling it. It would be almost inconceivable that those God called to love the Jews back to Himself would not only have a lack of love for them, but would hate them enough to be the catalyst for their persecution. It is almost unimaginable that the body of the Jewish Messiah would have anything less than a broken heart for those of His kin according to the flesh, yet some of the most listened-to leaders in the church began to preach hatred toward the Jews. This is the place in time where Satan began to deceive believers into pulling up their own faith by the roots.

Let's take a look at some quotes from some of the most well-established church leaders of history. Most of these quotes, though well-documented in many places, were obtained from Ramon Bennett's book *When Day and Night Cease*. First I will mention John Chrysostom (A.D. 347–407). Chrysostom is considered one of the most authoritative, well-respected preachers of all time. To use a line from an old TV commercial, when this preacher spoke, people listened! This man was considered to be one of the great people of God, yet listen to how much he hated the Jews:

"How can Christians dare have the slightest converse with Jews, most miserable of all men, men who are . . . lustful, rapacious, greedy, perfidious bandits. Are they not inveterate murderers, destroyers, men possessed by the devil whom debauchery and drunkenness have given them the manners of the pig and the lusty goat? They know only one thing, to satisfy their gullets, get drunk, to kill and maim . . ."[7]

The synagogue? Not only is it a theatre and a house of prostitution, but a cavern of brigands, a "repair of wild beasts," a place of "shame and ridicule, the domicile of the devil, as is also the souls of the Jews." Indeed Jews worship the devil; their rites are "criminal and impure;" their religion is "a disease." Their synagogue, again, is "an assembly of criminals . . . a den of thieves . . . a cavern of devils, an abyss of perdition . . . I hate the synagogue also.[8]

God hates the Jews and always hated the Jews . . . I hate the Jews also.[9]

Bennett goes on to say, "It is no wonder that after some of Chrysostom's sermons in A.D. 388, his flock went out and burned down synagogues. But what caused his great hatred of the Jews?

---

[7] Ramon Bennett, *When Day and Night Cease* (Arm of Salvation, 1996), 235.
[8] Ibid.
[9] Ibid.

In Chrysostom's own words: Their odious 'assassination' of Christ . . . for this deicide, there is 'no expiation possible, no indulgence, no pardon . . . vengeance is without end.' Thus Chrysostom cemented into the mind of the Christian his own stereotype of the Jew-'Christ-killers.' His anti-Judaic onslaught lit a fire within the Christian church to which others constantly added more fuel.[10]

Augustine was from the same time period and is considered by some as one of the great church fathers. Read his words as we seek after the source of today's deception.

> Judaism, since Christ, is a corruption; indeed 'Judas is the im-age of the Jewish people, their understanding of the Scriptures is carnal, they bear the guilt for the death of the Saviour, for through their fathers they have killed the Christ. The Jews held Him; the Jews insulted Him, the Jews bound Him, they crowned Him with thorns, dishonored Him by spitting upon Him, they scourged Him, they heaped abuses upon Him, they hung Him upon a tree, they pierced Him with a lance.[11]

Of course, even a cursory reading of Scripture shows us that Augustine was not only inaccurately attributing the sins of some Jews to all the Jews, but he also attributes what some Romans did to Jesus to all of the Jewish people as well. Some of the Romans abused Jesus, and after crowning Him with thorns they beat Him, spat upon Him, and pierced Him. As we listen to these great church leaders shouldn't we ask the question, "Did Satan not join the church?"

If we in the body of Messiah want to lay blame for the death of Jesus we can find out who the culprit is in the word of God. Isaiah 53:5:

---

[10] Ibid.
[11] Ibid., 235–36.

But He was wounded for our transgressions, He was bruised for our iniquities; the chastisement for our peace was upon Him and by His stripes we are healed.

We are all responsible for the death of Jesus Christ, not just the Jews or the Romans for that matter. What do you want more than anything for committing this crime? I will tell you what I want; I want *Mercy*!

So speak and so do as those who will be judged by the law of liberty. For judgment is without mercy to the one who has shown no mercy. Mercy triumphs over judgment.

(James 2:12–13)

We had better show to the Jews the mercy that we would like to receive from the Lord Jesus!

The before-mentioned leaders are just a couple of many in the church that preached hatred of the Jews. Ephraim called the Jews "circumcised dogs."[12] Jerome, while asking Jews for Hebrew lessons, denounced them as "Judaic serpents of whom Judas was the model."[13] The most well-known anti-Semite is amazingly the one that has escaped recognition of the majority of the modern church for his hatred toward the Jews. In Ramon Bennett's book we see a quote pertaining to reformer Martin Luther.

He raged at them in a language that at least equaled in violence anything uttered against them before or after. With biting sarcasm and occasional scatological insult, he renewed all the old charges of the past: Jews are poisoners, ritual murderers, usurers; it is harder to convert them than Satan himself; they are doomed to hell. They are, in truth, the anti-Christ. Their synagogues should

---

[12] Ibid., 236.
[13] Ibid.

be destroyed and their books seized; they should be forced to work with their hands; better still they should be expelled by the princes from their territories.[14]

Some of the most influential church councils spread their hateful doctrines to the churches in many different geographical regions. Many of the atrocities Hitler used against the Jews were handed down from the church leaders and the Christian councils. Some of these include making the Jews wear a certain piece of clothing to identify them as Jewish for the purpose of different types of persecution, moving them into slums or ghettos, and other assorted physical abuses. Many of the quotes I have used from Ramon Bennet's book are from another book that chronicles these specific atrocities by the church against the Jews. Written by Ed Flannery, it is called *The Anguish of the Jews* and it is a must-read if you really want to know the truth about these matters.

One Christian council that we will mention by name is the council of Nicaea. This well-known gathering produced the Nicene Creed, and is considered as a great event in the history of the church. Listen to Constantine's words as they are shared with the bishops: "We desire to have nothing in common with this so hated people, for the Redeemer has marked out another path for us."[15] This and other councils spread their doctrine in the same manner that the apostles spread the truth. They treated it as holy writ.

"Hence, the Council of Nicaea (A.D. 325) established, among other edicts, that Christians would not be allowed to commemorate Passover but would observe the Resurrection on a new holiday called Easter. Easter would be observed on the Sunday after the Spring Equinox. Consequently, today many Christians have forgotten the intimate connection between the Resurrection and the Jewish holy days."[16] Isn't this appalling? The God of Israel who

---

[14] Ibid., 237

[15] Ibid., 238.

[16] Barney Kasdan, *God's Appointed Times* (Lederer Messianic Publications, 1993) 45.

called the Gentiles in the way that He did, in the time that He did, for the purpose of loving Israel back to Himself, has in part had a hateful, confused, and deceived anti-Semitic bride. For those who say that the Jews failed God and thus the church took their place, I hope they take this as instruction. Many in the church have failed God just as miserably. I personally have and I would guess that at one time or another you have too.

Dr. Michael Brown preached a message "All Israel Shall Be Saved" in which he speaks of documented anti-Semitism in the church. The well-known yet rarely discussed Crusades are a grisly reality of church history. In an attempt to liberate the holy places, the crusaders began to kill the Jews, as they were the "assassins of Christ." Of course the crusaders killed many Muslims as well. Brown says a popular saying was "Kill a Jew and save your soul." He speaks of a crusader army that was moving on Jerusalem in the year 1099. "With crosses on their uniforms they gathered all the Jews that were fleeing, and they were all herded together at the great synagogue in Jerusalem. As they took refuge in the synagogue the crusaders marched around the building they had set on fire, and marched around the building singing "Christ We Adore Thee." Brown goes on to speak of documented atrocities, some of which were forced conversions, which included a renouncing of any trace of Jewish practice or affiliation upon the threat of death and other terrible persecution.[17]

In Nazi Germany on November 10, 1938, *Kristallnacht* (night of broken glass) marked the beginning of the most horrible persecution of the Jews. The date chosen for this event was Martin Luther's birthday to commemorate the reformer's doctrines of hatred toward the Jews. I have a friend that works for a wonderful ministry called Jews for Jesus. He tells the story of a very surprising encounter that a young lady working for Jews For Jesus had while passing out gospel tracks in New York City. An elderly Jewish woman walked

---

[17] Michael Brown, *All Israel Shall Be Saved,* sermon at Brownsville Assembly of God, March 19, 2000.

up to her, and having determined the nature of her activity, rolled up her sleeve revealing the Nazi concentration camp number on her arm. She then accused the young lady that she was finishing Hitler's work. Why? The terrible acts of persecution committed against the Jews in the name of Jesus are the reason for her disgust with those who believe in Him. Something wonderful then took place. At Jews For Jesus they began praying for this woman. She later came to their office and gave her life to the Jewish Messiah Jesus! This glorious redemption is a bright light that shines through the shroud of hidden darkness in the Protestant church.

What has happened to our faith that its identity has become so anti-Jewish? Could it be that we have been robbed of our identity? Robbed by these men of old who have been labeled as the church fathers? Some of these men have deceived and motivated so many to persecute and even kill God's people in the name of their own Messiah. Today, Satan is using these doctrines of demons attempting to teach believers in Jesus to hate, or at least esteem lightly, God's chosen people in the name of their Messiah. Satan has used these men in an attempt to tear up our faith by the roots. Could it be that we have been robbed and, in some areas of our faith, given a counterfeit?

Is there a reason we should feel shame? The reason is that the hatred of Jews that I have identified is not limited to isolated incidences in history. This has been the way of thinking for many who claim Jesus' name throughout history and right up to this very minute! Quoting a Catholic priest's documentation of anti-Semitism in the church, Michael Brown says, "The pages of history that the Jews have memorized, Christians have torn out of the books."[18] We act as if the church has been a friend or, at worst, indifferent to the Jewish people. In large part, this is due to an ignorance of history. The reality of the matter is well said by Brown in another quote regarding the Jews being labeled as "Christ killers." "It thundered

---

[18] Ibid.

down through history: God hates the Jews!"[19] Should we not be ashamed?

In chapter 2 I shared an unpleasant experience about my friend the pastor. Do you remember what one of the anger-stirring issues was at his church? I was standing up for "those Jews who killed Jesus!" Things haven't changed much. Oh, I am greatly ashamed of such horrible notions by those who claim the same God that I serve. Friends, the acts of hatred I am writing of don't begin to scratch the surface of the many hateful deeds done to the Jews in the name of Jesus. Many good books have been written for the purpose of bringing to light this truth in greater detail, and I recommend that you search one out. As we learn the truth and humble ourselves, I believe the Lord will grant us repentance, and open our eyes to a more authentic understanding of our identity in Christ.

Many sins have been born out of the anti-Semitism of the early church. One is the terribly false doctrine of replacement theology. Replacement theology is based on the premise that, as a result of their rebellion to God, He has replaced the Jews with the church. This means that all of the promises to the Jews are now promises to the church. Of course the Jews are not left out all the way as they still get the curses and judgments. At this point when you see good things in the Bible that pertain to Israel, that really isn't Israel, that is the church. When you see Israel being judged and chastised by the Lord, that would be the real Israel. Hmm, makes a lot of sense, doesn't it? The more you dislike the Jews the more sense it makes.

Some subtle terms will identify replacement theology immediately. We have discussed one, which is "true Jews," meaning those in the church are now the Jews and the Jews are not. Another replacement term is "new Israel." The late Derek Prince wrote about this man-made label for Jesus' church.

---

[19] Ibid.

To recover the truth about the identity of Israel it is necessary to go back to the actual text of the New Testament and see how the apostles used the term *Israel*. This is the only legitimate basis for a scripturally accurate use of this term. Ever since the canon of Scripture was closed, no subsequent writer or preacher has been authorized to change the usage established by the apostolic writers of the New Testament. Any writer or preacher who introduces a different application of the term *Israel* forfeits the right to claim scriptural authority for what he or she has to say about Israel. I have discovered seventy-nine instances in the New Testament where the words Israel or Israelite occur. After examining them all, I conclude that the apostles never used *Israel* as a synonym for the church. Nor does the phrase *the new Israel* occur anywhere in the New Testament. Preachers who use that phrase should take care to define their use of it. They should also state that it is not found in the Bible.[20]

Replacement theology has confused the identity of Israel and the church in our minds, and can be identified by terms such as "new Israel."

What do the Jewish leaders or rabbis teach about believing in Jesus as it relates to Jewish identity? They, hoodwinked by the enemy, have attempted to make belief in Jesus Christ a Gentile thing to do. Tragically, by and large, the body of Christ has accommodated the teachers of Jewish faith in this effort, thus deluding the church even further.

There are three primary streams of Judaism, each having many arteries. They are Orthodox, Conservative, and Reform Judaism. In as much as these basic forms of Jewish thought contradict each other in many ways, there is one thing that unites them with great solidarity: "You cannot believe in Jesus and be Jewish!" Even with the liberal, in many cases, completely un-Jewish tolerances

---

[20] Derek Prince, *Prophetic Destinies* (Orlando: Creation House, 1992) 15.

that Reform Judaism expresses, they still cannot think of belief in Jesus as anything but a betrayal of the Jewish people. I heard one person say that "a Reform Jew can believe in Buddah, bicycling, or basket weaving, but can't believe in Jesus and be Jewish." This is their contribution to the lie "believing in Jesus is not for those who are Jewish."

To understand this strictly from a human perspective we must remember that the Jewish people who subscribe to these affiliations are for the most part descendants of those who have been tortured, persecuted, or at least disliked by many who profess the name of Jesus. From their perspective, the Jewish people have a pretty good excuse not to believe in Him. "Why should I believe in your God who used His people to kill my people." We also know the majority of them have descended from the Jews who rejected Messiah Jesus, and have no excuse before God (Romans 2:28–29). However, the Bible states the reality of a partial hardening over the hearts of the Jews until the time of the Gentiles is fulfilled (Romans 11:25). In basic terms this reveals some Jewish perspective on the source of confusion as it relates to the Jewishness of our faith in Jesus.

Interestingly, there is one religion that seems to understand the relationship between the Jews and the Gentile followers of Jesus more than both of these groups. Koran-believing, obedient Muslims understand more than most Christians the relationship between Israel and the true church. Here is a quote from a Friday service at a mosque in Yemen. "Oh Allah, finish off our enemies, who are enemies of our religion. The Jews and their friends the Christians are enemies of our religion. Let the ground shake under the feet of the Jews. Put fear into the hearts of Jews and Christians, and let their blood freeze in their veins."[21] As the Jewish holy day is Saturday and traditionally the Christian's is Sunday, Islam has a saying: "We will kill the Jews on Saturday and their friends the

---

[21] *Israel Today: Friday Sermons Incite the Arab Masses,* 9.

Christians on Sunday." You see, Islam understands that there is an undeniable relationship between the nation of Israel (people and land) and the church of Jesus Christ.

They have even perverted a beautiful word, which describes something God greatly cares about, into an ugly term in the eyes of the world. The word is *Zion*.

Zion is used over one hundred and fifty times in the Bible. Here is a fairly comprehensive definition from a Hebrew study resource. "Zion is the fortified mound between the Kidron and the Tyropean Valleys that David conquered from the Jebusites (2 Samuel 5:7). It became known as the City of David. With the building of the Temple to the North that hill later became known as Mount Zion. Zion may even refer specifically to the Temple vicinity or more generally to Jerusalem itself. Sometimes it includes the entire nation of Israel and the covenant community itself."[22] By the way, who is the covenant community? It is Israel and the Gentiles who believe in Jesus Christ.

That would be you and I! "Zion appears most frequently in Psalms and Lamentation. It refers to the political capitol of Judah but much more often stands for the city of God in the new age."[23]

We see here that depending on the context in Scripture, Zion refers to a few things. Zion refers to a geographical place in Israel, the Jewish people, or the Gentiles who believe in Jesus. Do you see what this means? When Zion is being attacked, the land of Israel, the Jewish people, and the church of Jesus are under attack. Why do I say that? The reason is that we are in the same covenant with Abraham!

---

[22] *Theological Wordbook of the Old Testament,* 764.
[23] Ibid.

As a result of the satanic deception of the world, and too often the church, we hear things like this: I am not anti-Jewish just anti-Zion. The world is rallying around this vehement disgust for biblical Zionism. The mosques across the globe and especially in the Middle Eastern countries are laden with Muslim clerics that spew their hatred for the Zionists. A radio program in Syria hosts a Muslim cleric: "Oh Allah, support our comrades in Palestine and on the Golan Heights and help them destroy the Zionists."[24] This propaganda is taking hold and most in the world are confused at best.

> *For God will save Zion and build the cities of Judah, that they may dwell there and possess it.*
>
> (Psalm 69:35)

May we attempt to understand not only the source, but the reality of the identity crisis in the body of Christ, so that we can accurately appraise the authenticity of our faith. Jesus said in John 4:23:

> *But the hour is coming, and now is, when the true worshipers will worship the Father in spirit and truth; for the Father is seeking such to worship Him.*

Oh, that we would worship King Jesus in spirit and truth!

---

[24] *Israel Today*, 9.

CHAPTER 8

The Effect of Deception

. . . who exchanged the truth of God for the lie,

(Romans 1:25)

The deception that infected the church, regarding the Jewish heritage of Christianity, has been woven into the very fabric of our beliefs. Every facet of our Christian, or Christ-centered existence, has been affected. Our understanding of God including who He is, who we are, and our responsibilities to Him and others, has been altered by God's enemies (the world, the flesh, and the devil). In our minds God's order that helps us define and structure the local church has been drastically changed. Our identity has been stolen from us, and to a great degree replaced with a counterfeit.

One of the pilfered treasuries is the glorious word of God revealed in the Jewish Scriptures. I would not have imagined that I had any replacement theology in my interpretation of the Bible. Then I recognized the wrong interpretation of Isaiah 52:7–8 that we discussed in chapter 6. Surprisingly, I received this error from a church where, by and large, people supported the Jews. You may remember this church from my testimony at the beginning.

Why did these supporters of Israel teach me to change the meaning of Isaiah 52:7–8? It had purposely been reinterpreted years ago, handed down through the church age, received by my friends as truth, and then given to me. The intention by those who changed the meaning was to remove the Jewishness from the Scriptures. We are being taught the Bible from an ethnically cleansed identity. This is robbery!

We have been taught to understand the Scriptures devoid of our true roots, and have been given distorted glasses through which to observe, interpret, and then apply the Bible to our lives. The problem with wrong thinking about Israel and our relationship has taken on many forms, which has sullied the authenticity of our faith in ways that are difficult to imagine. An understanding of our Jewish spiritual heritage determines much of our ability to accurately know the God of the Jewish Scriptures.

One reason for the skewed vision that impairs our understanding of the Bible is that we are reading the Bible through Greco-Roman glasses. There are many good resources available that will explain this in great detail, one of which is a book by Marvin Wilson, *Our Father Abraham*. There is a relationship between this book and the Center for Judaic Christian Studies based out of Dayton, Ohio, which also has balanced resources for gaining understanding of our Jewish roots. Another book, which is more anecdotal, is *Echoes of His Presence* by Ray Vander Laan. The Bible is an Eastern book that we have been interpreting with Western glasses. I will give an example:

In Matthew 11:29–30 Jesus said,

"Take my yoke upon you and learn from Me, for I am gentle and lowly in heart, and you will find rest for your souls. For My yoke is easy and My burden is light."

Most in the church have been taught that the yoke of Jesus is simply a reference to the farm instrument that harnesses animals together. After all, that is the meaning in other places of Scripture. Yet, in this passage of Matthew, the only way to fully understand this reference is to understand the social culture of that day, which would include faith in the context of our Jewish heritage. We must understand and be nourished by our own Jewish roots. Let's look at Matthew 11:29–30 through a pair of Jewish lenses.

In the Jewish faith, during the time of our Lord's earthly ministry, there were many traveling rabbis. By the way, what human occupation had the Lord Jesus been given by His Father? Was it not that of a traveling rabbi? As rabbis would travel about the countryside, certain Jewish young men would decide to follow them. These traveling rabbis would not only teach their disciples the writings of Moses, but also their own personal interpretation and application of the over six hundred laws therein. My, what a task to learn and then live out in one's life.

In Acts 15:10 we see the difficulty of keeping the law as Peter was discussing how to deal with the new Gentile converts to this new sect of Judaism (sect of the Nazarenes, Acts 24:5):

> Now therefore, why do you test God by putting a yoke on the neck of the disciples which neither our fathers nor we were able to bear?

Here we see a reference of the yoke of the law, much the same as these traveling rabbis would teach.

Can you imagine how burdensome it was to not only keep these laws, but then to apply them according to the interpretation of assorted traveling rabbis? The followers of a particular Jewish teacher were called his *talmudim*, or disciples as we know them. There was a term used to describe the decision to follow or become a disciple of a rabbi. It was *to take on his yoke*. So Jesus, the traveling rabbi, told them to "take His yoke upon them," meaning that compared to any other yoke, or rabbi's disciplined teaching, His yoke was easy and His burden was light. Why? This was not an ordinary itinerant rabbi with ordinary teachings of the Law of Moses. This was the Messiah whose yoke is the law of the Spirit, which is also called the law of liberty in the second chapter of Jacob (James). This rabbi and this law bring liberty from the law of sin and death (Romans 8:2).

The authentic Jewish perspective gives clarity to the passage. This is the perspective from which the Scripture was written. Here we see an authenticity that results from a true interpretation that is seldom taught today. Are there other places like this in the Bible? The answer is yes. There is so much of our faith from the Jewish Scriptures just waiting to be understood with greater accuracy. This is a small example of much that the Lord desires to show us. When we receive this genuine perspective, we will be dazzled with the renewed brilliance of His word. Though we have read the words, there is an unmined treasure we have never known!

In Dwight Pryor's teaching, *Our Hebrew Lord*, he discusses another commonly misinterpreted passage. In Matthew 6:22–23 Jesus says:

> *"The lamp of the body is the eye. If therefore your eye is good, your whole body will be full of light. But if your eye is bad, your whole body will be full of darkness. If therefore the light that is in you is darkness, how great is that darkness!"*

This Scripture has often been interpreted and taught to mean that if a person doesn't have pure or single-minded devotion to Christ, the person is deceived by the supposed light he or she possesses. However, Jesus is actually talking about something completely different. In reality He is talking about greed. The Jewish way of thinking understood an evil eye that was full of darkness to be one of greed. Proverbs 28:22:

A man with an evil eye hastens after riches, and does not consider that poverty will come upon him.

So many have simply been taught this Scripture from a Western understanding of the words in the text.

Like an article of tarnished silver that has been polished, this more accurate understanding gives brilliance to the Scripture that was hidden by the dinginess of Western misinterpretation. These are just a couple of many examples that demonstrate the importance of appreciating and understanding the Jewishness of our faith. The alternative is a Bible interpretation that is tarnished at best, and dangerously erroneous at worst. In John 4:23, God's word tells us the Father is looking for those who will worship Him in spirit and in truth. Wouldn't you like your understanding of God to be more genuine?

What does God's word say about correct Bible interpretation?

Be diligent to present yourself approved to God, a worker who does not need to be ashamed, rightly dividing the word of truth.
(2 Timothy 2:15)

These may seem like small nuances to some, but realize there are a multitude of places in Scripture that have suffered over sixteen hundred years of westernizing. From years past, those who had the motive of unearthing our Jewish roots in Jesus have damaged our understanding of God's word. Remember what the devil said to Eve: *Hath God said?* The purer understanding of the Bible will come from understanding our Jewish heritage in Jesus.

Philosophies of the great Western civilizations of Greece and Rome began to creep into the church as our Jewish roots were severed. Greek philosophy is commonly the antithesis of Hebrew, or biblical Hebraic thinking. It is also the antithesis of God Himself. The Greco-Roman mind places selfish man at the center of the universe. We know that the Lord is to be the star of the show. The many different strains of Greek, or any other humanistic philosophy, usually get it backward in that they exalt man, creation, or both. Let's look at this mind-set to see if we can detect it in the modern church age.

One way the Greek thinker exalts himself is by great emphasis placed on his superior ability to seek after, then attain knowledge and wisdom. In 1 Corinthians, Paul speaks of the Greeks' appraisal of the message of the cross as "foolishness," as they were seeking for human wisdom. He also addresses them as the debaters of this age, and in the power of the Holy Spirit Paul rebukes the wisdom of man. We see the wisdom of man on a collision course with the wisdom of God in 1 Corinthians 1:10–3:23. Listen to this strong word from Isaiah quoted in 1 Corinthians 1:19:

> *For it is written: "I will destroy the wisdom of the wise, and bring to nothing the understanding of the prudent."*

We also see that man's wisdom is foolishness to God.

> *Has not God made foolish the wisdom of this world?*
> *(1 Corinthians 1:20b)*

To whom was Paul addressing these sharp admonitions? It was to those of the Greco-Roman mind-set, which dominated most of the earth at the time the apostolic epistles were written. It is simply the worship of man on the altar of the acquisition of knowledge.

Of course, God's word commands us to seek after knowledge and wisdom.

> *The fear of the LORD is the beginning of knowledge, but fools despise wisdom and instruction.*
> *(Proverbs 1:7)*

Grace and peace be multiplied to you in the knowledge of God and of Jesus our Lord, as His divine power has given to us all things that pertain to life and godliness, through the knowledge of Him who called us by glory and virtue . . .

(2 Peter 1:2–3)

In basic terms, knowledge is information, while wisdom pertains to the most excellent application of that knowledge. So we see that to seek after knowledge and wisdom is of the Lord.

However, in God's word we are instructed that not all knowledge and wisdom is good. For example, was the knowledge that Eve desired good knowledge? She was promised the wisdom and knowledge of God, yet that is not at all what she got. Her motivation was lust of the flesh, lust of the eyes, and the pride of life. The wisdom we are to seek is God's wisdom. Where do we find it? In the Jewish Scriptures and the ancient Jewish heritage into which we have been grafted. The wisdom of God is tangibly different than man's; as God's wisdom bears good fruit. James 3:17–18:

But the wisdom that is from above is first pure, then peaceable, gentle, willing to yield, full of mercy and good fruits, without partiality and without hypocrisy. Now, the fruit of righteousness is sown in peace by those who make peace.

As we continue to form a basic appraisal of Greco-Roman thinking, using God's word as the standard, we see that this pursuit of mental assent by human knowledge and wisdom is futile, as it exalts man and not God. It makes one proud, aloof, or puffed up as Paul says in 1 Corinthians 8:1–3:

*Now concerning things offered to idols: We know that we all have knowledge. **Knowledge puffs up, but love edifies.** And if anyone thinks that he knows anything, he knows nothing yet as he ought to know. But if anyone loves God, this one is known by Him.*

These Scriptures show us what happens to a church that is working with a Greco-Roman mind-set. It is in danger of becoming puffed up with an acquisition of knowledge motivated by the promotion of self. There is even a term given to one who is aloof and a bit untouchable, with a continuous, possibly intimidating, deep and thoughtful look on his face. This person might be all tangled up in his own little world of knowledge and thought. What would he be called? He would be labeled *stoic*, named after one of the ancient Greek philosophers.

Has this unhealthy brand of desiring knowledge truly been handed down from generations by our so-called church fathers? One of the titles given to John Chrysostym was a Doctor of the Church.[25] I know many humble, meek, and godly pastors and leaders who are called doctors of theology today. The pastor who is also a doctor is rather common in American Christianity. I am very thankful for some of the more scholarly in Christ's body, as they have helped, and I am sure will continue to assist, some of the less scholarly like me along profoundly. I know a dear pastor with three earned doctorates, and in terms of his demeanor, you would never know it from talking to him. I get the impression that he is more thankful to be known as a pastor than a doctor.

Yet, I also know some who might as well have their doctorate on a large gold necklace and wear it on their chest. It is a great doctor mentality which espouses, "You can't question what I say about the things of God. Don't you know I am a doctor?" These with a head knowledge, that know much about God but really don't personally know Him very well, are our inheritance from the Greco-Roman intrusion into Jesus' body.

Again, the word of God is clear that we must seek after knowledge and wisdom. And there are many who are seeking these degrees of higher learning with pure motives.

---

[25] *When Day and Night Cease,* 234.

However, when men place more prestige on the title of doctor, which man gave, and less on the title of the calling of pastor teacher, which God gave, then we have a Greco-Roman smudge on the garments of Jesus' righteous bride.

We must remember what we are talking about here is the wisdom of man. It is this great desire for knowledge so that one can know more, and the subtlety is very dangerous. The motivation that causes church leaders to get enamored with themselves from the knowledge they are attaining has an unhealthy emphasis on learning that isn't motivated by godly incentives. Remember that the Lord judges the heart. Hebrews 4:12:

> *For the word of God is living and powerful, and sharper than any two-edged sword, piercing even to the division of soul and spirit, and of joints and marrow, **and is a discerner of the thoughts and intents of the heart.***

God knows whether we are operating under man's wisdom or God's wisdom.

Also, there is a spiritual reality that I believe many leaders have forgotten. If the knowledge that we have in our mind about God hasn't been communicated by God's Spirit to our spirit, and then illuminated to our mind, it is dry, hollow, head knowledge. Speaking of the things of the Spirit, God shows us this in 1 Corinthians 2:10–14:

> *But God has revealed them to us through His Spirit. For the Spirit searches all things, yes, the deep things of God. For what man knows the things of a man except the spirit of the man which is in him? Even so no one knows the things of God except the Spirit of God. Now we have received, not the spirit of the world, but the Spirit who is from God, that we might know the things that have been freely given to us by God. These things we also speak, not in words which*

man's wisdom teaches but which the Holy Spirit teaches, comparing spiritual things with spiritual. But the natural man does not receive the things of the Spirit of God, for they are foolishness to him; nor can he know them, because they are spiritually discerned.

Here, the natural man is the unsaved. Yet, beloved, when a man walks in human wisdom, which is the futility of his own mind, his knowledge *about God* becomes irrelevant. Knowing about God is insignificant unless we are abiding in Him. Today, the majority of Christians in the modern Western church know *about* the Lord Jesus, but have little, if any, relationship *with* Him.

Has this Western mind-set trickled down from the modern leadership into the body? I would like to share a story about a woman who was a madam of a house of ill repute. She was gloriously saved and became a world-wide evangelist. Her testimony was powerful and she was invited to speak at many places.

One place was a very prominent church about which many in Christian circles have heard. After speaking and spending some time there she was reported to have noticed how knowledgeable everyone was. They had concordances, lexicons, and other Bible interpretation study helps. There was only one thing, or better said, one Person missing. His name is Jesus! She was heard to have said: "They were so deep that they were sunk." The great search for learning was alive and well, but they weren't. Why? This great prominent church, as many are today, was operating like the Greek philosopher. I can speak on this with great authority, as I have been so deep that I have been sunk in my walk, or lack thereof, with Jesus. So, yes, this thinking has become a great factor in modern faith in Jesus.

The Western form of thought would have some other implications. Remember that we are trying to determine if, and if so, in what detectable way, this Western seed of man's wisdom has been sown into the modern church. One shoot, or growth, from this seed would be less emphasis on relationship and more on philosophical or doctrinal understanding. Don't get me wrong: God's word is clear that accurate Bible doctrine is essential for the integrity of the faith. What I am talking about is the unbalanced confidence in mental assent and quest for knowledge for the sake of exalting self and not to glorify and serve the Lord Jesus. Let's look at the implications of that type of thinking on a church.

This type of learning would not produce a collective group of individuals with a love *for* Jesus Christ as much as it would create those who knew a lot *about* Him. This would not be a holy place. It would be very worldly, though surprisingly it might have teaching that is sound. Only those who are abiding in Jesus can live the spiritual life of Christ.

In John 15:5 the Lord says:

"I am the vine, you are the branches. He who abides in Me, and I in him, bears much fruit; for without Me you can do nothing."

At that point you wouldn't see people caring for the needs of others. Why? Remember, man's love cares first for himself. If the Greek mind-set were in the church today, it wouldn't make for a body of believers that is operating biblically in the spiritual gifts. Instead there would be a room full of people who want to know more information. In many cases the extent of relationship and understanding people would have with their spiritual family would be that which could be realized from looking at the back of someone's head from the pew behind them on Sunday morning. The order of this philosophy would facilitate a place where one person got up to teach everyone else information, so they could learn what they should know. Yet, because so many don't love or know Jesus very well, the consequences would be extremely noticeable.

Of course if this worldly mind-set were being employed it would produce hearers not doers. They would be people who have

111

learned much but don't do what they have learned. Why? There are a lot of reasons, but here are a few. This church has grieved God so terribly that He isn't filling her with His Spirit so that people have an unction to do what they have learned. To a great degree it is a wealth of useless head knowledge. All the while there would be much human activity in the name of Jesus. However, they wouldn't sense that dying to themselves and living for Jesus is all that important. After all, they have fulfilled their religious responsibilities by going to church every week, doing church activities, and giving their money in some cases. The most dangerous characteristic is they would think they were just fine even though they wouldn't have a love relationship with Jesus. They would resemble the Laodicean church.

Revelation 3:14–19:

"And to the angel of the church of the Laodiceans write, 'These things says the Amen, the Faithful and True Witness, the Beginning of the creation of God: "I know your works, that you are neither cold nor hot. I could wish you were cold or hot. So then, because you are lukewarm, and neither cold nor hot, I will vomit you out of My mouth. Because you say, 'I am rich, have become wealthy, and have need of nothing'—and do not know that you are wretched, miserable, poor, blind, and naked—I counsel you to buy from Me gold refined in the fire, that you may be rich; and white garments, that you may be clothed, that the shame of your nakedness may not be revealed; and anoint your eyes with eye salve, that you may see. As many as I love, I rebuke and chasten. Therefore be zealous and repent."

Here is a great example of the Greek philosophy thriving in the modern church. I was sitting in a pastor's office talking with him about matters of faith and the current condition of the church in America. As we were discussing the average American Christian's lack of holiness and denying self to follow Jesus, the pastor said something that startled me. He said something like this: "We tell them the truth; if they don't listen that's their problem." You see, he believes that his responsibility is to give information, and that the people in the body's responsibility is to get and then use that information. The problem is that Jesus told us as ministers to leave the ninety-nine to go and rescue the one. Church is more than a lecture class at a seminary! This is the body of Christ, and if one is held captive by the enemy then we are all being attacked! The human shepherds that Jesus placed in leadership must feed the sheep. That means more than giving information on Wednesday nights and Sunday mornings.

If God's children are in rebellion and not listening to God's word, they first need to be approached in love and admonished (Galatians 6:1–2; 1 Thessalonians 5:12–13). If admonishment is rejected they must be disciplined so that there will be restoration and healing. This will also keep the cancer of sin from spreading through the body (Matthew 18:15–20; 1 Corinthians 5; Hebrews 13:7, 17). There seems to be some evidence that supports the claim that there is a wrong way of thinking in the body of Messiah. Many shepherds are not shepherding.

In the thirty-fourth chapter of Ezekiel, the Lord warns the shepherds to watch over God's flock. Though this specific reference is to Israel, I believe there is a legitimate application for the leaders of the New Covenant flock as well. Ezekiel 34:4:

The weak you have not strengthened, nor have you healed those who were sick, nor bound up the broken, nor brought back what was driven away, nor sought what was lost; but with force and cruelty you have ruled them.

The Lord gives a reference in the new covenant of such leaders:

"I am the good shepherd. The good shepherd gives His life for the sheep. But a hireling, he who is not the shepherd, one who does not own the sheep, sees the wolf coming and leaves the sheep and flees; and the wolf catches the sheep and scatters them. The hireling flees because he is a hireling and does not care about the sheep."

(John 10:11–13)

Could the Western mind-set be producing hirelings?

There are quite a few characteristics that Western thought might produce were it in our modern church. The last one I will discuss is an inappropriate affection for the things of this world. Why? Remember, the man of worldly wisdom has a worldly admiration for things created. God calls it idolatry.

As the Holy Spirit breathes the word of judgment to the Gentiles onto the pages of Romans 1:22–25, could we be hearing a warning for a great number in church today?

Professing to be wise, they became fools, and changed the glory of the incorruptible God into an image made like corruptible man—and birds and four-footed animals and creeping things. Therefore God also gave them up to uncleanness, in the lusts of their hearts, to dishonor their bodies among themselves, who exchanged the truth of God for the lie, and worshiped and served the creature rather than the Creator, who is blessed forever. Amen.

The Complete Word Study Dictionary by Spiros Zodhiates defines *creature* in this passage as: "denotes a particular created thing."[26] The apostle John warned us in 1 John 2:15:

---

[26] Spiros Zodhiates, *The Complete Word Study Dictionary: New Testament* (Chattanooga, TN: AMG Publishers, 1992) 897.

*Do not love the world or the **things** in the world. If anyone loves the world, the love of the Father is not in him.*

In the first chapter of Romans, Paul warns the Gentiles of judgment according to the wicked propensities toward which they gravitate. He does the same with the Jews in chapter 2.

God divides the whole world's population in two ways. Romans 1:16:

*For I am not ashamed of the gospel of Christ, for it is the power of God to salvation for everyone who believes, for the **Jew** first and also for the **Greek**.*

The term *Greek* refers to non-Jewish or Gentile people. Why the term *Greek*? The Roman Empire, ruling most of the "civilized" world at that time, worshiped Greek philosophy to the extent that it became a driving force in the thinking of the Gentile world. God is pronouncing judgment on the Gentiles, and this Greek philosophy is a significant factor that angers the Lord. We see worship of that which is created provoking a holy God to judgment.

There is a modern term for the unhealthy admiration and desire for the things of this world. What is worse is that the American church is up to its neck in the quagmire of this ancient iniquity with a new name: materialism. It is so pervasive in America that there are doctrines of demons flourishing in the church today asserting the notion *God wants you to be rich*. If you aren't rich it is because of your sin, ignorance of your new covenant rights, or unbelief. It is so crazy that I won't even spend any paper from this book addressing it. In some churches it is not so blatant, yet there is a subtle undercurrent of thinking that *always* equates worldly beauty and the acquisition of things with blessings from God. We in the church must understand that the sin of idolatry is very serious to God, and with it comes consequences that, sadly, many have not considered. An entire book could be written about this Greco-

Roman characteristic that plagues the church today. For our purposes we will just identify it and draw toward a conclusion.

And what is the conclusion? I believe the evidence speaks for itself. We have briefly discussed the Greco-Roman mind and how it has adversely affected the church. We have seen the following: tampering with correct interpretation of Scripture, in great part for the purpose of replacing Israel with the church; man's knowledge and wisdom for the purpose of exalting self; many who are knowledgeable about Jesus but don't love Jesus; humanistic churches without the Spirit of the Messiah; individuals in a crowded building instead of living members of Jesus' body; lecture hall leaders instead of shepherds; and worship of the created instead of the Creator.

Is the Greco-Roman philosophy driving the church in America? I will depart from this chapter with a Scripture:

> *Beware lest anyone cheat you through philosophy and empty deceit, according to the tradition of men, according to the basic principles of the world, and not according to Christ.*
>
> (Colossians 2:8)

CHAPTER 9

Traditions of Men

For when one says, "I am of Paul," and another, "I am of Apollos,"
are you not carnal?

(1 Corinthians 3:4)

Of all the chapters in this book, this and the next one I write with the greatest apprehension. For the sake of truth written in these chapters, I am risking the popularity of this book, and consequently the number of people who will read and then be helped by it. However, my highest priority is serving King Jesus. I trust that the fruit from pure motives will be of a higher quality than that of my human reasoning, which would produce a more-palatable, yet less-truthful book. Please be ready to handle the truth and be set free!

If the root of our faith is Jewish and the thinking in the church is Greco-Roman—which has damaged our faith—then exactly how was this wrong thinking handed down to us today? In what vehicle did these man-made philosophies travel to arrive at our doorstep?

The first thing Satan did in this regard was to deceive the men we have already spoken of into hating the Jewish people. One of the goals of this strategy was to damage the foundation of Jesus' church. As Paul is writing to the church in Ephesus, he addresses the Gentile believers as those adopted into the commonwealth of Israel, and clarifies the nature of the foundation of the church.

Now, therefore, you are no longer strangers and foreigners, but fellow citizens with the saints and members of the household of God, having been built on the foundation of the apostles and prophets, Jesus Christ Himself being the chief cornerstone.

(Ephesians 2:19–20)

Of course, in time there were Gentile prophets in the churches as well. But those who God first chose to establish His body were Jews, including the chief cornerstone, Messiah Jesus.

As we established earlier, the Lord planted two trees, which are found in Romans 11:16–24:

For if the firstfruit is holy, the lump is also holy; and if the root is holy, so are the branches. And if some of the branches were broken off, and you, being a wild olive tree, were grafted in among them, and with them became a partaker of the root and fatness of the olive tree, do not boast against the branches. But if you do boast, remember that you do not support the root, but the root supports you. You will say then, "Branches were broken off that I might be grafted in." Well said. Because of unbelief they were broken off, and you stand by faith. Do not be haughty, but fear. For if God did not spare the natural branches, He may not spare you either. Therefore consider the goodness and severity of God: on those who fell, severity; but toward you, goodness, if you continue in His goodness. Otherwise you also will be cut off. And they also, if they do not continue in unbelief, will be grafted in, for God is able to graft them in again. For if you were cut out of the olive tree which is wild by nature,

118

and were grafted contrary to nature into a cultivated olive tree, how much more will these, who are natural branches, be grafted into their own olive tree?

The first is a natural cultivated olive tree, which represents Israel. The other is a wild olive tree that illustrates the Gentiles. The root of the natural tree is Abraham, Isaac, and Jacob. The branches are the Jewish people. Here, God's word teaches that the original faith of the Jewish people literally holds up the faith of the church. Have you ever heard of the term the Judeo-Christian faith? What does that term mean? It refers to the faith that started with the faith of Abraham, Isaac, and Jacob. This tree of Jewish faith then had Gentile branches grafted into it from the second of two trees. This tree of faith needs its Hebrew root to nourish the trunk and the branches. Remember from one of the above Scriptures: *You do not support the root, but the root supports you.*

Why do the Gentile branches need nourishment from the root of the host tree? The reason is that now they are grafted into the Jewish tree, with Gentile branches, and are no longer a part of the Gentile tree. When you graft a branch from a tree into another one, it is an obvious fact that it cannot be part of the former tree. The branches of the two trees that are maintained from the root of the covenant God made with Abraham, Isaac, and Jacob have become one tree with a Jewish root system.

We see this in Ephesians 2:11–16:

Therefore remember that you, once Gentiles in the flesh—who are called Uncircumcision by what is called the Circumcision made in the flesh by hands—that at that time you were without Christ, being aliens from the commonwealth of Israel and strangers from the covenants of promise, having no hope and without God in the world. But now in Christ Jesus you who once were far off have been brought near by the blood of Christ. For He Himself is our peace,

*who has made both one, and has broken down the middle wall of
separation having abolished in His flesh the enmity, that is, the law
of commandments contained in ordinances, so as to create in Himself
one new man from the two, thus making peace, and that He might
reconcile them both to God in one body through the cross, thereby
putting to death the enmity.*

Now, this is not to say that a Gentile who believes in Jesus stops
being a Gentile physically and culturally, to the extent that it isn't
former sinful behavior, and somehow becomes Jewish. What it does
say is that the person's soul-saving faith and spiritual identity has a
Jewish heritage, which is a tangible element to the life of the Gentile
convert. The covenants, and the Messiah (Christ) are Jewish. If the
two—Jews and Gentiles in Jesus—become one, then how can there
not be a Jewish influence in spiritual identity?

Thus, there is necessary life-giving nourishment, which can
only be obtained through abiding in that authentic biblical faith.
Remember, the Father is looking for those who will worship in
spirit and in truth. In plain speech this means that to pretend our
faith doesn't have Jewish roots, which nourish us as the branches,
is extremely damaging to our faith. What happens to a tree that has
damaged roots? The rest of the tree including the branches (that is
us) suffers tremendously. The predominantly Gentile church must
recognize that our faith has been damaged as a result of being ripped
up by the roots and given a counterfeit root system.

Deceived men rose up and attempted to sever us from and
graft us into another tree. Remember, from the eleventh chapter
of Romans, that God planted two trees, not three. Don't look in
the Bible for this third tree it's not there. Men attempted with great
success to plant a third tree; or lay a new foundation.

*For no other foundation can anyone lay than that which is laid,
which is Jesus Christ.*

(1 Corinthians 3:11)

Jesus warned us that many would come in His name, which is what these men did when they tried to lay a new foundation or plant a third tree. This new tree was planted with the purposeful goal to erase any Jewish-ness from our faith in Jesus the Jewish Messiah. *You will see a diagram of this third tree later in the book.* You may remember this quote of Constantine, founder of the Catholic Church, from earlier in the book. "We desire to have nothing in common with this so hated people, for Christ has marked out *another path* for us." This other pathway is not that of the Lord.

In Acts 20:29–31 the apostle Paul warned us of Mr. Constantine:

> *For I know this, that after my departure savage wolves will come in among you, not sparing the flock. Also from among yourselves men will rise up, speaking perverse things, to draw away the disciples after themselves. Therefore watch, and remember that for three years I did not cease to warn everyone night and day with tears.*

Constantine and his new religion did draw many disciples after himself. Many of his contemporaries did the same thing as they assaulted the faith with horrible error in the name of Jesus. We have seen this in earlier quotes. I am not saying he invented anti-Semitism or replacement theology. However, he was very influential in making it and other horribly false doctrines part of mainstream Christianity.

In 1 John 2:18–23 we see the person and spirit of Antichrist:

> *Little children, it is the last hour; and as you have heard that the Anti-christ is coming, even now many anti-christs have come, by which we know that it is the last hour. They went out from us, but they were not of us; for if they had been of us, they would have continued with us; but they went out that they might be made manifest, that none of them were of us. But you have an anointing*

from the Holy One, and you know all things. I have not written to you because you do not know the truth, but because you know it, and that no lie is of the truth. Who is a liar but he who denies that Jesus is the Christ? He is antichrist who denies the Father and the Son. Whoever denies the Son does not have the Father either, he who acknowledges the Son has the Father also.

Antichrist not only means *against Christ*, it means *another Christ*. One tactic of the spirit of antichrist is to present itself *as Christ* to lead people away *from Christ*. The demonic spirit does this in believers and similarly uses the same scheme on the lost to keep them from receiving Jesus Christ. The effect on the believer is deception, rendering their faith less of a threat to the kingdom of darkness, and bringing destruction into the life of the child of God. Of course the most serious consequence of this false spirit for the lost is it leads to an eternity in the lake of fire (Revelation 20:11–14).

Some would say that Constantine didn't deny the Father or the Son. To them I say, "What about others that believe in the Father and the Son, such as Jehovah's Witnesses? They believe in the Father and the Son but their Jesus isn't God. He is created, not Creator. Have they not denied the Son? What about the Mormon who believes that Jesus is the half brother of Satan? Have they not denied the Son? What about Catholic dogma that promotes a way of salvation other than being born again? Do those who hold to a works-based religion founded by Constantine not deny the Son? The reason they have that belief is because the human father of their religion very likely wasn't born again!

Am I saying that there were not, and are not, born-again Catholics? No, there are variations of Catholicism with many beliefs under one name. The Protestant denominations, which are branches from this third tree, are also very fragmented, though there are more of them, thankfully, which teach that we must be born again to be part of God's family. Many of them also teach a literal interpretation of the Bible and are much closer to the truth in terms of doctrine than the Catholic dogma. I am confident that there are born-again Catholics and unregenerated Protestants and vice-versa. However, I am also confident that what is going on in Jesus' name in so many churches, including the Protestants, is less than authentic faith in the Holy One of Israel.

The purpose of this book is not to point a finger at any particular group, because quite frankly all of us need to get back to a more authentic biblical faith in Jesus. I will say that if anyone teaches we don't have to be born again, or that there is any other way to heaven than being forgiven by repentance of sin resulting from faith in Jesus, God the Son, they are preaching another gospel (Luke 24:46–47; John 3:3; Galatians 1:8–9). That would classify them as a cult, not a denomination of the body of Jesus Christ. One of the primary points of this book is that our faith has been uprooted, and we are branches that aren't receiving nourishment from the root of our original tree. I am hopeful that the truths found in these pages will be helpful to you, the seeker of Jesus Christ, in bringing you into a closer and more vibrant walk with the Lord.

Anyway, the Catholic Church, initially headed by Constantine and the Roman Empire in the fourth century, made Christianity the state religion. It also became a conglomeration of many different religions all in the name of Jesus. I will discuss this briefly in the next chapter. Due to the focus of this book, I will not spend a great deal of time or go into great detail regarding church history. There are a number of good resources that have been published on the subject. Maybe these chapters will challenge you to seek for the truth regarding the history of the church. At any rate, the Roman religious system became so corrupt that God raised men up to lead His sheep from it.

You have probably heard of men like Huss, Knox, Wycliffe, Tyndale, Calvin, and the Huguenots. The Lord continued to raise men up after the Reformation. Men like the Wesleys, Whitfield,

Spurgeon, and Moody. Some of these and many others, men and women, all of whom would be impossible to mention, underwent great suffering and many paid the ultimate price, their very lives! What were they doing? They were working out their own salvation in fear and trembling (Philippians 2:12). These are people who would not be denied worshiping Jesus in spirit and truth. They paid the price of discipleship, and after running their race have handed the baton to us! Like the saints of old, they truly were men and women of whom this world was not worthy! (see Hebrews 11:27–28).

So, what have we done? Instead of following their great commitment by working out our own salvation in fear and trembling, we have built monuments to them and taken on their names as our religion. Luther (the Lutheran Church), the Wesleys (the Methodist Church), Knox and Calvin (the Presbyterian Church), the founders of the Ana Baptist (the Baptist denomination); the Pentecostals came up following men such as John Fletcher, Edward Irving, and others. We have dropped the baton and made idols out of these men.

There is a phenomenon of nondenominational churches that are attempting to get away from this system. In all honesty, there is also a directionless characteristic about many of these entities, which tends to make them a mixed bag of tricks. I will attempt to suggest some solutions to these issues with the help of God's word. Another problem, which is really the same problem, is that modern Western churches are full of people following the pastor, or pastors, instead of following Jesus for themselves.

There is a star-power attraction in churches today that follows many pastors. They are the star of the church instead of Jesus Christ. If they left, the church would fold. Why? One reason could be that many are looking for a human king like the Israelites who rejected God in the first book of Samuel. The Jews wanted to be like the ungodly nations and have a human king instead of God as their king. Could it be that things haven't changed much? It is much easier to just let the pastor seek after God, let him hear from the Holy Spirit, and then do what the preacher says, than to deny yourself, take up your cross, and follow Jesus for yourself. Sadly, I must point out that many nondenominational churches have a lot of the same trappings as the denominations that were inherited from the idolized men from the past.

How did this happen? We need only look to the carnal church in Corinth for the answer. There was a division that could potentially divide the body into sects based on their unhealthy esteem, or following of one man or another. Paul addressed it in the first letter to the Corinthians. Are we not guilty of this sin?

> *Now I say this, that each of you says, "I am of Paul," or "I am of Apollos," or "I am of Cephas," or "I am of Christ." Is Christ divided? Was Paul crucified for you? Or were you baptized in the name of Paul?*
>
> (1 Corinthians 1:12–13)

Then later in the same letter Paul continues addressing this division.

> *I fed you with milk and not with solid food; for until now you were not able to receive it, and even now you are still not able; for you are still carnal. For where there are envy, strife, and divisions among you, are you not carnal and behaving like mere men? For when one says, "I am of Paul," and another, "I am of Apollos," are you not carnal?*
>
> (1 Corinthians 3:2–5)

Today, we instead say, "I am of Luther," "I am of Wesley," "I am of Calvin," and so on. The denominations in the church today are a result of God's people many years ago esteeming men in an unhealthy manner, becoming spiritually lazy, and not leading. Is it possible that we have been so concerned about keeping this religious system intact that we haven't risked the uprooting of these false foundations for the love of that which is stable, familiar, and comfortable? Doesn't that sound like the same problem some of the Pharisees had?

Am I speaking against God's leaders? No, I believe God has raised many of them up for such a time as this! I believe that many of them will recognize that they are men of valor, will have zeal for God's truth and stand therefore! Though we have accepted the mediocrity of running others' races by following after the achievements of mere men of the past; I believe God for great things of His appointed leaders! I am also confident that some are not called by God to the positions which they hold, and this will be revealed by their leadership or lack thereof.

You see, when these men we call the reformers left the Catholic system, they were just men who loved God, and were moving toward a more authentic walk with the King of kings! They went out at any cost, denied themselves, took up their crosses, and followed Jesus. They wanted to get as far away as they could from what they rightly deemed a wicked system. They did in fact re-establish truthful doctrines, some of which were: salvation from grace through faith, not salvation by adhering to Catholic dogma; the Bible is the final authority, not the Catholic hierarchy; we are individual priests unto God, not led by one priest who is a mediator between God and man; and many other glorious truths. Yet the reformers were mere men like you and me. They weren't supersaints that we should worship from a time gone by. These men and women had a super God and so do we! They loved Jesus and worshiped Him as God in their lives.

The result was that God honored these men and women, who stood for godly reforms, with grace and power to lead many to righteousness. They did much in their lifetimes for the kingdom of God! They accomplished a great deal in their lifetimes. They hated what is evil and loved what is good to the extent of leaving behind many ungodly traditions to worship the living God. However, though their faith was more authentic than the wicked system they came out of, it was not the authentic belief system from before the perversions of the third and fourth centuries.

The reformers brought much of the ungodly stuff from the Roman system with them when they came out. One of those dark, ungodly doctrines was replacement theology. God not only honored their sincerity but also their new, fresh authenticity. But there was, and is, a long way to go. We (the church) instead of taking up where they left off, camped around, and got comfortable with their achievements. I want to ask you an exciting question that is more like a bold proposal. Brethren, who wants to go forward from there?

Therefore we also, since we are surrounded by so great a cloud of witnesses, let us lay aside every weight, and the sin which so easily ensnares us, and let us run with endurance the race that is set before us, looking unto Jesus, the author and finisher of our faith, who for the joy that was set before Him endured the cross, despising the shame, and has sat down at the right hand of the throne of God.

(Hebrews 12:1–2)

Don't you see that now we have, on different levels, and in many areas of the body, an ungodly system? The Lord is requiring us to work out our own salvation in fear and trembling, and the Father is looking for us to worship Him in a more authentic way. He is tired of the traditions of men on which we are living! He wants us to get the leaven of false religion out of our hearts, lives, and churches. In the modern Western church we, by and large, have become a powerless, watching souls going to hell, not advancing the kingdom of righteousness religion! I for one, thankfully because of what King Jesus is doing in my heart, am ready for a change!

127

What we can do now, hundreds of years later, is take up the baton where it was dropped, and start paying the price like they did to worship the Father in spirit and truth! Let's not only shake off the ungodly remnants of the wicked system that they came out of, but also the ungodly traditions they brought with them. We must also shed the ones we have picked up along the way under the banner of the reformers' names that are not authentic faith in Jesus Christ. Trust me, that is what they would want us to do! I have already mentioned some of these significant ungodly traditions and wrong doctrines that are still with us today. They affect our understanding of our very identity in Jesus Christ. I will address a couple more for which you will need to brace yourself and be ready to handle the truth. Let's stop following dead men, and start following the living God. Let's do so by living by His Holy Spirit and His holy, living word!

But wait a minute. What should most do, as they are currently involved in a denominational church of some kind or another? Or if I am a member of a nondenominational church that is having problems like those mentioned earlier? The first thing to do is ask King Jesus. He may lead you elsewhere. If He wills that you stay, then by all means stay. Then like Dwight Pryor says, using an old saying: "Don't look at the cup as half empty and complain about it, look at it as half full and let God use you to fill it up more."

As the Father conforms more individuals to the image of His dear Son (and isn't that what grace is?) then all who are submitted to King Jesus will benefit from it. The result will be that those called out to worship the King will begin to change as a body. What I am saying is, Jesus doesn't want us to go hide somewhere as He blesses us with a more authentic faith, He wants it to spread through His body. He desires believers in the denominational and nondenominational churches to grow together as a body.

God will raise the leaders up to direct the body in this effort. They will equip the saints with the truth in love, and the body will grow up in all things being conformed to Him, according to the desire of the head, King Jesus! The Lord Jesus will also raise up healthy followers of Jesus to help the leaders accomplish this worthy task.

At the church my family attends, a pastor recently spoke on being a good follower. I was greatly impacted by the message. He told a story of a young person who was filling out a college attendance application. The chances were not great for this person to be selected. One question was, "Are you a leader or a follower?" With thoughtful deliberation the hopeful candidate answered truthfully that he or she, was a follower. (I don't remember if it was a young lady or man.) The student thought that in today's society the absence of leadership ability would be a negative, disqualifying factor. However, to the surprise of the not-so-hopeful student, the school answered that of the fourteen hundred applicants, all were leaders, and they were in need of some good followers. Thus this truthful, potential follower was accepted.

And He Himself gave some to be apostles, some prophets, some evangelists, and some pastors and teachers, for the equipping of the saints for the work of ministry, for the edifying of the body of Christ till we all come to the unity of the faith and of the knowledge of the Son of God, to a perfect man, to the measure of the stature of the fullness of Christ; that we should no longer be children, tossed to and fro and carried about with every wind of doctrine, by the trickery of men, in the cunning craftiness of deceitful plotting, but, speaking the truth in love, may grow up in all things into Him who is the head—Christ—from whom the whole body, joined and knit together by what every joint supplies, according to the effective working by which every part does its share, causes growth of the body for the edifying of itself in love.

(Ephesians 4:11–16)

Some might look at me, and say, "There goes a radical," as I am addressing some sacred cows in the church. I believe I am just another member that is functioning for the good of the body, and following the head, King Jesus Christ! By the way, the prophets, apostles, and Jesus Christ were all considered radical. Anyway, whether you are a leader in the body with speaking gifts, or a member that has gifts leaning more toward helps or service, we are all to *lead* others to King Jesus, take up our cross, and *follow* Him! (Romans 12:5–8; 1 Peter 4:11; 1 Corinthians 12:15–31; 2 Corinthians 5:20, 21; Luke 9:23)

I do have a warning for you. As I have identified some ungodly traditions that we have inherited, turned from them, and moved toward a more biblically authentic fellowship with the Father, I have experienced resistance from the most improbable place and people that you might imagine. Before I tell you from where and whom, I will ask you a question: Who do you think persecuted the great reformers more than anyone? To give you a hint I will ask another question: Who led the persecution of Jesus Christ? It was those blinded by religion and all that accompanied it. Things such as power, prestige, money, sinful doctrines and lifestyle, traditions, and so on, were at risk when Jesus hit the scene.

The established church persecuted the reformers the most. Again, I say things haven't changed much. The place from which Jesus and the reformers received some of the most trouble is the same from which we will also if we become radical as they were for truth. Jesus told us to expect persecution as we follow Him, so don't be surprised even if it is friendly fire. There is good news with this warning:

> *Blessed are those who are persecuted for righteousness' sake, for theirs is the kingdom of heaven. "Blessed are you when they revile and persecute you, and say all kinds of evil against you falsely for My sake. Rejoice and be exceedingly glad, for great is your reward in heaven, for so they persecuted the prophets who were before you."*
> (Matthew 5:10–12)

As we are falsely accused and treated wrongly for seeking to live by truth, we will be in good company!

CHAPTER 10

Pagan Rituals and Traditions

"You shall not worship the LORD your God with such things."
(Deuteronomy 12:4)

Whatever forms the philosophies of man or pagan religions take, they can be traced back to an ancestry that God pronounces judgment on from the beginning of the Scriptures to the end. Whether these philosophies are labeled ancient Greco-Roman or modern-day humanism, they all come from one religious center. This religious, economic, and governmental power is going to face the wrath of God; sadly, much of the body of Christ is in love with its trappings. It is identified by God in Revelation 17:5b as ". . . THE MOTHER OF HARLOTS AND OF THE ABOMINATIONS OF THE EARTH." The name of this place is Babylon.

Remember the tower of Babel? This is the place where all of mankind united to accomplish great things. There was only one big problem. They were purposely excluding the Creator of the universe. Instead of building their great city and tower to the glory of God, their endeavors were for the purpose of making a name for themselves (see Genesis 11:4). We know that they all spoke one language, and had incredible potential to accomplish amazing feats in their pursuit of human achievement. However, God halted the building project by confusing their languages. We have a term of derision with us today that helps us remember the futility of man's initiative without the Creator Jesus. Of course it is used to identify useless, nonsensical speech, which we call "babble."

Later, this place would become the epicenter of false religion and paganism. Look at a few quotes regarding Babylon. "Enuma Elish, the early Babylonian Genesis, mentions a pantheon of gods and goddesses. Even as late as the first century A.D. John referred to the religious system, Babylon, as the Mother of Harlots and of the abominations of the earth" (Rev 17:5).[27]

"There were patron gods and goddesses, of each city-state as well as gods representing such things as the **sun**, moon, and stars, the weather, crops, rivers and the land."[28]

Yes, Babylon truly is the Mother of Harlots, and God has revealed in Scripture how important it is to stay clear of fornicating with her gods.

Let's first take a look at her gods and then see if the church of Jesus Christ is abstaining from this dangerous paganism. We know that the Israelites were commanded to have nothing to do with these false deities and the idolatry accompanying them. We are also aware from Scripture that as Israel disobeyed in this regard they were severely judged. We look back and ask, "How could they have been so rebellious to their true and living God?" Maybe we need to ask ourselves the same question.

One of the primary gods of Babylon was Semiramis. She was immortalized in Babylonian legend and became known as the

---

[27] *Theological Workbook of the Old Testament,* vol 1, 198.
[28] *World Book Encyclopedia,* vol. 2 (World Book Inc., 2003), 14.

Queen of Heaven. Here are some excerpts from a very interesting article. "Nimrod was so reprehensible, ancient writings say, that his own mother, Semiramis, bore him a child. Semiramis would become known as the Babylonian Queen of Heaven or Goddess Mother."[29] We see the Jews refusing to repent of worshiping the queen of heaven in Jeremiah 44:17–19, 25.

> *But we will certainly do whatever has gone out of our own mouth, to burn incense to the queen of heaven and pour out drink offerings to her, as we have done, we and our fathers, our kings and our princes, in the cities of Judah and in the streets of Jerusalem.*
>
> (Jeremiah 44:17)

The article continues: "Gradually, through trade, influence of Babylon spread to other nations as they incorporated its government and religious system."[30] It also says, "Many monuments in Babylon show her (Semiramis or the queen of heaven) with a child in her arms. As the Babylonians dispersed throughout the known world, they carried their mother-child deity worship with them. Surprisingly, many nations were already worshiping a mother and child before the Savior of men was born!"[31]

Another aspect of this pagan worship is that the child became accepted as Nimrod resurrected, and was named Tammuz. As God was sending Ezekiel to warn Israel of coming judgment, one form of their idolatry was worship of Tammuz.

> *So He brought me to the door of the north gate of the LORD's house; and to my dismay, women were sitting there weeping for Tammuz.*
>
> (Ezekiel 8:14)

---

[29] *The Real Story of Christmas*, from Yahweh's Assembly in Messiah, 401 N. Roby Farm Rd. Rocheport, MO 65279, 4.
[30] Ibid., 5.
[31] Ibid.

Semiramis and Tammuz were the mother goddess and the son god. Ever heard of the mother of god in any popular Western religions? Ever seen any statues of Mary holding the baby Jesus? This understanding of the God of the Bible is a Babylonian perversion.

As the powerful Babylonian Empire exported its cultural influence, including its pagan worship, by means of trade, military expansion, and occupation, the gods of Babylon became widely accepted and worshiped by the nations of the world. They took on different names, yet their characteristics are evidence that they are the same gods and goddesses. Remember the Lord confused the languages at Babel. These gods and goddesses are with us today. As much as that probably doesn't surprise you, when you find out who and where they are, you not only may be surprised, but you will be faced with a decision that you may find very unpleasant. Jesus told us that to follow Him we must deny ourselves, take up our cross, and follow Him. So what does that have to do with us and Babylonian worship?

The "Christ Mass"

Most Bible-believing Christians would agree that Jesus Christ wasn't born on December twenty-fifth. It would be difficult to find a Bible scholar that would tell you that this was anywhere near the date of Jesus' birth. I would also challenge you to find in the Bible where God commands that we are to celebrate His birthday. Before you waste your time, I will just tell you, it's not there. So how did this celebration become what it is today in our society and churches?

What of the name of this celebration, and the history of this holiday? As I began to research this it astounded me what turned up.

The word Christmas derives from the Old English *Christes-Masse,*
a Catholic mass that grew out of a feast day established in the

year 1038. A mass is a prayer for a dead person. Why is it applied to the birth of the Messiah? Perhaps the answer is found in the Encyclopedia Americana, 1942 edition, Vol. 6, p. 623: "Christmas was according to many authorities not celebrated in the first centuries of the Christian Church as the usage in general was to celebrate the death of remarkable persons rather than their birth. A feast was established in the memory of the birth of the Savior in the Fourth Century. In the Fifth Century the Western Church (Roman Catholic) ordered it to be celebrated forever on the day of the old Roman Feast of the birth of Sol (the sun)."[32]

The *Encyclopedia Britannica,* 1946 edition, says, "Christmas was not among the earliest festivals of the church." For the first three hundred years, the religious writers are silent regarding the Christmas observance. An Armenian writer of the eleventh century states that the Christmas festival was first celebrated in Constantinople in 373. In Egypt the Western birthday festival was opposed during the early years of the fifth century, but was celebrated in Alexandria as early as 432. In 1644 the English Puritans forbade any merriment or religious services by act of Parliament on the grounds that Christmas was a heathen festival.[33]

Did you see that the Christ Mass was a celebration of a dead man and has origins that go back to the supposed birth of the sun? I wonder if Satan gets a laugh every time we celebrate the resurrected Savior, who is *Creator,* God the *Son,* with a tradition that originated with a ritual associated to a dead man, and was celebrated to worship the *created sun.* What is this birth of the sun that is being spoken of here?

Is there a link to Babylon with such a celebration? If there is, should we who follow Jesus be concerned?

---

[32] Ibid., 4.
[33] Ibid.

Let's trace this chain of false gods and their worship to see where it goes. "Semiramis is also known as Rhea. Her child from Nimrod is referred to in Scripture as Tammuz (Ezekiel 8:14). In this verse 'Yahweh,' [which is translated LORD in most English translations], is condemning Israelite women who professed to be worshiping Him but in secret were actually worshiping Tammuz. In the next few verses Yahweh denounces **sun** worship, part of the Babylonian 'abominations' in the worship of Nimrod and Tammuz."[34] So we do begin to see a link to Babylon. The links of the chain continue.

First look at how seriously the Lord takes this sun worship.

So He (the LORD) *brought me into the inner court of the LORD's house; and there, at the door of the temple of the LORD, between the porch and the altar, were about twenty-five men with their backs toward the temple of the LORD and their faces toward the east, and they were worshipping the **sun** toward the east. And He said to me, "Have you seen this, O son of man? Is it a trivial thing to the house of Judah to commit the abominations which they commit here? For they have filled the land with violence; then they have returned to provoke Me to anger. Indeed they put the branch to their nose.* [A term meaning 'spurning' or 'openly rebelling'.] *Therefore I also will act in fury. My eye will not spare nor will I have pity; and though they cry in My ears with a loud voice, I will not hear them."*

(Ezekiel 8:16–18)

God pronounces wrathful judgment on Babylonian sun worship. God also apparently is more offended by the men of Judah's pagan worship than that of the women. Could it be that they were responsible to keep that garbage out of the camp?

Anyway, remember that it was not uncommon for the same gods to have different names depending on language and culture.

---

[34] Ibid., 5.

"Interestingly, the Greeks adopted this son of Semiramis and gave him the name Bacchus, the deity of wine and revelry. His birthday was at the winter solstice (mid-December) and its celebration was marked by orgies in honor of the "son of the mother god."[35] There are other names of gods worth examining to follow the chain.

Mithras was another name for the sun god. "Mithraism the worship of Mithra, the Iranian (Persian) god of the **sun**, justice, contract, and war in pre-Zorastrian Iran. Known as Mithras of the **second and third century Rome**. Before the sixth century B.C. the Iranians had a polytheistic religion and Mithra was the most important of their gods. Mithra is invoked as the god of oath. Whenever men observed justice and contract they venerated Mithra."[36] This means that they would swear by, or make an oath by, the name of Mithra. "**In short, Mithra may signify any kind of communication between men and whatever establishes good relations between them**. The Greeks and Romans considered Mithras as a sun god. He was also the god of kings."[37]

This is very interesting. What did the Lord tell the Israelites about associating with and making oaths with the other nations or their gods?

> *Therefore be very courageous to keep and to do all that is written in the Book of the Law of Moses, lest you turn aside from it to the right hand or to the left, and lest you go among these nations, these who remain among you. You shall not make mention of the name of their gods, nor cause anyone to swear by them; you shall not serve them nor bow down to them, but you shall hold fast to the LORD your God, as you have done to this day.*
>
> (Joshua 23:6–8)

---

[35] Ibid.
[36] *Encyclopedia Britannica: Macromedia Ready Reference*, vol. 8 (2002), 197.
[37] Ibid.

The Lord tells them not to make mention or swear by their gods like Mithras. What God is saying is to have nothing to do with their false gods. Today, do we venerate the sun god by saying "Merry Christmas?"

There was another pagan celebration in Rome called the Saturnalia (worship of Saturn) celebrated for a week in December. In Deuteronomy 17:3 the Lord commanded the children of Israel not to worship the sun, moon, or any of the host of heaven. So, we have the Saturnalia bash, Bacchus's hoo hah, and the birthday of Mithras, in the month of December. All of these are pagan, drunken festivals, which is how many still celebrate the Christ Mass today. I am coming to the realization that those who mark Christmas in a drunken, pagan fashion today are more accurately celebrating the Christ Mass than we who believe in Jesus Christ. Why would I say such a thing? Mithras was also celebrated at the same time in Egypt as the birth of Osiris, which was another name for Tammuz. The date, of course, was December twenty-fifth. That is the truth about the date and origin of the celebration that we call Christmas. It was a conglomeration of wicked festivals, based on the worship of Babylonian false gods then, and I believe from the perspective of God it still is.

Wait! Before you close the book, and throw it into the yuletide fire, please let me tell you about the blending of truth with the lie, the mistletoe, the holly, the tree, and the baby Jesus.

First we will observe the blending of truth with the lie:

The Catholic Church wanted to eclipse the festivities of a rival pagan religion that threatened Christianity's existence. The Romans celebrated the birthday of their sun god, Mithras during this time of year. Although it was not popular, or even proper, to celebrate people's birthdays in those times, church leaders decided that in order to **compete with the pagan celebration** they would themselves order a festival in celebration of the birth of Jesus

Christ. Although the actual season of Jesus' birth is thought to be in the Spring, the date of December 25 was chosen as the official birthday celebration as Christ's Mass so that it would compete head on with the rival pagan celebration. Christmas was slow to catch on in America. The early colonists considered it a pagan ritual. The celebration of Christmas was even banned by law in Massachusetts in colonial days.[38]

Indeed, the Catholic encyclopedia confirms the merger. "The well known solar feast of Natalis Invivti (The Nativity of the Un-conquered Sun) celebrated on 25 December, has a strong claim on the responsibility for our December date" (vol. 3, p. 727).[39]

Do you ever notice church programs that appear too worldly to be of Jesus Christ, but are justified by the number of people that they bring in to hear the message? Ask yourself if the quote in the next paragraph demonstrates that we have inherited a horrible legacy of compromise.

Then how did December 25 become connected with the birth-day of the Messiah? Alexander Hislop explains: "Long before the fourth century, and long before the Christian era itself, a festival was celebrated among the heathen at that precise time of the year, in honor of the birth of the son of the Babylonian queen of heaven; and it may fairly be presumed that, **in order to conciliate the heathen, and to swell the number of the nominal adherents for Christianity,** the same festival was adopted by the Roman Church, giving it only the name of Christ" (*The Two Babylons*, p. 93).[40]

Once again, things haven't changed much.

---

[38]*The Symbols and Traditions of Christmas,* http://wilstar.com/xmas/xmassymb.htm
[39] *The Real Story of Christmas,* 9.
[40] Ibid.

Folks, God didn't tell us to compete with or be like the world. He told us to come out from it!

Do not be unequally yoked together with unbelievers. For what fellowship has righteousness with lawlessness? And what communion has light with darkness? And what accord has Christ with Belial?"

(or Semiramis, Nimrod, Tammuz, Bacchus, Mithras, Christ Mass)

Verse 15 continues:

Or what part has a believer with an unbeliever? And what agreement has the temple of God with idols? For you are the temple of the living God. As God has said: ". . . Come out from among them and be separate, says the Lord. Do not touch what is unclean, and I will receive you."

(2 Corinthians 6:14–17)

The world cannot compete with the One who is in the born again children of God! His name is Jesus Christ and I don't need to be like the world. On the contrary, I must be like Jesus so that God can use me to call others out of this lost and dying world! Do we want to throw a rope down to those who are dying in the quicksand of sin, or climb down into it with them?

Take a look at other trappings of the Christ Mass and I hope it makes you a little uncomfortable. The tree, mistletoe, and holly were associated with the goddess of love, and thus became symbols of fertility. The tree was used to represent the resurrected Nimrod in Tammuz.

According to *The Encyclopedia of World Religions,* Tammuz was the god of vegetation. "Every year a festival was held at which his death and resurrection was celebrated (Nimrod). The vegetation god was believed to die and rise annually, and in the myths of the descent of the mother goddess into the land of the dead there is a dramatic image of the search of the mother for her lost son and lover, the search of the earth for the temporarily lost fertility which the new spring restores." To depict his resurrection, the Babylonians believed that an evergreen tree sprang out of a dead tree stump. The old stump symbolized the dead Nimrod, and the new evergreen was Nimrod resurrected in Tammuz. Green holly, popular at Christmas, has long been a symbol of eternal life and it played an important role in portraying the rebirth of Nimrod.[41]

"Groves" is the Hebrew *asherah*, meaning to be erect or upright. It was either a living tree with the top cut off and the stump carved into a certain shape, or it was artificially fashioned and set erect in the ground. Connected with Baal worship, the practice of Asherah was to worship or sacrifice to idols among these "groves" of trees.[42]

They also built for themselves high places, sacred pillars, and wooden images on every high hill and under every *green tree*.

Now having heard of the origination of the Christ Mass tree, wouldn't you agree that it was an idol? Would putting Jesus' name on it make it less of an idol? In that light, see what God says about decorating an idol and setting it up with a stand.

Hear the word which the LORD speaks to you, O house of Israel. Thus says the LORD: "Do not learn the way of the Gentiles; Do not be dismayed at the signs of heaven, for the Gentiles are dismayed at them. For the customs of the peoples are futile; for one cuts a tree from the forest, the work of the hands of the workman, with the ax.

---

[41] Ibid., 9–10.
[42] Ibid., 17.

They decorate it with silver and gold; they fasten it with nails and hammers so that it will not topple. They are upright, like a palm tree, and they cannot speak; they must be carried, because they cannot go by themselves. Do not be afraid of them, for they cannot do evil, nor can they do any good."

(Jeremiah 10:1–5)

The reason Jeremiah tells them that the idol can do no evil or good is that the people were afraid of what the false god would do to them if they didn't pay homage to an idol made in its image. Isn't it interesting how they would decorate it and put a stand under it to hold it up?

The Lord speaks to Israel commanding them to destroy the pagan instruments of idolatry and have nothing to do with their form of worship, including inserting His name on their wickedness.

*"These are the statutes and judgments which you shall be careful to observe in the land which the L*ORD *God of your fathers is giving you to possess, all the days that you live on the earth. You shall utterly destroy all the places where the nations which you shall dispossess served their gods, on the high mountains and on the hills and under every green tree. And you shall destroy their altars, break their sacred pillars, and burn their wooden images with fire; you shall cut down the carved images of their gods and destroy their names from that place. You shall not worship the L*ORD *your God with such things.*

(Deuteronomy 12:1–4)

There are two things I would like to point out. One is that the evergreen tree was a source of pagan worship. See the above quote given in reference to the green tree in Deuteronomy 12:2. "In 11 passages of Scripture, scattered throughout the Bible, the green tree is associated with idolatry and harlotry. Because all trees are green part of the year, the special mention of 'green' trees probably refers to some form of evergreen tree (Deuteronomy 12:2; 1 Kings 14:23;

2 Kings 16:4, 17:10; 2 Chronicles. 28:4; Isaiah 57:5; Jeremiah 2:20, 3:6, 3:13, 17:2; Ezekiel 6:13)."[43] The other point of interest seen in Deuteronomy 12:4 is that God warns His people not to worship in a pagan manner in His name.

Is that not what we do with the Christ Mass? The evidence we have seen points to a different Jesus. The baby from the Babylonian mother-son worship is the baby that was celebrated long before the baby Jesus. The Catholic system blended Babylonian religion with the truthful gospel accounts of the birth of Jesus Christ. I have a challenging question for you: Have you ever seen anything that is truly of the God of the Bible that the world loves as much as it does the celebration of Christmas? Why? The reason is that it is a celebration of the world! Hear the convicting, powerful word of the King: 1 John 2:15 says:

Do not love the world or the things in the world. If anyone loves the world, the love of the Father is not in him.

As we look at the evidence in this chain, from the first link to the last, everything points to the fact that there is a great amount of Babylonian worship associated with Christmas. This evidence leaves us all with a decision. Will we compromise and go along with the flow of modern Christianity, or will we make the tough choices and turn away from such things to follow after King Jesus?

There are those who seek to legitimize the celebration of the Christ Mass by saying that the early Christians celebrated Jesus' birth in A.D. 250–300 before the pagan celebrations were adopted. They assert that the true and even suffering Christians were sincerely celebrating what they thought was the actual date of His birth. I strongly doubt it, but let's say for the sake of discussion that it is true. Friends, Satan doesn't enter into people's lives with a pitchfork and a red suit. He enters with seemingly harmless and

---

[43] Ibid., 15–16.

sometimes noble tactics, and then deceives people into idolatry. He also provokes people to scoff at those who identify him. I am confident that if the Christians were celebrating Jesus' birth in an unbiblical manner, which wound up defiling so much of Jesus' body, that it isn't of the Lord. That leaves only one spiritual entity for the introduction of this holiday, and I know he doesn't like us!

While having lunch, a church leader and I were discussing this issue. He disputed that the Christ Mass was no longer pagan because so many in the church don't know that it's pagan. My observation is that I am sure the women in Israel had a problem discerning that worshiping Tammuz was sin, as the men of Judah were bowed down on their knees to the sun. Who is responsible for this ignorance in the church? Who is accountable to God for teaching His sheep? The Lord will judge them with a more strict judgment, says James 3:1.

I was having this discussion on another occasion and the fellow said, "But those gods don't exist anymore in these times." Where do you think they went? They are a manifestation of demons and yes, they do! When indicting the Israelis for sacrificing their children to pagan gods, the Lord likens their gods to demons.

> They served their idols, which became a snare to them. They even sac-
> rificed their sons and their daughters to **demons**, and shed innocent
> blood, the blood of their sons and daughters, whom they sacrificed
> to the idols of Canaan; and the land was polluted with blood.
> (Psalm 106:36–38)

The Bible instructs us that the warnings in the Old Testament are in effect today and for good reason (see 1 Corinthians 10:1–7; Romans 15:4; 2 Timothy 3:16).

For me two years ago the decision, though initially difficult, became very clear and simple. My mother's side of the family is Jewish, yet I had been celebrating Christmas since I could remember. My Gentile family's tradition was the more accurate version of Christmas with a bit of drinking and revelry. Then, after being saved by Jesus, Christmas for me was a time of exciting worship. My wife had been celebrating it all her life and, like many, had lifelong memories attached to it. Yet, when I began to realize how absolutely pagan it is, I had to forsake it.

Another pagan worldly goddess was and is from Babylon. Her name in modern English is Easter. Some of her other names, many of which God calls abominations in the Bible, are Eostare, Aphrodite, Asherah, Ashtoreth, Astarte, Ishtar, Semiramis, Venus, Diana, and Isis.[44] That is right, Easter is a Babylonian pagan holiday that was morphed into the celebration of the resurrection of Jesus Christ. Here is another revealing quote: "It is not a Christian name, but is derived from an idol goddess, the Queen of Heaven. The Saxon goddess Eastre is the same as the Astarte, the Syrian Venus, called Ashteroth in the O.T. It was the worship of this woman by Israel that was such an abomination to God (1 Samuel 7:3; 1 Kings 11:5, 33; 2 Kings 23:13; Jeremiah 7:18, 44:18, 25)."[45]

The traditions of bunnies and eggs, Good Friday, hot cross buns, fires, and Lent are all Babylonian, abominable forms of worship that we are clearly commanded in Scripture to, as my dad would have said, "stay so far away from it that it would cost eleven dollars to send me a postcard."

Jesus probably wasn't crucified on Friday. The Bible says that He would be in "the heart of the earth" for three days and three nights (Matthew 12:40). The crucifixion took place on the Preparation Day for the Passover Sabbath. It most likely was not on Friday. The day began at dusk on Wednesday, which would make more sense to us if we understood our Jewish roots. If you count from

[44] Timothy A. and Kimberly B. Southall, *The Truth about Easter* from http://www.bright.net/~lwayonly/easter.html.
[45] Finnis Jennings Dake, *Dake's Annotated Reference Bible* (NT), 1963, 137

there, we see that Jesus resurrected after the Friday Sabbath on Saturday evening, which began the first day of the week. By the way, the Father gave us a biblical celebration to commemorate this day. There is great evidence to suggest that Jesus resurrected on the Feast of Firstfruits. It is a good thing to celebrate His resurrection. Let us celebrate it in spirit and truth.

As we look at the sheer number of Christians who have these holidays embedded into their lives, we have a big problem here. However, if you understand the meaning of the diagram of the trees at the end of this chapter, you will see that these celebrations aren't the problem. They are symptoms, or branches, of the real issue, or root. We have become accustomed to dealing with symptoms instead of the sickness that is causing the symptoms. What we must do is recognize that the root of the problem, as I have stated earlier, is the robbery of our true identity and its replacement with a counterfeit. The solution is found in authentic worship of the Father. Jesus Christ is our only hope.

> Jesus said to him, "I am the way, the truth, and the life. No one comes to the Father except through Me."
>
> (John 14:6)

Let's not look at the symptoms but appraise accurately the problem and turn to the Jesus of the Bible for the solution.

Here is something else to consider. Believers in Jesus are to provoke the Jewish people to jealousy. I mentioned Romans 10:19 earlier, in which Paul quotes Moses' warning from the Lord to the Jewish people.

> But I say, did Israel not know? First Moses says: "I will provoke you to jealousy by those who are not a nation, I will move you to anger by a foolish nation."
>
> (Romans 10:19)

Please remember that Paul challenges us in the next chapter of Romans to provoke the Jews to jealousy. How will we accomplish this if we are celebrating the same pagan gods that landed them in so much trouble with the Lord?

I have talked to Jewish people and read books on Judaism that identify the pagan behaviors and rituals in Christianity. Do you want to know the tragedy of what they are saying? It is true. It is enough that someone stumbles from their own hardness of heart. Yet, I don't want to be responsible before God for laying a stumbling block in front of them. This would be true for Jew and Gentile.

> Then He said to the disciples, "It is impossible that no offenses should come, but woe to him through whom they do come! It would be better for him if a millstone were hung around his neck, and he were thrown into the sea, than that he should offend one of these little ones."
>
> (Luke 17:1–2)

At the same time consider the fruit from celebrating their God! Just think of how a Jew feels when you tell them how good their Messiah is. Consider what curiosity is aroused when a Gentile says "Happy New Year" at Rosh Hashanah, or shares the glory of the Passover seder that they enjoyed as a Gentile follower of the Jewish Messiah.

One night close to Passover I told my unbelieving Jewish grandmother that I was leading the Passover celebration at our church. She is one that thinks of persecution and bloodshed when she hears the name of Jesus. I asked her what she thought of my Passover plans, and with a bit of a chuckle of surprise she said, "I think it sounds nice." That may be insignificant to some, but for me that is a miracle! I also was privileged to share with her that eight Gentile friends were going with me to celebrate the Feast of Tabernacles in Israel to support the Jewish people. I have shared Jesus with her in the past and I am still praying that the Lord reveals His Messiahship to her!

147

The Lord engineered it so that one night I sat in one of the biggest yeshivas (schools of Judaism) in Jerusalem. I was invited by a student to talk about Yeshua (Jesus). His goal was to bring this poor misguided lamb back into the fold of rabbinical Judaism. You should have seen it. There we were, four Gentile brothers and me with yarmulkes (skull caps) sitting in this Jewish school. As I began debating the rabbi, the Lord filled me with His Spirit and I began preaching the gospel from the Old Testament. At one point I stopped and proclaimed, "Don't you see, I am loving your God and He is loving me!"

Why did I say that? My desire, like Paul's, is that they would be provoked to jealousy and be saved!

Possibly and even likely, you are having trouble handling some of these truths. Maybe a look at the earthly father of our faith that King Jesus gave as an example will help you right where you are. What is *true* worship? True worship begins in the Bible when a man takes something he loves and is prepared to sacrifice it to God. The first time the word *worship* is used in Scripture is when Abraham is commanded by the Lord to take his son Isaac and offer him as a burnt offering.

For me to follow Jesus Christ has required, does require, and will require me to forsake many things that I hold dear and that have been, are, and will be important to me. There is a question that I have heard pastors ask. "What is your Isaac?" the question goes. At a number of junctures in my life in Christ, I have been faced with the reality that I had to let go of an Isaac. By the more-than-abundant grace of God I have realized that I am not my own and that I have been bought with a price.

Knowing that you were not redeemed with corruptible things, like
silver or gold, from your aimless conduct received by tradition from

your fathers, but with the precious blood of Christ, as of a lamb
without blemish and without spot.

(1 Peter 1:18–19)

The choice to turn away from false religious influences is much easier when I remember that I am no longer my own. I must do whatever it takes to follow my Redeemer Jesus!

Though the Lord was not going to relent of His judgment on Judah, He mercifully raised up a godly king to spare the Jewish people for a season. His name was Josiah, and he did something to stay the Lord's hand.

And the king commanded Hilkiah the high priest, the priests of the
second order, and the doorkeepers, to bring out of the temple of the
LORD all the articles that were made for Baal, for Asherah, and for
all the host of heaven; and he burned them outside Jerusalem in the
fields of Kidron, and carried their ashes to Bethel. Then he removed
the idolatrous priests whom the kings of Judah had ordained to burn
incense on the high places in the cities of Judah and in the places all
around Jerusalem, and those who burned incense to Baal, to the sun,
to the moon, to the constellations, and to all the host of heaven. And
he brought out the wooden image from the house of the LORD, to the
Brook Kidron outside Jerusalem, burned it at the Brook Kidron and
ground it to ashes, and threw its ashes on the graves of the common
people. Then he tore down the ritual booths of the perverted persons
that were in the house of the LORD, where the women wove hangings
for the wooden image.

(2 Kings 23:4–7)

Oh, that we would have such a reformation! May the Lord Jesus appraise us as He did the Thessalonians.

For from you the word of the Lord has sounded forth, not only in
Macedonia and Achaia, but also in every place. Your faith toward

God has gone out, so that we do not need to say anything. For they themselves declare concerning us what manner of entry we had to you, and how you turned to God from idols to serve the living and true God.

(1 Thessalonians 1:8–9)

Man-made Third Tree (see diagram from chapter 4)

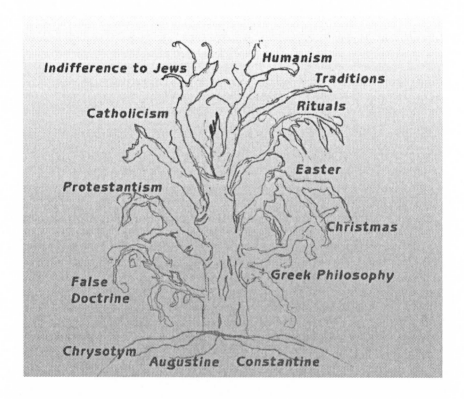

CHAPTER 11

Authentic Faith

"Look to Abraham your father . . ."

(Isaiah 51:2)

By the time the Lord brought the prophet Isaiah on the scene the children of Israel had sinned themselves into a terrible state. Their country had been divided, they were under great chastening from the Lord God and the worst was yet to come. God's nature consists of a perfect balance between all of His attributes. In Isaiah's time His perfect abundant patience was giving way to His also-perfect characteristic of holiness reflected in justice. In short, the Jewish people were in big trouble with the God of the universe!

We in the Western modern church are in not so different circumstances. Oh, most who claim the name of Christ in the contemporary church don't see our pitiful condition, yet isn't blindness one of the characteristics of judgment? We will address this principle in greater detail later. In this book we have established that the church is involved with the same idolatry that generated so much of God's anger with the children of Israel and Judah. The book of Isaiah largely deals with the Lord judging them for their persistent iniquity. The tribes of Israel loved the way of the nations and their gods so much that the Lord was announcing to them through His prophet that they would get all of the pagan worship they could stomach during their future captivity in Assyria (the northern ten tribes) and Babylon (the southern two tribes).

In case you have some doubts about where we are as a church in America, listen to some statistics that have given me a reality check.

"In 1996, a survey conducted by the Alan Guttmacher Institute in New York found that eighteen percent of abortion patients describe themselves as born-again or evangelical Christians. That is, of those who murdered their own child, nearly one in five professed faith in Jesus Christ."[46] Remember, in their deception, the Israelites sacrificed their children to the pagan god Molech. Today, there are women professing Jesus Christ who are sacrificing their own babies on the altar of lust and convenience.

It gets worse: "In 1994, the Barna Research Group found further evidence that all is not well in the contemporary Church. A survey revealed that one in four American adults who said they were born-again believe Jesus 'sinned' while He was on the earth."[47] How can one believe that the Father sent His Son, with sin, to be an acceptable sinless sacrifice? How can someone be born-again and blaspheme God so horribly? In the book of John, as well as many places in the Bible, we see that Jesus is God. Has God sinned? It is quite appalling. The same research group showed that only ten percent who profess Jesus in the contemporary American church really live as if they were born-again.

A small number of those who claim the name of Jesus actually are committed to prayer, read the Bible on a regular basis, and are

---

[46] Ray Comfort, *Revival's Golden Key* North Brunswick, NJ: Bridge-Logos, 2002), 11–12.
[47] Ibid., 12.

involved in the good works commanded by Jesus. "Another Gallup poll found '. . . very little difference in the behavior of the churched and un-churched on a wide range of items including lying, cheating, and stealing.' We are told that ninety-one percent lie regularly at work or home, eighty-six percent lie regularly to parents, and seventy-five percent lie regularly to friends (*The Day America Told the Truth*). A massive ninety-two percent own a Bible, but only eleven percent read it daily. Surveys also show that ninety percent of Americans pray, but eighty-seven percent do not believe in all of the Ten Commandments. To top it off, according to the Roper Organization, sixty-one percent believe that 'pre-marital sex is not morally wrong.'"[48]

If this one doesn't shake us I don't know what will. In 2003 the American Anglican Church ordained the first homosexual, or to be more accurate, sodomite priest! Romans 1:18–32 is one of many places that deal with this iniquity. When that which is holy is profaned, *God will judge!*

Here is the most current statistic indicator I have seen that should make the point. Barna Research posted a December 1, 2003, article that sums it all up. "The research indicated that everyone has a worldview, but relatively few people have a biblical worldview—even among devoutly religious people. The survey discovered that only nine percent *of born again Christians have such a perspective on life.*"[49] This indicting survey was based on six criteria: Jesus lived a sinless life, God is the all-powerful and all-knowing Creator of the universe and He stills rules it today; salvation is a gift from God and cannot be earned; Satan is real; a Christian has a responsibility to share their faith in Christ with other people; and the Bible is accurate in all of its teachings. Folks, this is extremely serious!

---

[48] Ibid., 13.
[49] Bama Research, http://www.barna.org/cgi-bin/bin/PagePressRelease.asp?PressReleaseID=154&Reference=F

We are in a dangerously woeful situation in the modern Western church. Many tend to shrug this all off with the notion that somehow God, because of His great mercy, compassion, patience, and love, will just overlook the wickedness in the church. They forget about His holiness, justice, wrath, judgment, and discipline. Upon hearing this some would say, "But God will not pour out wrath on those who are born again." Yes, but Jesus said that those who enter heaven and escape His wrath are those who do the will of the Father (Matthew 7:22). We must remember that God is, first of all, *holy, holy, holy.*

Maybe these words will be helpful in bringing us to a right thinking about persistent iniquity in the church.

> *Because the sentence against an evil work is not executed speedily, therefore the heart of the sons of men is fully set in them to do evil.*
> (Ecclesiastes 8:11)

We see here that there is a natural inclination in humans to seemingly take advantage of God's patience by the folly of following our flesh.

1 Peter 4:17 speaks directly to the church:

> *For the time has come for judgment to begin at the house of God; and if it begins with us first, what will be the end of those who do not obey the gospel of God?*

God will purge His church of wickedness, and before any of us get too comfortable, that would also include lukewarmness. In Revelation 3:15–18 King Jesus says:

> *"I know your works, that you are neither cold nor hot. I could wish you were cold or hot. So then, because you are **lukewarm**, and neither cold nor hot, I will vomit you out of My mouth. Because you say, 'I*

am rich, have become wealthy, and have need of nothing' —and do not know that you are wretched, miserable, poor, blind, and naked—I counsel you to buy from Me gold refined in the fire, that you may be rich; and white garments, that you may be clothed, that the shame of your nakedness may not be revealed; and anoint your eyes with eye salve, that you may see . . ."

There are times when the first step to receive the love of Jesus is to receive His rebuke. The very next verse (Revelation 3:19) tells us:

"As many as I love, I rebuke and chasten. Therefore be zealous and repent."

May we repent, receive His loving rebuke and chastening, and then judge ourselves lest we be judged.

Thankfully, in judgment God offers mercy. One of His methods is to give life-saving principles of correction. He did this with the Jewish people during the time of Isaiah, though not many reached for the lifeline. The Jewish people were receiving merciful instructions from the Lord. They were given correct steps to take to avoid painful destruction. Could the lifeline that He threw to them possibly help us out of the quicksand today? Romans 15:4 gives us the answer:

For whatever things were written before were written for our learning, that we through the patience and comfort of the Scriptures might have hope.

Remember, their identity had been robbed by the same devil that steals from us today. Consider this foundational concept that the Lord offered the Jewish people in their time of iniquity and identity crisis.

*"Listen to Me, you who follow after righteousness, you who seek the
LORD: Look to the rock from which you were hewn, and to the hole
of the pit from which you were dug. Look to Abraham your father,
and to Sarah who bore you; for I called him alone, and blessed him
and increased him."*

(Isaiah 51:1–2)

Why did the Lord tell them to look to Abraham and not to
God Himself? In other places of Isaiah's writings He did, yet their
problem required something that we are in desperate need of today.
They needed to know from whence they came. What I mean is that
they had no ability to follow God anywhere, as they didn't know
who they were or from where they had come. Their identity had
been so erased that they had no concept of a starting place. If you
look at a map to travel across the country, you need to accurately
know where you are coming from for it to be possible to reach your
destination. Like us, the Jewish people had no concept of their own
heritage. They had no concept of what God had originally called
them to be. That is the purpose of telling them to look to Abraham.
The foundation of their faith, or the root, had been so damaged
that they needed to start back at the beginning, as do we.

The Jewish people's understanding of God was so skewed that
they had no capacity to just pick up and start following God from
where they were. They had no concept of the fear of the Lord,
God's holy character, a sense of being a community of believers
in the true and living God, or their responsibilities regarding being a light to the nations. Does that not sound like the church in
America? As we have observed the deteriorated foundation or the
damaged roots of the modern Western church, should we not also
look to Abraham our father? Like those in Isaiah's time, we have
a mess on our hands, and with Jesus' help, I believe I can share
reasons why this principle would revolutionize and begin to restore
the church today!

Abraham was the first Hebrew, or as we know today, the first Jew. Abraham is the father of the Jewish faith, and also of the true church of Jesus Christ. We have seen in Galatians 3:7 that those who are of faith are sons of Abraham. Remember, when we sing the children's song in church, how does it go? *"Father Martin Luther had many sons, many sons had Martin Luther, I am one of them and so are you, so let's all praise the Lord."* No, the song rightly speaks of Abraham as one of the actual human fathers of our faith. The other two are Isaac and Jacob (Romans 9:4; 11:28; Psalm 105:8–10).

God refers to Abraham approximately thirty-nine times in the New Testament from Acts to Revelation. I did not count the gospels, as many of these references were from or directed to the Jewish people by King Jesus. I make this distinction because I am pointing out that Abraham is the earthly spiritual father of the church. Though some references in the book of Acts, and others, were directed to the Jews, they were preached from believers in Jesus Christ. Abraham is a constant through the New Covenant as the father or patriarch of our faith.

There is a great hall of faith in Hebrews 11 in which God accounts to Abraham eleven verses. This is a considerable ratio more than anyone else in this dynamic chapter of faith in the Bible. God uses Abraham to instruct us how to be a follower of Jesus. Is our faith today like that of Abraham? Remember, Abraham believed the gospel of Jesus Christ and is the patriarch of the predominantly Gentile church.

When the Lord made a covenant with Abraham He told him that through his descendants (seed) the nations of the world would be blessed (Genesis 12:1–3). It is through Abraham's seed that you who are born from above, or born again, have been grafted into a line or heritage of royalty.

Therefore it is of faith that it might be according to grace, so that the promise might be sure to all the seed, not only to those who are of the law, but also to those who are of faith of Abraham, who is the father of us all (as it is written, "I have made you a father of many nations") in the presence of Him whom he believed—God, who gives life to the dead and calls those things which do not exist as though they did.

(Romans 4:16–17)

So we see that you are in a spiritual sense the seed of Abraham.

There is an interesting Scripture that I would like us to see. I am developing something here, so stay with me. First John 3:9 reads:

Whoever has been born of God does not sin, for His seed remains in him; and he cannot sin, because he has been born of God.

The Greek word for *seed* here is *sperma*, which of course is the origin of the English word *sperm*. We see here that God has placed His *sperma* or *seed of faith* in believers in Jesus Christ. This gospel seed was given through the covenant God made with Abraham, passed down physically and spiritually through Isaac, and Jacob who God named Israel. This seed is then passed down through the Jewish people. In the fullness of time God honored this covenantal seed of faith with His very own physical presence into the womb of a Jewish woman descended from Abraham!

The Jewish people in large numbers reject the Messiah and the gospel *seed* is spread around the earth germinating in the hearts of the Gentiles. Look at Romans 11:11–12 in that light:

I say then, have they stumbled that they should fall? Certainly not! But through their fall, to provoke them to jealousy, salvation has come to the Gentiles. Now if their fall is riches for the world, and their failure riches for the Gentiles, how much more their fullness!

Isn't it amazing how big our God is that He has planned this from before time began?

> . . . just as He chose us in Him before the foundation of the world . . .
>
> (Ephesians 1:4a)

God anticipated, or engineered, as Oswald Chambers would say, all of these events so that the seed of Abraham would go all over the world!

Paul, addressing God's foreordained plan for Jew and Gentile, speaks of fathers Abraham, Isaac, and Jacob as he voices his wonder and awe of God in Romans 11:28–33:

> Concerning the gospel they are enemies for your sake, but concerning the election they are beloved for the sake of the fathers. For the gifts and the calling of God are irrevocable. For as you were once disobedient to God, yet have now obtained mercy through their disobedience, even so these also have now been disobedient, that through the mercy shown you they also may obtain mercy. For God has committed them all to disobedience, that He might have mercy on all. Oh, the depth of the riches both of the wisdom and knowledge of God! How unsearchable are His judgments and His ways past finding out!

Behold the majesty and mercy of our God as He saves those of Abraham's seed all over the globe!

We see the soul-saving seed of God's word in the book of James:

> Therefore lay aside all filthiness and overflow of wickedness, and receive with meekness the implanted word, which is able to save your souls.
>
> (James 1:21)

We also see that the Jews who receive Jesus will have the spiritual seed, as the gifts and calling of God are irrevocable. Many of the Jewish people will be grafted back into their own tree.

And they also, if they do not continue in unbelief, will be grafted in, for God is able to graft them in again.
(Romans 11:23)

Since we have been grafted into the family of Abraham, we have quite a heritage. This Jewish heritage is the only true biblical root or foundation of faith in Jesus Christ. Don't let anyone fool you; it is a rich royal heritage for which you should be thankful. Even those who weren't Jews—such as Ruth—converted to the Jewish faith appreciating their new-found spiritual lineage. Remember Ruth, this physical picture of the church, told Naomi, "Your people will be my people."

How was this rich heritage established, nurtured, and then handed down from the Jews to us? God, through Abraham, Isaac, and Jacob (Israel), created a physical people to represent Him to the entire earth. Imagine, as the population of the world was worshiping idols, and wandering aimlessly in the futility of their own minds, God created a people with which He would communicate personally and exclusively. He would call them His own special people. God speaking to Moses says:

"'And you shall be to Me a kingdom of priests and a holy nation.' These are the words which you shall speak to the children of Israel."
(Exodus 19:6)

The Hebrew people were hand picked by God, starting with Abraham, as a people to represent Him to the rest of the earth.

When God created this special people He taught them how to think. He created a social order that was based on the worship of the God of the universe. He taught them to know the ways of God.

Of course, many didn't take advantage of this knowledge, but the Jews that had the faith of Abraham gave their very lives so that we could know how to think about the God of Israel. Why their very lives? The reason is that God engineered their lives, not only for His glory and their blessing, but also to be a source of nourishment to us. Their lives show us how to follow Jesus Christ!

I believe that Hebrews 12:1–2 is one of the most misinterpreted Scriptures in the Bible:

Therefore we also, since we are surrounded by so great a cloud of witnesses, let us lay aside every weight, and the sin which so easily ensnares us, and let us run with endurance the race that is set before us, looking unto Jesus, the author and finisher of our faith, who for the joy set before Him endured the cross, despising the shame, and has sat down at the right hand of the throne of God.

Most have been taught that this means that there is a heavenly grandstand of passed-on saints watching us down here. Here is another interpretation that I think is better.

These witnesses being spoken of are those who have gone on before us. They were running a race. Their lives were a witness of this powerful faith in the Lord of the universe to a lost and dying world. They are our example of how to be a witness to the lost and dying world of our time. They have handed the baton to us. They have finished their race and we have them as a pattern of how to finish our course and be a witness for the Lord Jesus Christ. Some of them made terrible mistakes and then regained their witness. Most of these witnesses came through the loins or the seed of faith of Abraham, Isaac, and Jacob. The examples of our spiritual ancestors' lives are a source of nourishment for us today.

The Jewish faith started with Abraham; one of the first things we see is a seventy-five-year-old man leaving his former life behind to follow this true and living God:

161

So Abram departed as the LORD had spoken to him, and Lot went with him. And Abram was seventy-five years old when he departed from Haran.

(Genesis 12:4)

We see that God was not only faithful to Abram, but through Abram's faith was teaching us to sojourn in this life and, in faith in the God of Abraham, to never look back.

By faith Abraham obeyed when he was called to go out to the place which he would receive as an inheritance. And he went out, not knowing where he was going. By faith he dwelt in the land of promise as in a foreign country, dwelling in tents with Isaac and Jacob, the heirs with him of the same promise; for he waited for the city which has foundations, whose builder and maker is God.

(Hebrews 11:8–10)

And truly if they had called to mind that country from which they had come out, they would have had opportunity to return. But now they desire a better, that is, a heavenly country. Therefore God is not ashamed to be called their God, for He has prepared a city for them.

(vv. 15–16)

Is that the life of the average believer in Jesus in America? Are we sojourning here in obedience to God's holy word on our way to a heavenly country? Or are we looking at Jesus as our cosmic genie, and in madness summoning Him to make things as comfortable as possible in this world system that we love? Do our lives say, "Yes, I am a follower of Jesus, but I will not leave my life to follow Him." Sounds a bit like nonsense, doesn't it? Oh, that our eyes were on God's upward call like father Abraham!

By the way, this upward call on Abraham didn't have him gazing up into the sky and waiting to go to heaven. He lived the spiritual reality of heaven in his life on earth. The Jewish person was taught to live holy for God here and now. So many Christians are waiting for the rapture or the next life as a way to escape the difficult realities of this life. It is because we have inherited a mind-set that doesn't understand "Thy kingdom come, Thy will be done on earth as it is in heaven." We are to cooperate with God to bring the reality of His glorious kingdom into this earth. That is what God chose Abraham's children to do. Sadly, most who are dying and on their way to hell don't see the reality of the kingdom of God in the church in America.

Father Abraham would obey God at any cost because of a characteristic that few in the American church seem to have. As Abraham was going to offer up, in God's eyes, his only son as a burnt sacrifice as per the Lord's command, there was a spiritual attribute that God was cultivating in this faithful follower. We know that the Lord had no intention of having Abraham go through with the sacrifice. What was God nurturing in Abraham? What is this trait that is important enough to test Abraham in this way? We find out as the angel of the Lord intervenes:

> *And He said, "Do not lay your hand on the lad, or do anything to him; for now I know that **you fear God**, since you have not withheld your son, your only son, from Me."*
>
> (Genesis 22:12)

Through Abraham, Isaac, and Israel we learn the importance of fearing the Lord. The fear of the Lord is a bedrock principle that is handed down to us from our roots. The fear of the Lord is another constant in the Jewish Scriptures. We would understand that if we would look to Abraham, Isaac, and Israel.

What about the many times the Jews forsook the fear of the Lord. How true! We can look to the mistakes they made, benefit from their lives, and not have to learn in the same difficult fashion as a result. What a wonderful opportunity for us; at the expense of others we can take instruction. The fear of the Lord has been given to us through our wonderful heritage!

There are different levels and a variety of applications of the fear of the Lord. You have probably heard the term referred to as an awe and reverence of God. This is true, yet in our Christian society that has an entirely different meaning than it did in the Bible. Today the world's use of the word *awesome* is very common and describes things that are not really very awesome. People say to each other, "Man, that was awesome!" about a Monday night football game. Regrettably, the church accepts the watered-down worldly application of awe, as today the awe and reverence of God produces very little respect for, and obedience to, the Lord Jesus Christ.

Compare the word *awesome* used for the center-fielder that makes a diving catch, to what you will see when you are lying facedown before Jesus Christ.

> *His head and hair were like wool, as white as snow, and His eyes like a flame of fire; His feet were like fine brass, as if refined in a furnace, and His voice as the sound of many waters; He had in His right hand seven stars, out of His mouth went a sharp two-edged sword, and His countenance was like the sun shining in its strength. And when I saw Him, I fell at His feet as dead.*
> (Revelation 1:14–17a)

Remember, this is the apostle John who had walked the shores of the Galilee with Jesus. Now, John sees King Jesus as we will, in all of His glory, and he falls to his face as he sees something truly awesome!

That is why Paul, the Jewish apostle, commanded those in the Philippian church to work out their own salvation in fear and trembling. This didn't mean that they could work for their salvation, yet we who claim Jesus' name, are to do everything possible to cooperate with the Lord's work in us, which demonstrates our reverence to Him. I want you to know that the thought of how *holy* and *awesome* He is makes me tremble. Dwight Pryor, teaching from his *Haverim* series recently said, "Awe and reverence should produce action and results."[50]

In this series he spoke of a psalm that impacted me greatly when I received the Lord Jesus. Because of the nature of my life-style before Christ, everything had to change. I didn't exactly know what to do in terms of how to think and speak, the employment I was to take on, how to be a husband and a father. From the time I was fourteen years of age until my thirty-second year of life, the only time I hadn't been on drugs was the couple of years I spent in prison. All I knew was that this Lord and King wouldn't have my old ways in this new life.

I sensed not only His great unexplainable love but His holiness, His unmatched power, and that I feared Him greatly! He began to communicate with me regarding the way I should behave, the places I should go, and the type of person He desired for me to become. I was so thankful that I could understand the spiritual thoughts of the Most High, yet at the same time I was trembling with the understanding that *someone like Him was talking to someone like me!* This psalm revealed what God was doing in my new life.

The secret of the LORD is with those who fear Him, and He will show them His covenant.

(Psalm 25:14)

Only with the Lord could it be possible to have such wonderful memories of the most difficult times. There were times when it seemed that we as a family, or I personally, was going under the deep waters of life because of financial trials or other assorted

---

[50] Dwight Pryor, "Fear of YHWY and Hebrew Spirituality," audio cassette, Center for Judaic Christian Studies, Haverim, October 2003.

difficulties associated with trying to carry your cross. God would speak to my spirit and bring me through by revealing Himself to me. He had given me this wonder, awe, and reverence of Him that carried me through, and praise Jesus, it still does! Oh, what so many are missing in that they don't fear the Lord! That lack of reverence for God grieves Him to the point that He doesn't speak to that heart of deception. To know Him is to fear Him!

In this same teaching Pryor also read a quote that was very interesting. Earlier we spoke about the Greco-Roman mind-set and its ungodly motivations that promote seeking after knowledge. Listen to this quote: "The Greeks study to comprehend; the Jews study to revere." You see, the Jewish perspective on learning isn't simply the acquisition of knowledge. Learning is a form of worship motivated by the awe and reverence that they have for the King of kings! Knowledge is for the purpose of understanding how to revere the Lord!

Pryor, also teaching on the difference between Greek thinking and Jewish thinking, discussed holiness from the two perspectives. He said that the Greeks would worship the holiness of beauty, while the Jews worshiped the beauty of holiness. You see, the Jewish mind-set was formed by God and in its purest form is a right way of thinking; while that of Greco-Roman is completely the opposite, and is on a collision course with the Creator, Messiah Jesus. The biblical Jewish mind-set would place one near to God, and the Greco-Roman would leave one far off. Which mind-set do you want to employ?

In this light we can better understand Ephesians 2:12–13. As Paul is addressing the Gentile believers in Messiah he says:

> . . . that at that time you were without Christ, being aliens from the commonwealth of Israel and strangers from the covenants of promise, having no hope and without God in the world. But now in

Christ Jesus you who once were far off have been brought near by the blood of Christ.

By the gospel seed of faith in Jesus, those who thought like the pagans are now saved and can have their minds renewed to think like father Abraham, Isaac, and Israel!

We have observed that the Lord created a physical people from the patriarchs to be a kingdom of priests to Him. By His Spirit, through His Jewish prophets and His word, He gave them a God-centered philosophy in order that He could be represented in a people to the entire world. In the Jewish people He planted an understanding of worship from which an entire culture grew.

This would be an appropriate time to be reminded of the Jewish olive tree in Romans 11. From this holy (meaning *set apart* for God) society's roots sprouted forth the understanding of every aspect of life for the person who desires to take up his cross and follow the Lord. We must not forget that the Creator calls Himself the God of Israel. Speaking of Israel's glorious rebirth:

You shall rejoice in the LORD, and glory in the Holy One of Israel.
(Isaiah 41:16b)

This holy tree of the people of faith contains the potential nourishment to build us up and give us necessary sustenance. The list of these nutrients includes, yet isn't limited to, right thinking of God, ourselves, and others; healthy congregating; being a light to the nations; and the word of God penned in human language.

Paul gives us a list in Romans 9:3–5:

For I could wish that I myself were accursed from Christ for my brethren, my countrymen according to the flesh, who are Israelites, to whom pertain the adoption, the glory, the covenants, the giving of the law, the service of God (temple service), *and the promises;*

167

of whom are the fathers and from whom, according to the flesh, Christ came, who is over all, the eternally blessed God. Amen.

Entire books have been written on any one of the great life-giving items on this menu that the Lord has served us through His people. Sadly, the church has missed out on this health food, and is malnourished and fragmented as a result.

The Lord intended this physical and spiritual legacy to be the foundation of our faith. Here is another Scripture that demonstrates this:

Now, therefore, you are no longer strangers and foreigners, but fellow citizens with the saints and members of the household of God, having been built on the foundation of the apostles and prophets, Jesus Christ Himself being the chief cornerstone, in whom the whole building, being fitted together, grows into a holy temple in the Lord, in whom you also are being built together for a dwelling place of God in the Spirit.

(Ephesians 2:19–22)

Friends, you don't have to be a structural engineer to know that if the foundation of a building isn't sound, the rest of the structure isn't either. One of those foundational pillars is the prophets, of which much of the church understands little.

We are to cooperate with the Father by following Jesus' example and building on that foundation described in Ephesians. Let me ask you a question. When was the last time you studied Obadiah, Isaiah, Micah, Joel, Zechariah, or Ezekiel? Does your heart weep for the Jewish people and the wayward church, like the God who spoke through Jeremiah in the first verse of the ninth chapter? Satan has damaged our foundation. We need to repent, and look to Abraham our earthly spiritual father. We must ask the heavenly Father in the name of King Jesus to help us set our spiritual house on a truthful, balanced foundation. That, my brothers and sisters, is called restoration!

The baton has been handed from the Jewish people to us. We are now to run the race much like that of our spiritual ancestors. In 1 Peter 2:9–10 the Lord calls us to royalty. It is now our time to be a royal priesthood, and a holy nation. We have attained royalty for such a time as this. We who once were not a people are now the people of God and are the only light for the nations. Will we follow the people who tried to reinvent God's wheel, or will we look to Abraham? Will we realize that the root of Abraham, Isaac, and Israel hold up our faith?

Like the world, will we view the Jewish people as "those stubborn people who killed Jesus?" Will we see them as a small insignificant people that are causing the world's problems? Will we look at them as a people that God has a mysterious plan for later, but really have little to do with us? Instead, will we appreciate them, identify with the Jewish people, and learn from our royal Hebrew legacy?

Just to give you an idea of God's perspective, let's close this chapter by looking at Isaiah 49:22–23 as God clearly states the future of Israel:

"Behold, I will lift My hand in an oath to the nations, and set up My standard for the peoples; they shall bring your sons in their arms, and your daughters shall be carried on their shoulders; kings shall be your foster fathers, and their queens your nursing mothers; they shall bow down to you with their faces to the earth, and lick up the dust of your feet. Then you will know that I am the LORD, for they shall not be ashamed who wait for Me."

This is the Jewish nation of Israel being served by human kings and queens during Christ's thousand-year reign on earth. The Jewish people who receive Jesus will be restored to a position of royalty.

These are just a few examples of the many branches that shoot forth from the root that makes up the tree of faith we have been grafted into as the church of Jesus Christ. I pray that this has been enough to send you on a mission to know the truth more clearly. May we look to Abraham, Isaac, and Israel to discover with greater clarity the Jewish Messiah, Jesus Christ.

Again, what is the purpose of looking to Abraham, Isaac, Israel, and having our foundations restored? Is it so we can be more Jewish? Oh, God forbid! The goal is to fulfill the call to have authentic faith in King Jesus! On this journey it would be natural to take on a degree of Jewish identity, as our Savior and spiritual ancestors are Jewish. Yet, the primary responsibility that you, myself, and Jesus' body are given is to follow after our glorious Savior, and worship His Father, by the Holy Spirit in truth. Isn't that what Jesus called us to do?

As some of the Pharisees confidently boasted to Jesus of their righteousness, based on their lineage from Abraham, what did Jesus say?

If you were Abraham's children, you would do the works of Abraham.

(John 8:39b)

May we learn and do the works of father Abraham. Amen.

CHAPTER 12

The Law? A Necessary Distinction

But his delight is in the law of the LORD . . .

(Psalm 1:2)

One of the most controversial Bible doctrines (teachings about God) is the application of what we have come to know as the Mosaic law. This would include all of the Levitical statutes, including the Ten Commandments.

To some degree it is a line of division between the predominantly Gentile congregations and the predominantly Jewish Messianic congregations. It also tends to divide those in the messianic movement from one another. Here we are again, with contention resulting in division. Do you see a theme yet? Are you beginning to understand that the enemy of God is making us enemies of each other? How? By perverting the word of God and using disagreements to drive us apart instead of drawing us together on our knees in humble pursuit for the truth.

Could it be that we are so busy defending our positions that we aren't seeking after Jesus with all of our heart, mind, soul, and strength for our own necessary adjustments? If this is the case and we don't repent, the same empty, dry, ineffective, unpleasing-to-God culture of faith that we call Christianity, which in America is quickly becoming just another religion, will be our lot. Could it be that we need to humbly repent of having our own agenda and look at the beam in our own eye (Matthew 7:3–5)?

Guess how I learned to ask you that question. That's right, the Lord Jesus convicted me of the 'California Redwood' in my own eye. I thought I had this Christian-Jewish thing down so well that I didn't need to make any adjustments. Then the Lord stepped in and showed me that I knew not what I thought I knew. In no uncertain terms He humbled me and I was quite undone, as Isaiah said in his sixth chapter.

Much like some of the other divisions, the shame of this one (application of the law) is that it is quite unnecessary. God spends so much time and energy using His prophets and apostles through His unchanging word to prevent it. The Lord constantly and comprehensively spells it out for us, so that we can know the truth and be set free. The problem is that there are agendas, traditions, and demonic extremes that must be identified, and from which we must turn away.

I will give you examples in a moment, yet I must first share why understanding God's truth on this issue became a matter of extreme importance for me. I had been saved a very short time. The Lord gave me these wonderful Gentile people that loved the Jews and began teaching me what it meant to be Jewish. I went to Israel with them and was having a lovely time, when people also very close to me began instructing that I needed to be more Jewish. They preached that it was necessary for me to keep some of the Levitical laws, such as keeping kosher and observing the Sabbath. I had trouble understanding why I should only keep some of the laws, but we will discuss that later. I really wanted to obey Jesus with all of my heart, so I needed to know what to do.

My dilemma began to manifest soon after I came back from Israel, as my second baby was born and my wife was in the hospital recovering. She asked me to order her a pepperoni pizza, which after having a baby shouldn't be such an unreasonable request. However, I told her, "No, we are not going to break God's laws." Thankfully, she was quite patient with me as I went on a search for the truth regarding the understanding of the law. Praise Jesus, if we really are seeking, He will reveal the truth!

Lord willing, what I will do with a little help from Hebrew and Greek resources, is to first make biblical distinctions on the word *law*. Then I will seek to establish through Scripture how God intends for us to apply it. Then we will see that the Lord establishes, in most circumstances, that we are not to divide over one's thinking on this issue. There are healthy divisions, which the Scriptures identify and confirm. I will seek to establish the one instance we are to divide over this issue to protect the flock. Prayerfully, we then will have the leading from the Holy Spirit to follow Jesus in applying the law.

To the detriment of Jesus' body, the church has traditionally been taught a fractional meaning of the word *law*. The way the church has been taught to understand the word *law* would be like describing to a child the world's most beautiful merry-go-round, with majestic, multicolored horses with lovely painted ornaments, accompaniment by the most festive music, as merely a ride that goes round and round. Quite purposely, I believe, the divided body of Messiah has been handed different partial teachings on the law.

You see, the Hebrew word for *law*, which is generally transliterated *torah*, means so much more than commandments or laws as we think of them. The word more accurately means "teaching" or "instruction." Here are some quotes from a Jesus-centered Hebrew resource.

The word *tora* means basically "teaching" whether it is the wise man instructing his son or God instructing Israel. The wise give insight into all aspects of life so that the young may know how to conduct themselves and to live a long blessed life (Proverbs 3:11). So too God, motivated by love, reveals to man basic insight into how to live with each other and how to approach God. Through the law God shows his interest in all aspects of man's life, which is to be lived under his direction and care. **Law of God stands parallel to word of the Lord** to signify that law is the revelation of God's will (e.g. Isa 1:10). In this capacity it becomes the nation's wisdom and understanding so that others will marvel at the quality of Israel's distinctive life style (Deut 4:6).[51]

Here we see that the word *law* refers to the wise counsel of God Himself. In most Christian circles we have been taught to think of the word only as it relates to the Levitical statutes, which then justifies in the minds of many the dismissing of the need for torah in our lives. For one moment, try to forget how the *isms* and *ists* have primarily interpreted the word *torah*. Temporarily forget that Judaism is thought to define it as only the first five books of Moses, while the Methodists, Baptists, and other Christian denominations define it only as the Levitical commandments. If we just become followers of King Jesus it gets so simple to understand. The Lord gave us His torah to teach us His ways and to reveal Himself to us.

Does this mean that the word does not speak of God's commandments? No, in a number of places in Scripture, torah does specifically speak of the statutes that are administered by the descendants of the Israeli tribe of Levi. Hence, the statutes are known as those of the Levitical priesthood. "Specifically law refers to any set of regulations; e.g., Ex 12 contains the law in regard to observing the Passover. Some other specific laws include those for the various offerings (Lev 7:37), for leprosy (Lev 14:57) and for jealousy (Num 5:29). In this light

---

[51] *Theological Workbook of the Old Testament,* vol. 1, 404.

law is often considered to consist of statutes, ordinances, precepts, commandments, and testimonies."[52] I might add that this would include the Ten Commandments.

So we see that one of the narrow or specific definitions of torah is the Levitical law, but we also have necessary teaching that we in so many cases dismiss as done away with and obsolete from the Old Testament doctrines. This has resulted in a people that don't have the necessary tools of wisdom and understanding to function in this New Covenant!

May I explain? Soon after I got saved I became a sponge, attempting to soak up the knowledge and understanding of the truth of King Jesus. I was listening to many Bible teachers, studying, praying, fasting, and attending services. The church I was attending introduced a ministry that God used to change my life. It is called Precept Ministries, and a majority of the Bible teaching is presented by a woman of God named Kay Arthur. In case some of you have concerns, her husband is a spiritual authority over the ministry, and our pastors were overseeing the teaching. Anyway, just the definition of the word *precept* that was given from this ministry began to change my life. So much of the truth that is transforming me into a man that can truly follow King Jesus is from principles that came from what we call the Old Testament, including the first five books, which are called the Law of Moses by Jesus (Luke 24:44).

You see, I learned that a *precept is God's standard by which His children are to live.* The children of God the Father who aren't living by these precepts are living substandard lives. Beloved, that is the state of most in the body in America!

I will give you a few examples. For most of my life I had been, among other things, a fornicator. I repented when I received Jesus, but had no practical knowledge to help me live out my desire to

---

[52] Ibid.

remain clean before God. Then, I learned some of God's precepts. I learned that God commands His children to be holy as He is holy. What are some precepts or principles that will help me to accomplish this? One that I use to this day is found in Job 31:1:

"I have made a covenant with my eyes; why then should I look upon a young woman?"

This principle sets the standard for my life.

I, Don Schwarz, made a covenant with my eyes as soon as I understood this principle. For me not to look away when there is a potential temptation involving the opposite sex is sin and a violation of God's precepts regarding holiness and purity. Is it always easy? Do I ever face temptation? No, it isn't easy, and of course, I still battle my flesh, this world of iniquity, and the devil. However, I have learned how to overcome by applying God's torah (instruction) by making no provision for my flesh, which we see in the New Covenant in Romans 13:14.

The Lord has given me the power to honor this covenant with my eyes. The reason that so many today are becoming casualties of horrible sins of sexual perversion is because they don't know these simple-to-understand precepts of God, thus they live substandard lives. I apply this to the television, the computer, the places I go, the people with whom I associate. When I cannot avoid being in the presence of temptation, I pray and seek Jesus to help me see the desperate need of a person's soul, not their flesh which they flaunt in ignorance.

Why does this sound like puritanical nonsense to most Christians in America? It is because they don't understand God's precepts. Here is another one. The Lord told Israel to utterly destroy the enemies in the land. I learned that as the Lord commanded the children of Israel not to *compromise* with the enemies in their land, I am not to compromise with my enemies today. Of course,

Jesus told us to love our enemies (Matthew 5:44). The enemies that I am speaking of in this New Covenant are my own flesh, the world system set against God, and the devil. All we need to do is simply look at the plight of Israel, as they compromised with the pagan world around them to see our own destiny if we won't put to death the deeds of our own flesh, and our compromise with the world and the devil.

We, in the power of the Holy Spirit, are to destroy any pride, anger, lust, lying, greed, and any other sin that will continually gain ground in our lives. If not, the Midianites, Philistines, or the Amalekites, which wouldn't have been there had they obeyed the Lord, eventually will rise up and take us into bondage. One place we see this is in the book of Judges.

Before looking at Judges though, I would like to first ask a question. In the Law of Moses (the first five books of the Bible), and the prophets, do we see a fairy tale where people live happily ever after? No, we see the real life of a people set apart for God, most of whom disregarded Him and suffered horrible consequences. That which is meant to be holy can be perverted. It can become useless to God, and also useful for God's enemies to blaspheme the Lord. This set-apart people of God (the Jews) became evil and greatly angered the Lord. Judges 2:10–15:

> When all that generation had gathered to their fathers, another generation arose after them who did not know the LORD nor the work which He had done for Israel. Then the children of Israel did evil in the sight of the LORD, and served the Baals; and they forsook the LORD God of their fathers, who had brought them out of the land of Egypt; and they followed other gods from among the gods of the people who were all around them, and they bowed down to them; and they provoked the LORD to anger. They forsook the LORD and served Baal and the Ashtoreths. And the anger of the LORD was hot against Israel. So He delivered them into the hands of plunderers who de-spoiled them; and He sold them into the hands of their enemies

177

all around, so that they could no longer stand before their enemies. Wherever they went out, the hand of the LORD was against them for calamity, as the LORD had said, and as the LORD had sworn to them. And they were greatly distressed.

A repeated Scripture was one of the themes of the times of the Judges in Israel, Judges 21:25:

In those days there was no king in Israel; and everyone did what was right in his own eyes.

This is one of the darkest periods in Israel's history, as they had forgotten the Lord and became their own king. What about us? Do we act as though there is no king in our lives, and do what is right in our own eyes? What is the opposite of doing what is right in your own eyes? The answer is obeying the teaching, or instruction, which is the torah of the Lord.

In Judges the Jewish people were again in terrible trouble with God, which was their plight then and still is today. What does this have to do with God's torah (teaching), precepts, and principles? Today, we have a nation of church people that really don't *know* Lord Jesus. They know His name, and a lot about Him, but most don't know Him. They don't know His covenants, precepts, principles, and worst of all they haven't experienced Him in their lives. Sadly, they know religion, not Jesus. Without the *knowledge* of God's precepts, we will certainly wind up in trouble with God.

Seeking after the knowledge of the Lord is another precept (2 Chronicles 1:10; Proverbs 1:4, 7, 22, 2:10–11, 10:14; Hosea 4:6). Where did King David, the man after God's own heart, tell us to get knowledge?

Blessed is the man who walks not in the counsel of the ungodly, nor stands in the path of sinners, nor sits in the seat of the scornful; but *his delight is in the **law** of the LORD, and in His **law** he meditates day and night.*

(Psalm 1:1–2)

What word here is used for law? That's right, it is *torah*, and refers not only to the Mosaic laws, but also to God's teaching, most of which at that time had come from the books of Moses. We need to humbly appreciate and learn the precepts, instruction, and principles that the Lord has given us, and follow His teachings (torah) to do so.

What good is knowledge without wisdom? One of the things wisdom provides is the ability to use knowledge. If we have knowledge that we can't properly use, what good is the knowledge? The best definition I have ever heard of the word *wisdom* is from the Hebrew word *chokmah* or *khok-maw,* as it is transliterated into English. It is the Hebrew word used for wisdom in most of the Old Testament. It means "Mastering the art of living in accordance with God's expectations." Isn't that a great precept?

How do we get knowledge and wisdom?

The fear of the LORD is the beginning of wisdom, and the knowledge of the Holy One is understanding.

(Proverbs 9:10)

Having a genuine, reverential awe of God facilitates the receiving of useful knowledge, wisdom, and understanding. This type of awe provokes us to action and produces results. Where do we find God's wisdom? Where would Solomon tell us to look?

*For the commandment is a lamp, and the **law** a light; reproofs of instruction are the way of life, to keep you from the evil woman, from the flattering tongue of a seductress.*

(Proverb 6:23–24)

179

Here we are taught by God, not only the torah as commandments, but also torah as God's instruction. The torah gives us wisdom as it instructs how to avoid the seducer. Look at all of these rich precepts!

Some would say that since we have the New Covenant, we don't need to tap into, and then obey the principles given to Moses or the prophets. My, I can't understand why so many believe in evolution today. Having completed a house to the tenth floor you don't then rip out the foundation and justify it because you have a building built upon it. It is quite a scary concept! Yet, so many unknowingly live in the Leaning Tower of Pisa, and a great number of them are pastors and leaders in the church!

I do have much good news! Today we have men and women who have learned from the torah of God. They are people of valor like Joshua, whose name in Hebrew is an incredibly close spelling to a man who never compromised in battle, namely King Jesus! Those like Caleb, Ruth, Deborah, Joseph, and of course, many others who are alive and well today! We have contemporary lovers of Jesus, who are living by God's precepts and principles. Many of these precepts are directly from the first five books of Moses and the rest of what we call the Old Testament. Many don't even know that they love the law of the Lord, or how Hebraic their lives really are. They just love Jesus and His word, and God is doing the rest! Isn't this good news?

I think of the teachings of Moses, the prophets, the rest of the Old Testament writings, and the precepts, principles, and judgments therein, as another facet of God's great loving-kindness toward me. You see, I am greatly thankful and hopeful. With love and mercy God took a hopeless, dying man like me, and picked me up like a piece of bubblegum that had been stuck to the bottom of the world's shoe. Then King Jesus mercifully taught me, and is teaching me of Himself by these glorious truths! If there is hope for me, there is hope for anybody! I will move on to the more-debated definitions of the law in just a moment. But first I must add one more precept that will change your life. No matter what, even when times are tough, especially when times are tough, rejoice in Jesus!

> *Though the fig tree may not blossom, nor fruit be on the vines; though the labor of the olive may fail, and the fields yield no food; though the flock may be cut off from the fold, and there be no herd in the stalls—yet I will rejoice in the LORD, I will joy in the God of my salvation.*
>
> (Habakkuk 3:17–18)

Praise Jesus for His torah!

The longest chapter in the entire Bible is about what? It is torah, the teachings of God's word exalted in Psalm 119:

> *I will never forget Your precepts, for by them You have given me life.*
>
> (Psalm 119:93)

Amen!

CHAPTER 13

Should We Then Keep the Law?

. . . Judah is my lawgiver.

(Psalm 108:8)

I would like to move on now, and inform you how the Lord Jesus stepped into my quandary regarding the observation of the Levitical statutes such as the Ten Commandments, Shabbat (the Sabbath), and the Feasts of the Lord. Around the same time this confusion was troubling me, I was introduced to Precepts Ministries. I enrolled in a twelve-month journey in the book of Romans. I committed myself to study on average thirty to forty-five minutes every day, which was required to fully participate. It was amazing! We studied line upon line, cross-referenced through the whole Bible, and did Hebrew and Greek word studies to confirm the meaning of many verses. Did I mention that it was amazing?

King Jesus taught me so much as I participated with great zeal in the class. My wife and I were invited to lunch with the pastor of our church one Sunday. I almost fell out of my chair when he asked me to pursue certification from Precepts Ministries to teach their ministry material at our church. I was very thankful and sensed such a challenge to teach God's word that I spent a great deal of time on most of my lessons. I was still young in the

Lord and frankly, was quite overwhelmed. This challenged me to spend much time studying, praying, and relying in new ways upon the Lord Jesus.

I had almost completed the Romans study when I began to teach. We were in the spiritual gifts for twelve weeks or so. We then went into Judges for many weeks, then into a study on God's covenants for approximately six months. We also studied Titus and James line upon line. In the midst of this abundant, wonderful, life-giving knowledge of God, I was given the answers to the question of the Levitical observances. By the time we were through with the study of Hebrews, I had a clear understanding of God's will regarding the application of the law. The Lord my God met me in His word, and completely resolved my confusion. We studied Hebrews for nine months, and I will share with you a bit of what God has revealed from His word.

Before we can understand today's application of the Ten Commandments or the additional specific statutes and observances that the Lord issued, we must first understand something else: God created a thing called time. The great God of the universe exists above and outside of time. One of the reasons He created time is so that He could unfold His plans and purposes in human affairs through it. God has always existed and will always continue to exist. He is not getting old and neither will we after we physically die. In the first chapter of Genesis when the Bible says, "In the beginning," it is the beginning of what? It is the starting of the clock, or the calendar, for humankind.

I am going somewhere with this, so hang on. God factored into His plan that Adam would sin and kill the human race. We see that God had a plan of redemption before the foundation of the world.

*. . . just as He chose us in Him **before the foundation of the world,** that we should be holy and without blame before Him in love, having **predestined us to adoption as sons by Jesus Christ to Himself,***

*according to the good pleasure of His will, to the praise of the glory
of His grace, by which He made us accepted in the Beloved.*
(Ephesians 1:4–6)

Here is a Scripture that illustrates the curse on humans that
necessitates a need for redemption:

*Therefore, just as through one man sin entered the world, and death
through sin, and thus death spread to all men because all sinned—*
(Romans 5:12)

God knew about Adam's sin and the death of mankind before
such a thing called time. Having established that, let's move on
shall we?

God pronounced that one would come through the seed of the
woman that would give a crushing blow to the seed of the devil in
Genesis 3:15. This person of the seed of faith was handed down
through Noah, to Abraham, Isaac, and Jacob, and ultimately fulfilled in the Messiah Jesus Christ. Do you remember our discussion
regarding the seed? Genesis 3:15 is the place that the seed of Jesus
Christ is first pronounced in time.

We know that after the time of Abraham, Isaac, and Jacob, the
people of the seed of faith went into bondage in Egypt, as God told
Abraham they would (Genesis 15:13–16). In these passages we
also see that a period of time, four hundred years, would pass and
God would bring them back to Israel. These are not happenstances
that randomly take place in the lives of people. This is God's plan
being unfolded in time.

When (see the reference to time) God delivered the children
of Israel from Egypt, He stepped into time and met them at Mount
Sinai. God personally appointed a meeting with their representa-
tive that He selected named Moses. He then gave them a set of
commandments and observances including such things as the

Sabbath, the feasts of the Lord, the Ten Commandments, along with what totaled six hundred and thirteen laws. These were spiritual laws as well as civil laws, which is where much of our civil law in America originated.

Who gave these laws? Was it Moses? Of course not, it was the God of heaven. To whom did these laws pertain? They were only for the people of the seed of Abraham, Isaac, and Jacob. God was revealing Himself, at this *time,* to the Jewish people as they were the exclusive people of the seed at that *time.*

> *He declares His word to Jacob, His statutes* [or laws] *and His judgments to Israel. He has not dealt thus with any nation; and as for His judgments, they have not known them. Praise the Lord!*
> (Psalm 147:19–20)

God gave the laws and appointed a specific people from those of the seed to administer this body of statutes. Who were these ministers? They were those from the tribe of Levi, from which we get the term *the Levitical priesthood.* God established the highest position in this human priesthood, the high priest who of course is a human being.

However, there was another priesthood that already existed but was not yet being administered in human affairs at this time. It is called the priesthood of Melchizedek.

We first see Melchizedek in Genesis 14:18–20:

> *Then Melchizedek king of Salem brought out bread and wine; he was the priest of God Most High. And he blessed him and said: "Blessed be Abram of God Most High, Possessor of heaven and earth; and blessed be God Most High, who has delivered your enemies into your hand." And he* [Abram] *gave him a tithe of all.*

What does Scripture tell us about Melchizedek?

We see that he was the king of Salem, which means peace. Salem is ancient Jerusalem. He was king of the city of peace, and also a what? He was a *priest* of the Most High God. Here we see the introduction of the priesthood of Melchizedek. Who will later reign as King and be the High Priest from the city of peace named Jerusalem? That is right, our King Jesus Christ. This priesthood of Melchizedek appears later in time in Psalm 110:4:

The LORD has sworn and will not relent, "You are a priest forever according to the order of Melchizedek."

In this psalm there is a man declared to be the Priest of God forever, which is outside of time, according to the priesthood of Melchizedek. Was that priesthood operating in the affairs of Israel in David's time? No it wasn't. The Levitical priesthood was operating and demanding obedience.

Why wasn't this priesthood of Melchizedek being administered while the Levitical one was? Simply, it wasn't time for its administration yet. It was time for that of the tribe of Levi. If we want to follow Jesus in spirit and truth, we must look at the true Lawgiver and see what He is doing, and be ready to forsake the traditions of man. Does the Lawgiver come into the human race from the tribe of Levi?

Listen to this:

Gilead is Mine, and Manasseh is Mine; Ephraim also is the helmet for My head; Judah is My lawgiver.

(Psalm 60:7)

The lawgiver is one that would, in time, come from the tribe of Judah not Levi:

The scepter shall not depart from Judah, nor a lawgiver from between his feet, until Shiloh comes; and to Him shall be the obedience of the people.

(Genesis 49:10)

Who comes from the tribe of Judah that could also be a future King of Jerusalem, which would be God's Lawgiver and High Priest forever? Of course, it is Jesus the Messiah.

So *when* does this priesthood start? It already has! In the fullness of time Jesus came into the world, lived a sinless life, suffered on the way to and then on the cross. He rose again and is now the High Priest of our faith.

> *But when the fullness of the time has come, God sent forth His Son, born of a woman, born under the law, to redeem those who were under the law, that we might receive the adoption as sons.*
>
> (Galatians 4:4)

We will continue to look at the Scriptures that not only instruct us that this priesthood is operational today, but how to apply that instruction to our lives, as well as its relationship to that of Levi.

We observe in God's written word that the priesthood of Jesus is functioning today in the affairs of those who have repented and believed on Him. In Hebrews 5:5–6 we see the calling of Jesus to High Priest:

> *So also Christ did not glorify Himself to become High Priest, but it was He who said to Him: "You are My Son, today I have begotten You." As He also says in another place: "You are a priest forever according to the order of Melchizedek."*

Here is a New Covenant confirmation that Jesus Christ is the High Priest now in time.

Authors and teachers John McTernan and Louis Ruggiero wrote on the theocracy and priesthood of Jesus. While addressing the fact that Jesus would restore Israel, they wrote something very interesting. "Isaiah forty-nine unveils the Messiah's ministry set before Him by Almighty God. He would be called to complete all of the things that Israel failed to accomplish. Since Israel was called to be a kingdom of priests to the entire world, **the Messiah Himself would provide the priesthood that was taken away from Israel as a result of their sin.** In addition, He would reconcile the children of Israel before the Lord by providing atonement for their sins."[53]

The Bible tells us that the Father initiates a new priesthood in Jesus Christ. When in time does this happen? It happened when Jesus was resurrected. In the previous Scripture that says ". . . today I have begotten thee" we see the initiation of the priesthood of Jesus Christ. But doesn't *begotten* address His birth in Bethlehem? Well, that is partially what it means. Yet, there is Scripture that establishes that it also refers to the Resurrection.

I will give Scriptures to explain both meanings. In John 1:14 we see King Jesus begotten in the incarnation:

And the Word became flesh and dwelt among us, and we beheld His glory, the glory as of the only begotten of the Father, full of grace and truth.

We also see Jesus begotten of the Father in Acts 13:32–34:

And we declare to you glad tidings—that promise which was made to the fathers. God has fulfilled this for us their children, in that He has raised up Jesus. As it is also written in the second Psalm: "You are My Son, today I have begotten You." And that He raised Him from the dead, no more to return to corruption, He has spoken thus: "I will give you the sure mercies of David."

---

[53] King Messiah Series, *Part 1: Jesus of Nazareth* (Oklahoma City: Hearthstone Publishing, 2002), 71.

In this passage the initiation of the new priesthood is proclaimed by resurrection!

Let's continue in Hebrews, as this forever priesthood unfolds, and pick up at 5:9–11:

*And having been **perfected**, He became the author of eternal salvation to all who obey Him, called by God as **High Priest** "according to the order of Melchizedek," of whom we have much to say, and hard to explain, since you have become dull of hearing.*

There are four things I would like us to see here.

One is that Jesus didn't somehow need to become perfect, as it would appear at first glance, to someone who didn't know the context of the Scriptures. A man would have to live a sinless life over a period of time to become the acceptable sacrifice to pay for the sins of the world. Jesus, having never sinned over the time of His life, became that perfect acceptable sacrifice. Again, in the above Scripture, Jesus the author of eternal salvation, is the High Priest according to the order of Melchizedek.

The author of Hebrews then stops to share with these Jewish believers something that should cause self-examination. He tells them that he is hesitant to share the teaching of Melchizedek with them because they will have an unhealthy difficulty understanding this truth. The source of their difficulty regarding their understanding of the relationship between the priesthood of Melchizedek and Jesus Christ is their own dullness of hearing. This verse and the next few passages in Hebrews explain to us that we can become unable to understand the necessary meat of God's word. On some occasions when I have tried to explain the relationship of the Levitical commandments to the New Covenant to believers who have been saved for quite some time, it is like talking to a person in another language.

Why? The next verses give us the answer. Hebrews 5:12–14:

For though by this time you ought to be teachers, you need someone to teach you again the first principles of the oracles of God; and you have come to need milk and not solid food. For everyone who partakes only of milk is unskilled in the word of righteousness, for he is a babe. But solid food belongs to those who are of full age, that is, those who by reason of use have their senses exercised to discern both good and evil.

You see, today there are so many who have gone along with the flow of the world, that as a result of not discerning good from evil and then acting on that discernment, they have no spiritual sense. They have become, or remained, babes in Christ and cannot hear the meat of God's word.

How tragic to be a spiritual dwarf without the ability, or skill as Hebrews terms it, to hear from God regarding these meaty and necessary issues! How long have you been saved? Can you hear from God? Can you understand His word? In great caution I cry out to God and petition Him that I would never get to a place where I can't discern His voice and His word. Am I saying that we should understand everything in the Bible as we read it? No, what I mean is that we should be exercising our senses, discerning good from evil, and acting on what God shows us, so that we can then understand the things He desires to reveal to us in the proper time. If someone like me can understand these things in Christ, any child of God who really desires to surely can!

In the seventh chapter, the author of Hebrews continues the instruction of Melchizedek for the purpose of explaining the superiority of, and need for, a better priesthood. Like an artist painting a beautiful work, he brushes the canvas with the colorful explanation of why God uses Melchizedek to illustrate the priesthood of Jesus the Christ.

For this Melchizedek, king of Salem, priest of the Most High God, who met Abraham returning from the slaughter of the kings and blessed him, to whom also Abraham gave a tenth part of all, first being translated "king of righteousness," and then also king of Salem, meaning "king of peace," without father, without mother, without genealogy, having neither beginning of days nor end of life, but made like the Son of God, remains a priest continually.

(Hebrews 7:1–3)

The author shares with us that unlike the priests descended from the tribe of Levi this priest, who is called king of righteousness and king of peace, is without genealogy. The Scripture tells us that he hasn't a beginning of days or end of life, which would mean that he is, at the very least, a picture of one who operates outside of time and that he was made like the Son of God. He also remains a priest continually. Some interpret this to mean that this is the preincarnate Jesus Christ, while others say that Melchizedek is a picture, or a type, of Jesus. My position is not relevant to the point: The point being that this priesthood is superior to that of Levi, as Levi's priesthood is finite. The priests are men that have a beginning and an end, as does this priesthood. Not so with the priesthood of Melchizedek.

Hebrews chapter 7–11 goes on to confirm this. Let's cut to the chase with Hebrews 7:11–14:

Therefore, if perfection were through the Levitical priesthood (for under it the people received the law), what further need was there that another priest should rise according to the order of Melchizedek, and not be called according to the order of Aaron? For the priesthood being changed, of necessity there is also a change of the law. For He of whom these things are spoken belongs to another tribe, from which no man has officiated at the altar. For it is evident that our Lord arose from Judah, of which tribe Moses spoke nothing concerning priesthood.

Did you see that the Scripture teaches that there was a need for a change of law?

Friends, the Levitical priesthood was not perfect. It couldn't be, as its priests were mere men. This priesthood was passing away just like its priests.

Also there were many priests, because they were prevented by death from continuing. But He, because He continues forever, has an unchangeable priesthood.

(Hebrews 7:23–24)

The Levitical or Aaronic priesthood is over. There is no high priest officiating for that priesthood. The above Scriptures tell us that the priesthood has been changed to one that is officiated by a high priest from another tribe than Levi. Which one is it? In that light "Judah is my lawgiver" makes a lot of sense, doesn't it?

Hebrews 7:18–19 continues by explaining the annulling of the former commandments as we know them:

For on the one hand there is an annulling of the former commandment because of its weakness and unprofitable-ness, for the law made nothing perfect; on the other hand, there is the bringing in of a better hope, through which we draw near to God.

What I couldn't understand, as I mentioned earlier, is why those who instructed me to keep the commandments in the prior fashion before the time of the new priesthood, only partially keep the laws themselves. For example, why weren't they sacrificing a bull for atonement? The reason is that the final sacrifice has been made, which is the very reason that we have a new priesthood!

It is very simple, with a *new priesthood* comes *new priests, new commandments, and new spiritual applications to the old ones.*

These new spiritual applications can only be understood if the *Holy Spirit is residing inside a person*, enabling them to live out the *fulfillment of Jesus to the Old*. We should be very thankful for this new and living way in that *the old commandments demand justice for anything less than perfect obedience to them*. I will explain these Italicized words.

In John 13:34–35 Jesus is preparing His disciples to be the first priests in this priesthood. What does He tell them?

> *"A new commandment I give to you, that you love one another; as I have loved you, that you also love one another. By this all will know that you are My disciples, if you have love for one another."*

This new commandment was that they love one another, not like they previously had under the law, but as a priest in this new priestly order loves. They love with the love of the High Priest Jesus.

We must understand that in this new priesthood we who believe in Jesus are the priests of God. In the old priesthood the descendants of Aaron, who descended from Levi, were the priests (Exodus 28:1–4). First Peter 2:9,10 addresses the priestly responsibility of the New Covenant priests:

> *But you are a chosen generation, a royal priesthood, a holy nation, His own special people, that you may proclaim the praises of Him who called you out of darkness into His marvelous light; who once were not a people but are now the people of God, who had not obtained mercy but now have obtained mercy.*

We who once weren't God's people have been begotten into the priesthood with serious responsibilities.

Wait, how have we been brought into the priesthood? We have been adopted by the new birth into it. How are we saved? By being born from above or born again. As we are born again we *all* become priests unto God. Then we have New Covenant priestly responsibilities that are intensely different from those of the old priesthood. We need to be consecrated (set apart, holy) priests unto the Lord.

By the way, we should take instruction as God warns His priests in Hosea 4:6:

> *My people are destroyed for lack of knowledge. Because you have rejected knowledge, I also will reject you from being priest for Me; because you have forgotten the law of your God, I also will forget your children.*

The application for us is not the Levitical statutes, but the law of the Spirit that we are to walk in as New Covenant priests. We need to take our responsibilities as priests unto the Lord seriously.

Is your life holy? Are you set apart and living apart from the system of the world? Here is a new application to an old statute concept:

> *I beseech you therefore, brethren, by the mercies of God, that you present your bodies a living sacrifice, holy, acceptable to God, which is your reasonable service. And do not be conformed to this world, but be transformed by the renewing of your mind, that you may prove what is that good and acceptable and perfect will of God.*
>
> (Romans 12:1–2)

This means that since God has shown mercy to Jew and Gentile, in spite of their disobedience, through this glorious and unimaginable plan of grace through the ages, we should (at least) be living sacrifices to God. In the old way they killed the sacrifice and offered it to God; in this priesthood we the priests are to live our lives as a sacrifice to the Lord.

We are to be dead to ourselves in terms of our fleshly, earthly, carnal desires and pursuits by baptism into His death, and alive to His will no matter the cost, by the resurrection of His life! (see Romans 6). Do you see the replacing of the old, which is a sacrifice of a dead animal on the altar, with the new, which is a consecrated, resurrected life that gives God great glory and births others into the priesthood?

Only King Jesus can fulfill the requirements of the law in terms of perfect obedience to it. The commandments demand perfection.

> *For as many as are of the works of the law are under the curse; for it is written "Cursed is everyone who does not continue in all things which are written in the book of the law, to do them." But that no one is justified by the law in the sight of God is evident, for "the just shall live by faith." Yet the law is not of faith, but "the man who does them shall live by them."*
>
> (Galatians 3:10–12)

In Deuteronomy 31:26 Moses says something very interesting to the Levite priests:

> *"Take this Book of the Law, and put it beside the ark of the covenant of the LORD your God, that it may be there as a witness against you; for I know your rebellion and your stiff neck."*

Israel demonstrated that the statutes of the law are impossible for a sinful human being to keep. The law is a witness to the wickedness of the nation of Israel and to us all. The Bible teaches us that the law is a witness to and an agitator of our sin, which causes us to die all the more.

Does that mean that the law is not good? Paul answers in Romans 7:7–12:

What shall we say then? Is the law sin? Certainly not! On the contrary, I would not have known sin except through the law. For I would not have known covetousness unless the law had said, "You shall not covet." But sin, taking opportunity by the commandment, produced in me all manner of evil desire. For apart from the law sin was dead. I was alive once without the law, but when the commandment came, sin revived and I died. And the commandment, which was to bring life, I found to bring death. For sin taking occasion by the commandment, deceived me, and by it killed me. Therefore the law is holy, and the commandment holy and just and good.

Because the law is so holy and good it stirs up the evil that dwells in our sinful flesh. There is even a wicked saying about rules that demonstrates this principle: Rules were made to be . . . what? That's right, rules were made to be broken, is how the worldly saying goes, which emanates from the sin that dwells in us. There is a New Covenant principle that we must understand as priests unto the Lord. It is called the law of sin. Be ready for a lot of Scripture and please hang on.

Has then what is good become death to me? Certainly not! But sin, that it might appear sin, was producing death in me through what is good, so that sin through the commandment might become exceedingly sinful. For we know that the law is spiritual, but I am carnal, sold under sin. For what I am doing, I do not understand. For what I will to do, that I do not practice; but what I hate, that I do. If then, I do what I will not to do, I agree with the law that it is good. But now, it is no longer I who do it, but sin that dwells in me. For I know that in me (that is, in my flesh) nothing good dwells; for to will is present with me, but how to perform what is good I do not find. For the good that I will to do, I do not do; but the evil I will not to do, that I practice. Now if I do what I will not to do, it is no longer I who do it, but sin that dwells in me. I find then a law, that evil is present with me, the one who wills to do good. For I delight in the law of God according to the inward man. But I see another law in

*my members, warring against the law of my mind, and bringing me
into captivity to the law of sin which is in my members.*

(Romans 7:13–23)

Paul agrees that the law of God is good and just. He even speaks
of the fact that He delights in the law of the Lord. There is one big
problem. There is another law that is as real as the sun coming
up in the morning and the moon at night. Sin, which hates what
is good, dwells in the very members of our physical bodies. It is
defined as *our flesh* in the Bible, and it hates obedience to the law
of God. To ignore this principle, which is very customary in today's
Christian society, is a horribly tragic mistake.

We see here that the Mosaic commandments literally cause our
flesh, or the sinfulness in us, to be stirred and agitated. It upsets
Paul to a point that he says, *O wretched man that I am!* And he
cries out, *Who will deliver me from this body of death?* The Mosaic
commandments reveal and magnify the principle of sin and death
that dwells in us.

Paul then gloriously answers his own question, and shares
another law with we who believe in Jesus!

*I thank God—through Jesus Christ our Lord! So then, with the
mind I myself serve the law of God, but with the flesh the law of sin.
There is therefore now no condemnation to those who are in Christ
Jesus, who do not walk according to the flesh, but according to the
Spirit. For the law of the Spirit of life in Christ Jesus has made me
free from the law of sin and death. For what the law could not do
in that it was weak through the flesh, God did by sending His own
Son in the likeness of sinful flesh, on account of sin: He condemned
sin in the flesh, that the righteous requirement of the law might be
fulfilled in us who do not walk according to the flesh but according
to the Spirit.*

(Romans 7:25–8:4)

We see that the law of the Spirit is the end of the line for condemnation, and also for the law of sin and death. The commandments of the Levitical priesthood were to be adhered to for a time. That time is up! It is God's plan for the ages. The law stirs up fleshly passions that make my flesh want to sin. The law of the Holy Spirit delivers me as He makes me want to follow Jesus in this new priesthood. The law is weak because it can only demand perfection, which stirs up my flesh and kills me. Jesus, who is perfect, lived a sinless life and died for me, which fulfills the requirements of the law. He fills me with His Spirit, and I now follow Him as a priest in this new priesthood, which doesn't demand my perfection, but operates from and is upheld by His perfection.

God's Purpose for the Law

The commandments of the Lord under Levi's priesthood have not passed away, as some would say, though the priesthood has. It's not that they have passed away, more accurately they are passing away. Listen to Paul clarify this further in 2 Corinthians 3:7–11:

> But if the ministry of death, written and engraved on stones, was glorious, so that the children of Israel could not look steadily at the face of Moses because of the glory of his countenance, which glory was **passing** away, how will the ministry of the Spirit not be more glorious? For if the ministry of condemnation had glory, the ministry of righteousness exceeds much more in glory. For even what was made glorious had no glory in this respect, because of the glory that excels. For if what is **passing** away was glorious, what remains is much more glorious.

So, if the commandments of Moses haven't fully passed away, then what are God's purposes for them now?

I am glad you asked! God's purposes of the commandments today are specific and necessary. One place we find this is Galatians 3:21–25:

199

*Is the law then against the promises of God? Certainly not! For if there had been a law given which could have given life, truly righteousness would have been by the law. But the Scripture has confined all under sin, that the promise by faith in Jesus Christ might be given to those who believe. But before faith came, we were kept under guard by the law, kept for the faith which would afterward be revealed. Therefore the law was our **tutor** to bring us to Christ, that we might be justified by faith. But after faith has come, we are no longer under a tutor.*

The law is a necessary tool, given by our great High Priest Jesus, to be used in evangelism. The law is a tutor or instructor that points people to the Messiah. The commandments in the law show people how desperately they need a Savior. The commandments reveal our sin to us and drive our prideful, arrogant, self-sufficient souls to the cross in humility. Here are a couple of quotes from a book written by evangelist Ray Comfort: "Only those who can sing 'and grace my fears relieved' see grace as being amazing."[54] The chapter name from which this quote came is *Take Two Tablets and Call Me When You're Mourning.* Of course the two tablets are the Ten Commandments.

Another quote from the same book reads: "The Law's rightful purpose is simply to act as a mirror to show us that we need cleansing."[55]

Why use the law in evangelism? "Dr. Martin Lloyd Jones gives us the answer: 'A gospel which merely says "Come to Jesus," and offers Him as a Friend, and offers a marvelous new life, without convincing of sin, is not New Testament evangelism. (The essence of evangelism is to start by preaching the Law; and it is because the Law has not been preached that we have had so much superficial

---

[54] Comfort, *Revival's Golden Key,* 135.
[55] Ibid., 42.

evangelism.) True evangelism . . . must always start by preaching the Law.'"[56]

When talking to the average American about eternity, if you ask them where they are going when they die, what do they generally say? "I am going to heaven." Why? "Because I am a good person." Then when asked, "Have you ever heard of the Ten Commandments and have you broken them?" The answer is "Yes, of course, everyone has." When asked, "Have you ever stolen anything, lied, or said 'Jesus Christ' as a curse word," most would admit they are guilty. Then when instructed that they had just admitted to being a liar, a thief, and a blasphemer, they start to see that going to heaven as a good person is a losing proposition.

On one occasion I was speaking with a young lady who was a member of a denominational church that typically teaches a watered down gospel. When I asked her where she was going when she died, she predictably answered that she was going to heaven. I then asked her why, to which she answered, "Because I deserve to go to heaven." I shared the law with her and the conviction of sin made her become politely angry with me. My prayer is that the Lord reveals to her what she deserves before she gets it!

Oswald Chambers speaks of the law and the gospel in his insightful book *My Utmost for His Highest*:

> For whosoever shall keep the whole law, and yet stumble in one point, he is guilty of all.
>
> (James 2:10)

The moral law does not consider us as weak human beings at all, it takes no account of our heredity and infirmities; it demands that we be absolutely moral. The moral law never alters, either

---

[56] Ibid., 38.

for the noblest or for the weakest, it is eternally and abidingly the same. The moral law ordained by God does not make itself weak to the weak, it does not palliate our shortcomings; it remains absolute for all time and eternity. If we do not realize this, it is because we are less than alive; immediately we are alive, life becomes a tragedy.

> I was alive once without the law, but when the commandment came, sin revived and I died.
>
> (Romans 7:9)

When we realize this, then the Spirit of God convicts us of sin. Until a man gets there and sees that there is no hope, the Cross of Jesus Christ is a farce to him. Conviction of sin always brings a fearful binding sense of the law, it makes a man hopeless—'sold under sin.' I, a guilty sinner, can never get right with God, it is impossible. There is only one way in which I can get right with God, and that is by the Death of Jesus Christ."[57]

The law plows up the hard ground of the heart, so that the gospel seed can germinate in good soil. It drives sinners to the cross with their lives. Most today remove the tutor from the preaching of the gospel, and sadly, the result is a high percentage of false converts who think that they are saved, yet look to Jesus as a magic genie more than a great Redeemer. Hence, churches are full of false converts. Pastors, therefore, spend much precious time as keepers of the asylum instead of equippers of the saints. What could be crazier than a room full of people pretending to follow Jesus when they are truly following after their lost and carnal desires? Friends, welcome to the reality of American Christianity.

---

[57] Chambers, Oswald. My Utmost for His Highest, Barber & Co., Inc., 1935, p. 250, Dec. 1 entry.

If you ask most in church today they wouldn't tell you that they deserve hell. Why? They never had a schoolmaster point them to the Savior that died for their lawbreaking.

> *Whoever committeth sin transgresseth also the law: for sin is the transgression of the law. And ye know that He was manifested to take away our sins; and in Him is no sin.*
>
> (1 John 3:4–5 KJV)

Oh, how Satan wins when we ignore God's precepts.

> *Therefore by the deeds of the law no flesh will be justified in His sight, for by the law is the knowledge of sin.*
>
> (Romans 3:20)

We must see that the commandments in the Law of Moses are for the purpose of evangelism! Will you ask the Father to teach you how to use the tutor in leading people to Messiah?

We also see in Galatians 3:25 that we are released from the Levitical order, and no longer under those laws. We have been released to a new set of commandments, the law of the Spirit:

> *But after faith has come, we are no longer under a tutor.*

One way you know if you are interpreting a Scripture correctly is if it cross-references well. If the Bible states something in one place, it also states it in others, which is confirmation of the true meaning. Does the Bible teach that we are not under the law in other places?

In Romans 7:1–6 there is an analogy of a married woman who is bound to her husband. Yet, if the husband dies she is released to marry another. So it is when we become saved that we are released from the laws of Levi to be joined to the New Husband. Of course we know that in Jesus we are the bride of Christ.

> *Or do you not know, brethren (for I speak to those who know the law), that the law has dominion over a man as long as he lives? For the woman who has a husband is bound by the law to her husband as long as he lives. But if the husband dies, she is released from the law of her husband. So then if, while her husband lives, she marries another man, she will be called an adulteress; but if her husband dies, she is free from that law, so that she is no adulteress, though she has married another man.* **Therefore, my brethren, you also have become dead to the law through the body of Christ, that you may be married to another—to Him who was raised from the dead, that we should bear fruit to God.** *For when we were in the flesh, the sinful passions which were aroused by the law were at work in our members to bear fruit to death. But now we have been delivered from the law, having died to what we were held by, so that we should serve in the newness of the Spirit and not in the oldness of the letter.*
>
> Romans 7:1-6

Praise Jesus for our High Priest and the law of the Spirit!

Another purpose for the law is that it keeps sinful societies in order and restrains chaos. Have you noticed the attack on the Ten Commandments in our society? Have you noticed the chaos?

CHAPTER 14

Clarification, Disagreements, Divisions

But we know that the law is good if one uses it lawfully.

(1 Timothy 1:8)

There are long-standing, widely tolerated schisms in the body today over the interpretation and application of the Mosaic law. Some of these doctrines are additionally hindering, and unnecessarily keeping Gentile believers from receiving the truth regarding their relationship to Israel. For those of us with the burden for the church to have their identity restored, this should be something to identify and adjust. Concurrently, the Gentile church must learn that the Bible instructs, with specific New Covenant principles, appropriate thinking toward those in the body who have convictions to observe the law.

Some say that to recognize the instruction of God's word, and to make distinctions and adjustments to the new priesthood, is to advocate lawlessness. For example, while discussing the law, a man called me an Antinomian. This term, meaning *against law*, refers to a heretical doctrine promoted at the time of the apostle Paul, that basically taught "since grace abounds all the more where there is sin, the more you sin the more grace you get." In other words, this belief promotes lawless, sinful living, and attempts to justify it with the grace of God.

How could someone compare recognition of this change in priesthood, and then its application to one's life, with advocacy of iniquity? The New Covenant applications are more intrusive into the normal life of a human being than the old. By the way, I am quite thankful for the intrusion, which keeps me from dangerous sin. The New Covenant requires a higher degree of self-control, and is much more comprehensive in that these New Covenant commandments judge the very heart with more scrutiny. The bar of purity and holiness has been raised, not lowered. The law of liberty judges my heart at a higher standard than the law of Moses.

Jesus said in Matthew 5:27–28:

"You have heard that it was said to those of old, 'You shall not commit adultery.' But I say to you that whoever looks at a woman to lust for her has already committed adultery with her in his heart."

Previously, in Matthew, Jesus compared anger and hatred to murder; He then continued to speak of divorce, making oaths, loving not just friends but also enemies, and love and charity in a way that raises the standard from that of the statutes given to Moses. I fail to see the lawlessness of properly operating under the new priesthood.

Many use this Scripture to dispute the points that I have made:

"Do not think that I came to destroy the Law or the Prophets. [The Old Testament writings.] *I did not come to destroy but to fulfill. For assuredly, I say to you, till heaven and earth pass away, one jot or one tittle will by no means pass from the law till all is fulfilled. Whoever therefore breaks one of the least of these commandments,*

and teaches men so, shall be called least in the kingdom of heaven;
but whoever does and teaches them, he shall be called great in the
kingdom of heaven. For I say to you, that unless your righteousness
exceeds the righteousness of the scribes and Pharisees, you will by
no means enter the kingdom of heaven."

(Matthew 5:17–20)

Let's look at this. When Jesus said in verse 17 that He wouldn't destroy the law or prophets, He was talking about the message of the entire Old Testament. He informed them, since He is the Messiah, that He came to fulfill the Hebrew Scriptures. In verses 18–19 He specifically warned that not one jot or tittle will pass away from the law including the commandments, and that anyone who teaches people to break them will not enter heaven. The term "least in the kingdom of heaven" would have meant ineligible for heaven to the Jewish people at that time. To understand accurately the meaning of this passage we must not only know what He is saying but to whom King Jesus is speaking.

You see, some of the Pharisees pretended to be holy representatives of the kingdom of heaven. They however, were quite wicked and led people to actually break God's laws.

"But woe to you, scribes and Pharisees, hypocrites! For you
shut up the kingdom of heaven against men; for you neither go
in yourselves, nor do you allow those who are entering to go in.
Woe to you, scribes and Pharisees, hypocrites! For you devour
widows' houses, and for a pretense make long prayers. Therefore
you will receive greater condemnation. Woe to you, scribes and
Pharisees, hypocrites! For you travel land and sea to win one
proselyte, and when he is won, you make him twice as much a
son of hell as yourselves."

(Matthew 5:17–19)

Then in Matthew 23:23–24:

"Woe to you scribes and Pharisees, hypocrites! For you pay tithe of mint and anise and cumin, and have neglected the weightier matters of the law: justice and mercy and faith. These you ought to have done, without leaving the others undone. Blind guides, who strain out a gnat and swallow a camel!"

The corrupt Pharisees led the nation into lawlessness. Of course, their greatest transgression was leading many Israelites away from their own Messiah. That is why Jesus finishes the Scriptures we were discussing, regarding the law, in Matthew 5:

"For I say to you, that unless your righteousness exceeds the righteousness of the scribes and Pharisees, you will by no means enter the kingdom of heaven."

(Matthew 5:20)

Jesus is not saying that we are to keep the Levitical commandments; He is indicting the Pharisees. Please go back and read the controversial passage in that light, and see what King Jesus shows you. Their biggest transgression, of course, was to lead many in Israel to reject the One who gave the laws!

To those who teach that we are to keep the commandments in the first five books, I humbly direct them to 1 Timothy 1:5–11:

Now the purpose of the commandment is love from a pure heart, from a good conscience, and from sincere faith, from which some, having strayed, have turned aside to idle talk, desiring to be teachers of the law, understanding neither what they say nor the things which they affirm. But we know that the law is good if one uses it lawfully, knowing this: that the law is not made for a righteous person, but for the lawless and insubordinate, for the ungodly and for the sinners, for the unholy and profane, for murderers of fathers and murderers of mothers, for manslayers, for fornicators, for sodomites, for kidnappers, for liars, for perjurers, and if there is any other thing that is contrary to sound doctrine, according to the glorious gospel of the blessed God which was committed to my trust.

What is the definition of the word *law* spoken of in 1 Timothy 1:8? *The Complete Word Study Dictionary* states: "The Law, i.e., a code or body of laws. In the NT used only of the Mosaic code."[58] It goes on to list the Scriptures this definition is applied to, one of which is 1 Timothy 1:8. This passage addresses the lawful use of the law and its exclusive application to unbelievers.

These passages tell us that there is a lawful use of the Mosaic commandments under the priesthood of Jèsus Christ. We have discussed that purpose. It is to lead the lost to Jesus and to keep a sinful society in custody until the sinners receive Him. When they receive Messiah Jesus they are released from the law into another law. We have seen that it is called the law of the Spirit. Again Galatians 3:24–25 makes it clear:

Therefore the law was our tutor to bring us to Christ, that we might be justified by faith. But after faith has come, we are no longer under a tutor.

The truth is that a believer in Jesus Christ has been completely released from the Levitical commandments.

Some would say that the laws don't save us but we are still supposed to keep them. That is contrary to the Scriptures that I have just cited. We are no longer under them, and it is not profitable to live by laws that we won't be judged by as believers. The Bible teaches that we will be judged by a different law by which it is wise to live.

---

[58] *The Complete Word Study Dictionary, New Testament,* 1016.

So speak and so do as those who will be judged by the law of liberty.

(James 2:12)

What is the law of liberty? It is the law of the Holy Spirit, which we discussed in terms of being released from the Law of Moses, then to the Spirit in Romans 7–8. What does 2 Corinthians 3:17 tell us?

Now the Lord is the Spirit; and where the Spirit of the Lord is, there is liberty.

Since I have been released to, and will be judged by, the law of liberty, I will live by that law, not another.

One noticeable discrepancy, based on my discussions with my brothers and sisters in the Messianic Movement, is the use of the word *law.* On different occasions some have told me that it means teaching, and rightly so. It means teaching where it means teaching. The problem is that in some cases, like those I cited in Galatians, 1 Timothy, Romans 7, and others, the Bible makes specific references to the commandments or statutes such as the Ten Commandments, feasts, and Sabbaths, as being for an earlier season for believers. They, in most circles, don't accept this, which facilitates the teaching that we are still required to adhere to the law, meaning observance or obedience to at least some of the Levitical statutes.

I would give, what I believe to be, reasons for this, but at the risk of judging my brother, who is observing out of conviction, I will not. I have been so blessed by so many that hold to these convictions, that I truly don't make any observations based on anything but love for the word of God and for Jesus' body.

Again let's say, for the sake of honest discussion, that you have been keeping the commandments, Sabbaths, or feasts, from a conviction of faith and at the very least a perceived obedience from God. For you to change right now, as a result of an intellectual understanding from reading this book, would be sin. To clarify, if God hasn't revealed a truth that promotes change, you must continue in faith. But, if you take this information to the Lord Yeshua and He reveals this to be truth, then you must make adjustments in order to operate from faith. Only the Lord Jesus by the Holy Spirit is to make the changes in our hearts and lives.

The apostle Paul is addressing clean versus unclean foods, in the middle of Romans 14:22–23:

Do you have faith? Have it to yourself before God. Happy is he who does not condemn himself in what he approves. But he who doubts is condemned if he eats, because he does not eat from faith, for whatever is not from faith is sin.

Paul is saying that for the believer to change his dietary conviction as a result of what he hears from man and not God, is not operating in faith, but from compulsion of man.

What is my position to be if you (remember "you and me" is for the sake of discussion) don't change your position on this issue? What if you continue to sense a conviction to worship on Saturday, or to eat kosher, or to keep commandments?

Paul answers us earlier in Romans 14:5–12:

One person esteems one day above another; another esteems every day alike. Let each be fully convinced in his own mind. He who observes the day, observes it to the Lord; and he who does not observe the day, to the Lord he does not observe it. He who eats, eats to the Lord, for he gives God thanks; and he who does not eat, to the Lord he does not eat, and gives God thanks. For none of us lives to himself, and no one dies to himself. For if we live, we live to the Lord; and if we die, we die to the Lord. Therefore, whether we live or die, we are the Lord's. For to this end Christ died and rose and lived again, that He might be Lord of both the dead and the living.

But why do you judge your brother? Or why do you show contempt for your brother? For we shall all stand before the judgment seat of Christ. For it is written: "As I live, says the LORD, every knee shall bow to Me, and every tongue shall confess to God." So then each of us shall give account of himself to God. Therefore let us not judge one another anymore, but rather resolve this, not to put a stumbling block or a cause to fall in our brother's way.

The Scriptures are clear that not only should we not divide over such issues, but that we should respect the convictions of others with these matters. The Lord will judge in a much purer way than you or I. This is not something we are to offend one another with in terms of our relationships.

However, there is a breaking of God's principles, which is called sin, that occurs when a believing observer of the law imposes that conviction on others. I have been approached by some, mostly Jewish believers, and made to feel like a substandard Jew, or worse a substandard follower of Yeshua, because I didn't live up to the standard they had for me regarding adherence to, or celebration of, certain Levitical observances. Some of these people were very close to me, which made the whole thing very difficult. To be fair, I am sure I have been difficult to them on a number of occasions as well. Thankfully, I know who I am in Messiah, and what His word instructs regarding these matters.

In the fifteenth chapter of Acts, the Jews had debates about the implementation of this new priesthood. One thing they were forced to grapple with was whether or not to impose the law on the Gentile converts. Some said that circumcision and keeping the Law of Moses was necessary for salvation.

And certain men came down from Judea and taught the brethren, "Unless you are circumcised according to the custom of Moses, you cannot be saved."

(Acts 15:1)

These were Judaizers, false prophets who taught a works-based gospel. Then others who were actually saved taught that it was necessary to keep the law.

But some of the sect of the Pharisees who believed rose up, saying, "It is necessary to circumcise them, and to command them to keep the law of Moses."

(Acts 15:5)

What does the apostle Peter say? Acts 15:6–10:

Now the apostles and elders came together to consider this matter. And when there had been much dispute, Peter rose up and said to them: "Men and brethren, you know that a good while ago God chose among us, that by my mouth the Gentiles should hear the word of the gospel and believe. So God, who knows the heart, acknowledged them by giving them the Holy Spirit, just as He did to us, and made no distinction between us and them, purifying their hearts by faith. Now therefore, why do you test God by putting a yoke on the neck of the disciples which neither our fathers nor we were able to bear?"

You see, the Lord had revealed to Peter the transition from one priesthood to another.

Acts 15 continues in vv. 24–26:

Since we have heard that some who went out from us have troubled you with words, unsettling your souls, saying, "You must be circumcised and keep the law"—to whom we gave no such commandment—it seemed good to us, being assembled with one accord, to send chosen men to you with our beloved Barnabas and Paul, men who have risked their lives for the name of our Lord Jesus Christ.

Not only do the apostles teach that the message of mandatory observance of the law is not accurate, there is something else to consider.

Think about this point. The apostles in Jerusalem were sending word to the churches in Antioch, Syria, and Cilicia that they were not required to live by the statutes of the Mosaic law. It is also interesting that they disqualified the false message by disqualifying the messengers. How did the apostles do this? The apostles told the churches that the people teaching this doctrine didn't receive it from them, which disqualifies those teaching observance of the law and their false message. The apostles exercised the authority that Jesus gave them (Matthew 16:19).

We have the same standard today. The word of God clearly addresses this issue. If people instruct us that somehow there is a requirement binding us to the observances of the Levitical statutes found in the law, we receive the words of the apostles today just like those churches did. The word, of course, gives us further revelations after the time of the book of Acts that instruct us with greater clarity on this issue. As we have seen, much is said about observance of the law by the apostle Paul, as God unfolds His plan for the New Covenant in later writings, which we commonly call the epistles.

In Colossians 2:13–14, we see that the sin debt of our lawbreaking has been paid. We are not subject to the commandments.

And you, being dead in your trespasses and the un-circumcision of your flesh, He has made alive together with Him, having forgiven you all trespasses, having wiped out the handwriting of requirements that was against us, which was contrary to us. And He has taken it out of the way, having nailed it to the cross.

In Colossians 2:16–17, Paul equips us for the false imposition of the law:

So let no one judge you in food or in drink, or regarding a festival or a new moon or Sabbaths, which are a shadow of things to come, but the substance is of Christ.

214

There is a teaching out there that espouses that the festivals, new moons, and Sabbaths in this verse are pagan, not Levitical observances. I have a question for the teacher of that doctrine. Are pagan festivals, new moons, and Sabbaths a shadow of the things to come in Jesus? It just makes no sense.

By way of reminder, the feasts point us to holy New Covenant spiritual applications that most, Jew and Gentile, haven't considered. Here is an example. Paul is addressing the church in Corinth in his first letter to them. There is gross immorality in the church. The leaders are puffed up with counterfeit grace. What truth does Paul proclaim to them regarding their disregard for holiness, and high regard for false spirituality?

> *Your glorying is not good. Do you not know that a little leaven leavens the whole lump? Therefore purge out the old leaven, that you may be a new lump, since you truly are unleavened. For indeed Christ, our Passover, was sacrificed for us. Therefore let us keep the feast, not with the old leaven, nor with the leaven of malice and wickedness, but with the unleavened bread of sincerity and truth.*
>
> (1 Corinthians 5:6–8)

You see, the Feast of Passover and Unleavened Bread teaches us that we are to get the leaven out of our lives and churches, and challenges us to be who we are in Messiah. Of course, it pictures the Passover Lamb Jesus, and has many other symbols that are beautiful and wonderful to celebrate. However, there is a difference between celebrating and being compelled to observe. Anyway, what is one of the biggest problems in the American church? It is contaminated with leaven and has a disregard for holiness. This unholy virus spreads like leaven rises in dough if it isn't dealt with properly.

This wouldn't be taking place if we understood and obeyed the New Covenant application for the Passover! A high percentage of leaders today, because of the same false Corinthian spirituality, would never consider publicly turning someone over to Satan for the protection of the body and the restoration of those in flagrant, unrepentant sin. Again these biblical words sound like antiquated puritan language to so many today. Thankfully, there still are some that will obey God's word by applying the spiritual principle of the Passover.

We must remember that the Levitical observances are a shadow of Messiah. A shadow indicates something that hasn't already come. Yeshua has already come and fulfilled the shadow. Some would say that since all of the pictures of the new moons, feasts, and Sabbaths haven't been fulfilled, such as the reign of Christ on earth, that we are to continue in these observances. Though we know that these things also shadow things that haven't come, the context in Colossians is addressing someone judging us improperly here and now. The new moons, feasts, and Sabbaths are a shadow of Messiah. The substance of these things is Him. Now we are judged by our observance of the substance, which is Jesus Christ, not the shadow that has been revealed in Him.

Also during the reign of Messiah Jesus on earth there will be judgment for those that don't celebrate the Feast of Tabernacles. Zechariah 14:16–19:

*And it shall come to pass that everyone who is left of all the nations which came against Jerusalem shall go up from year to year to worship the King, the LORD of hosts, and to keep the Feast of Tabernacles. And it shall be that whichever of the families of the earth do not come up to Jerusalem to worship the King, the LORD of hosts, on them there will be no rain. If the family of Egypt will not come up and enter in, they shall have no rain; they shall receive the plague with which the LORD strikes the nations who do not come up to keep the Feast of Tabernacles. This shall be the **punishment** of Egypt and the punishment of all the nations that do not come up to keep the Feast of Tabernacles.*

So we see that there is no judgment in this age for not observing the Feast of Tabernacles, but there certainly will be in the age to come.

At this point some have said, "You are right, the Gentiles don't have to keep these laws, but Don, you are Jewish, so you must." But Ephesians tells us in the second chapter that the two (Jew and Gentile) have become one new man, as the barrier that separated us, which is the law, has been broken down! In Colossians 3:11, I am told that there is neither Jew or Greek, circumcised or uncircumcised, in Jesus Christ! Regarding the law there is no distinction. God doesn't have one requirement for Jews and another for Gentiles. Some say that the Jewish apostles still observed the law. Let's just say for the sake of discussion that this is true. What about a diaspora Jew (Jew living in the nations) that was a total pagan when he got saved. Does God *require* him to be more Jewish? I happen to be one of those, and though I appreciate and have grown from the understanding of my heritage, I can tell you humbly, yet confidently, the answer is no.

Here is a great quote that sums it up. "In short, don't let anyone make you feel like you're sinning if you don't observe the holy days, and don't pressure anyone else to do so. On the other hand, if it is useful to you and you understand that it is not something God requires of you, continue without guilt and without looking down on those who do otherwise. That is what I see in Scripture. (Also, not all of the Holidays celebrated by the Jewish people today are mentioned in the Bible at all. Some are of later origin)."[59] I would add that if you do sense a requirement from God to adhere to certain observances of the law, only the Lord is qualified to tell you to change. I am called to teach His word, and though I will share the Scriptures regarding the law in this area, I am required to be especially sensitive not to offend.

---

[59] American Messianic Fellowship, AMF International Mailbag, http://www.amfi. org/mailbag/keepholidays.htm, August 5, 2003.

With regard to dividing or separating from people due to their position on the law, I think the instances are rare and one is very necessary. If someone is making unbiblical judgments toward a believer in Jesus, such as those we just discussed, there may be valid occasions to separate. Of course, the Lord directs our paths and guides our steps in such matters. If I sense a compulsion from someone to keep the law, or to be more Jewish, at the least it strains our relationship. However, there have been cases in which God has shown me that love covers a multitude of sins, and those relationships are ongoing. There is another instance when, 100 percent of the time, we should separate. When someone ties these observances to salvation, they are preaching a false gospel, and need to be avoided like a bad virus (see Galatians 1:8–9).

I believe this would be an appropriate time to issue a word of caution. Just like anything else that God is doing, the enemy comes in with a counterfeit. There are many false doctrines that sound very spiritual, in the name of "the pursuit of our Jewish roots." One thing to remember is that currently, in very general terms, Jewish identity has become a conglomeration of many worldly, and in some cases, dangerous religions and philosophies.

To not recognize this would be very unwise. Everything presented with "Jewish or Israel" on it isn't of the Lord. Primarily, this is a result of the rejection of Messiah Yeshua. We see in Hebrews, Romans, and other places, the beginning of the false religious system that sprang up from rejection of Jesus.

> Brethren, my heart's desire and prayer to God for Israel is that they may be saved. For I bear them witness that they have a zeal for God, but not according to knowledge. For they being ignorant of God's righteousness, and seeking to establish their own righteousness, have not submitted to the righteousness of God. For Christ is the end of the law for righteousness to everyone who believes.
>
> (Romans 10:1–4)

Here we see the beginning of the false religious system that is established by a rejection of Jesus. It is modern-day Judaism.

Most of Israel's rejection of Messiah began, and much even to this day, is based on their wrong elevation and interpretations of the prophet Moses. Listen to Jesus' indicting words in John 5:45–47:

> "Do not think that I shall accuse you to the Father; there is one who accuses you—Moses, in whom you trust. For if you believed Moses, you would believe Me; for he wrote about Me. But if you don't believe his writings, how will you believe My words?"

And in John 6:31–33:

> "Our fathers ate the manna in the desert; as it is written, 'He gave them bread from heaven to eat.'" Then Jesus said to them, "Most assuredly, I say to you, Moses did not give you the bread from heaven, but My Father gives you the true bread from heaven. For the bread of God is He who comes down from heaven and gives life to the world."
>
> (See also Hebrews 3:1–6)

The Jewish people had exalted Moses and erroneously used him to reject their own Messiah. Many still do today. That is why Jesus attempts to correct them from the perspective of Moses. Another reason to be careful when interpreting the law is that some of the false teaching initiates from this mind-set. There is a spirit out there that uses good things to compel us to take our eyes off Yeshua.

From this point the Jewish identity continued to morph into a number and combination of different belief systems, many of which are extremely dangerous. It is important to be discerning. In a sincere attempt to learn the truth of our Jewish identity, we must be careful not to pick up dangerous doctrines. Again, it doesn't help me or anyone else if instead of throwing a lifeline to them I jump into the quicksand with them.

One helpful hint in measuring any philosophy is the centrality of God the Son, Jesus Christ. Does this identify me with the true Son of God? Does this keep Jesus in the center, or does it edge Jesus out? "Is this teaching Jesus plus something else?" is always a good question. Does this help me to identify with the faith handed down through the apostles, prophets and the chief cornerstone, Jesus Christ? It is always helpful to become more acclimated with their true teachings. The truth reveals a lie, but we must know the truth. I trust that King Jesus will make the way for you and I. Yet we must do our part and be awake and discerning.

May we not be guilty of judging or offending our brother. May we ask God to reveal anyone that we should go to in repentance. May we not alienate the predominantly Gentile church from the truth of their relationship to Israel with a legitimate grievance. May we be wise, sober, and alert as we seek after genuine faith regarding our relationship to Israel. Finally, may we take our priestly responsibilities seriously. Amen.

CHAPTER 15

Discerning the Times

. . . Let us watch and be sober.

(1 Thessalonians 5:6)

In Matthew 16:1–3 the great Son of Man, Jesus Christ, rails against the religious leaders of His day and identifies their blindness. We will discuss blindness and its place of origin in the last chapters. However, in this Scripture, there is another point to be made. You see, Jesus gives them a label that I never want given to me.

> *Then the Pharisees and Sadducees came, and testing Him asked that He would show them a sign from heaven. He answered and said to them, "When it is evening you say, 'It will be fair weather, for the sky is red'; and in the morning, 'it will be foul weather today, for the sky is red and threatening.' **Hypocrites!** You know how to discern the face of the sky, but you cannot discern the signs of the times."*

I am sure that one of the reasons He calls them hypocrites is that they were supposed to be the people of God. Would Jesus expect the Gentiles who weren't expecting a Messiah to recognize

Him? Would He call them hypocrites? No, it is those who had been instructed constantly through their Scriptures that a Savior would come and give the signs that would identify Him. He was fulfilling these prophecies right before them and they, God's chosen, couldn't discern the times in which they lived. There is a common question that I have heard since I became a believer. "How could they have missed Him after all that God did to reveal Himself to the Jews?" I have a better question. With great Bible prophecies that are fulfilling these days, how can believers in Jesus Christ not see where we are in time? Is this another tragic symptom of the church's identity crisis? Just like those religious hypocrites, are we in danger of not discerning the signs of the times?

Just before 1 Thessalonians 5:1–6 Paul had been addressing the Thessalonians' fear regarding the timing of the coming of the Lord. He then says in 5:1–6:

> But concerning the times and the seasons, brethren, you have no need that I should write to you. For you yourselves know perfectly that the day of the Lord so comes as a thief in the night. For when they say, "Peace and safety!" then sudden destruction comes upon them, as labor pains upon a pregnant woman. And they shall not escape. But you, brethren, are not in darkness, so that this Day should overtake you as a thief. You are all sons of light and sons of the day. We are not of the night nor of darkness. Therefore let us not sleep, as others do, but let us watch and be sober.

God instructs that as believers in Jesus, we are to know the time and season of the Day of the Lord, that is if we are watchful and sober. What will be the buzz words that will help us to identify the season of the Day of the Lord? Incidentally, the Day of the Lord refers to the seven-year tribulation period and culminates with the return of Jesus Christ. It continues with Him building His magnificent temple on Mount Zion in Jerusalem, from which He will reign over all the nations for one thousand years. The nations have had their day, which will change abruptly when the Lord begins to pour out His wrath on the earth (See Joel 2:1–2, 11; Zechariah 14; Revelation 20:4). First Thessalonians gives us the clue to look for regarding the season of the Day of the Lord. It is when they are saying "peace and safety."

I personally remember beginning to hear these words coming out of my television on a regular basis during the early 90s. The American President George Bush, and then Bill Clinton, and the Prime Minister of Israel Rabin and then Netanyahu were speaking these words frequently into my living room. The American presidents were twisting the arms of the Israeli prime ministers to buy these words, who were in turn selling them to the Israeli people. They were involved in a game, which I call, and am confident the Lord Jesus approves, *Let's Make a Deal with God's Covenant Land.*

On October 30, 1991, President Bush spoke in Madrid, Spain, in an effort to get the ball rolling in the dealing of Israeli soil for what? That's right, peace and security.

"Throughout the Middle East, we seek a stable and enduring settlement. We've not defined what this means. Indeed, I make these points with no map showing where the final borders are to be drawn. Nevertheless we believe territorial compromise is essential for peace."[60] From this point on, the Israelis were told and in large part bought into the lie that they were supposed to give up land for peace and security. Neither peace or security has come of this. However, this we can know. This is a sign of the times.

In Austin, Texas, the State House of Representatives opens the session with prayer. There was an unusual session opening on March 19, 2003. "As America moved closer to war with Iraq, a Muslim cleric for the first time gave the opening prayer at a session of the Texas House of Representatives on Tuesday. Iman Moujahed Bakhach of Fort Worth spoke of 'peace and security' in

---

[60] John McTernan and Bill Koenig, *Israel: The Blessing or the Curse* (Oklahoma City: Hearthstone Publishing, 2002), 61.

his three-minute invocation but made no mention of President Bush's ultimatum to Iraqi leader Saddam Hussein."[61]

Why doesn't that give you goose bumps? Are you watchful and sober? One of the most astounding phenomena in the world to me is the ease with which the followers of Jesus are deceived regarding the war for the land of Israel and the intent to destroy the Jewish race. Especially when the same instrument that is attacking them hit America with historical, brutal force on 9/11! It amazes me that we as believers in Jesus Christ, who would not allow the media to instruct us in terms of our philosophy regarding such things as abortion, homosexuality, or evolution, with great naiveté accept the media's portrayal of the battle for God's covenant land and the destruction of His covenant people. This is an area, like many others, in which the church has been lulled to sleep by our participation with the world.

I will digress a moment and expose a lie regarding the name given to God's covenant land. I challenge you to find *Palestine* anywhere in your Bible for the land God calls Israel. The reason you won't find it is because the Romans so named Israel Philistinia (after the Philistines) after they slaughtered many Jews during a Northern Israeli revolt, in the years A.D. 130–135. Palestine is the Anglo version of Philistinia. Before the twentieth century there never was a Palestinian. It is simply the world's propaganda, which you can choose to accept or reject. Shamefully, the term *Palestine* is in most study Bibles and has been widely accepted by church leaders for too long. Whenever I see Palestine in one of my study Bible's notes I scratch it out and write Israel.

Remember Colossians 2:8:

---

[61] Robert T. Garret, "Muslim Cleric Gives Opening Prayer at Texas House of Representatives." *Dallas Morning News,* March 19, 2003.

Beware lest anyone cheat you through philosophy and empty deceit, according to the traditions of men, according to the basic principles of the world, and not according to Christ.

The name Palestine for Israel is according to the world, not according to Christ. Please don't be deceived!

The reason most wouldn't see the significance of an Islamic cleric giving an opening prayer at the opening session of the Texas Legislature in the state that is called *the Buckle of the Bible Belt* is because we aren't watchful and sober. We are in large part clueless regarding the truth of Islam. Islam, far from being a tolerant, loving religion, is one of the most dangerous, powerful, anti-Christ spirited philosophies on the planet!

Here are some interesting Koranic quotes from a book called *Israel, God, and America*. The Koran is the Muslim holy book.

Sura 9:5 [Refers to Christians and Jews and to kill them] "Then when the sacred months have passed slay the idolaters [Christians and Jews] wherever ye find them, and take them captive and besiege them and prepare them for an ambush."

Sura 9:30 "The Christians say: The Christ is the son of Allah; these are the words of their mouths; they imitate the saying of those who disbelieved before; may Allah destroy them."

Sura 23:91 (The God who sent His Son into the world to save it cannot be the same god who inspired Muhammad to write)— "NEVER DID ALLAH TAKE TO HIMSELF A SON, and never was there with him any (other) god."[62]

This loving, tolerant religion is responsible for the death of approximately two million people, many of whom were Christians, in

---

[62] David Stein, *Israel, God, and America* (Zion Publishers, 2002), 167.

the Sudan over the last twenty years. Feel the love of Allah in this article titled "Islamists Burn to Death Christian Pastor, Family":

> Military forces led by Sudan's militant Islamist regime burned to death a Christian pastor and his family in a massacre of fifty-nine unarmed villagers, a relief group working in the area reported. Sudan's cleric-backed National Islamic Front regime in the Arab and Muslim north declared a jihad on the mostly Christian and animist south in 1989. Since 1983, an estimated two million people have died from war and related famine. About five million have become refugees. The militia also wounded fifteen and abducted ten children and six women. The forces used a combination of rocket-propelled grenade launchers, .50-caliber heavy machine guns and assault rifles. Many villagers were burned alive as they hid in their homes from the government-led forces, Servant's Heart said. Jacob Gatet Manyiel, pastor of the Presbyterian Church of Sudan, and his wife and four children were burned to death as government soldiers stood outside their house and threatened to shoot anyone trying to escape.[63]

Do you feel the love?

I want to clarify that to identify Islam for what it is does not articulate anything less than love for the Arab people, or any others that are held by its deceptive grip. Quite to the contrary. We should be broken for these chained souls headed for the lake of fire. The apostle John spoke about the spirit that is deceiving the adherents to Islam:

> *Who is a liar but he who denies that Jesus is the Christ? He is antichrist who denies the Father and the Son. Whoever denies the Son does not have the Father either; he who acknowledges the Son has the Father also.*
>
> (1 John 2:22–23)

---

[63] http://www.worldnetdaily.com/news/article.asp?ARTICLE_ID=32897

Having said that, when a Muslim cleric preaches peace and safety from an American pulpit, you can be sure that the signs of the times of the Day of the Lord are upon us!

Are There Any Other Signs to Be Looking for Regarding the Day of the Lord?

In Luke 21:5–6, Matthew 24:1–2, and Mark 13:1–2 the disciples of Messiah are expressing how impressed they are with the majesty of Herod's temple. With deflating words the Lord prophesies the destruction of the temple in Luke 21, Mark 13, and here in Matthew 24:1–2:

> *Then Jesus went out and departed from the temple, and His disciples came up to show Him the buildings of the temple. And Jesus said to them, "Do you not see all these things? Assuredly, I say to you, not one stone shall be left here upon another, that shall not be thrown down."*

Their focus naturally then goes from the buildings to the desire to know the time of this event:

> *Now as He sat on the Mount of Olives, the disciples came to Him privately, saying, "Tell us, when will these things be? And what will be the sign of Your coming, and of the end of the age?"*
> (Matthew 24:3–4)

They, being good Jewish boys, would know from their Hebrew Bible that this was referring to the end of this age and the beginning of the Messianic Age. This is a reference to the Day of the Lord. That is why they ask when the temple will be destroyed, and what will be the sign of His coming, and the end of the age. Messiah Jesus will reign in His temple, which will make Herod's look like a sandbox (Ezekiel 40–48).

What about the rapture or snatching away of the saints spoken of in 1 Thessalonians 4:16–17 and 1 Corinthians 15:51? This is when the church is taken up to be with the Lord as the great tribulation is underway. The answer is simple. The disciples had no concept of the rapture of the church. They didn't even know that there would be such a thing as the church, at least as we know it today. How could they have asked about such things? They were expecting Messiah to come and reign from David's throne (2 Samuel 7:9–12; Acts 1:6; Revelation 20:6).

Then, after giving a prophetic overview of world events, King Jesus specifically answers their questions of what will be the sign of the Day of the Lord:

"And there will be signs in the sun, and the moon, and in the stars; and on the earth distress of nations, with perplexity, the sea and the waves roaring; men's hearts failing them from fear and the expectation of those things which are coming on the earth, for the powers of the heavens will be shaken. Then they will see the Son of Man coming in a cloud with power and great glory. Now when these things begin to happen, look up and lift up your heads, because your redemption draws near."

(Luke 21:25–28)

Jesus says when these things begin to take place that He is coming! It would be accurate to say that most of these tumultuous world events have been taking place during every century of man's history. So how will we know when they qualify as signs of the Day of The Lord?

There are two sets of clues that Jesus gives that are helpful to understand the time of His return. These clues have jolted me and changed the way I live my life in Christ. As Jesus is giving His prophetic overview in Matthew 24:4–8, He talks about false Messiahs, wars, ethnic groups violently clashing, famines, pestilence, and earthquakes in various places. In the eighth verse He gives us a clue: *"All these things are the beginning of sorrows."* This Greek word for *sorrows* actually means *birth pangs*. Listen to this quote from a well-known study Bible as it clarifies the signs of the Day of the Lord:

> Matthew 24:8: *Sorrows*. The word means "birth pangs." Famines, earthquakes, and conflicts have always characterized life in a fallen world; but by calling these things "the beginning" of labor pains, He indicated that things will get notably and remarkably worse at the end of the era as these unique tribulations signal the soon arrival of Messiah to judge sinful humanity and set up his millennial kingdom.[64]

There are three characteristics of labor pangs in childbirth that will help us understand how these events are signs of the Day of the Lord. Toward the end of childbirth the labor pangs come in greater frequency. They also get much more severe. The only thing that stops them is the birth of the child. So it will be with the coming of the Lord. The difficulties and calamities in the world will come more often, with greater severity, and won't stop until the birth. But what is going to be birthed? That is the second clue, which we will discuss in a moment.

So the first clue we are looking at is the beginning of sorrows or birth pangs. Let's look at some articles from news services that cover part of the year 2003, many of which are secular and respected by most in our society. I will just offer a few to make the point. There are things going on that are very interesting. Keep in mind the signs of which Jesus spoke.

Lunar Eclipse to Turn Moon Red, Latest in String of Cosmic Shows (CNN, November 7, 2003).[65]

---

[64] *MacArthur Study Bible*, 1438.
[65] http://www.cnn.com/2003/TECH/space/11/06/lunar.eclipse.ap/

Dead Trees Pose "Apocolyptic" California Wildfire Threat (AP, October 30, 2003).

Sun on Fire, Unleashes Three Major Flares[66] (Space.com, November 3, 2003). The science writer from this article says, "I think the last week will go into the history books as one of the most dramatic periods of solar activity we have seen in modern time."

Sun Produces Monster Solar Flare[67] (BBC News, November 5, 2003).

Weird, Wild Weather From Denver to Delhi Stumps Climatologists: Rain or Shine, Indoors Seems the Place to be Worldwide[68] (The Christian Science Monitor, August 16, 2003).

World Alert on "Cars Of Death" Terror Attacks[69] (Guardian, November 22, 2003). In Matthew 24, Jesus warned about nation rising up against nation, which is better translated "ethnic group against ethnic group." Here is an article that identifies the situation today in terms of military hot spots. "Hot spot in 2003? The Earth, UN Says"[70] (New York Times, December 17, 2003).

Antarctica Witnesses Solar Eclipse: Hundreds of scientists and staff in Antarctica braved freezing temperatures Monday to catch a glimpse of the first total solar eclipse ever recorded on the icy continent"[71] (MSNBC, November 24, 2003).

---

[66] http://www.space.com/scienceastronomy/solar_flares_031103.html
[67] http://news.bbc.co.uk/2/hi/science/nature/3242353.stm
[68] http://www.sfnewmexican.com/mail.asp?SectionID=2&SubSectionID=8&ArticleID=31314
[69] http://www.guardian.co.uk/alquaida/story/0,12469,1090972,00.html
[70] http://query.nytimes.com/gst/fullpage.html?res=9E06E1D61E3CF934A25751C1A9659C8B63
[71] http://www.msnbc.com/news/996532.asp?0cv=CB20

13,600 Killed By Heatwave: Undertakers in France estimate the recent heat-wave killed more than 13,600 people[72] (Daily Record, August 21, 2003).

Ten 5.0 Higher World Earthquakes in 48 hours[73] (Koenig International News; USGS Earthquake Hazards Program, December 27, 2003).

Ten 6.0 and Higher World Earthquakes in Seven Days[74] (Koenig's International News, USGS Earthquake Hazards, December 28, 2003).

Whole Lotta Shakin' Going on in 2004: Seismologists Alarmed by Rash of Quakes Rattling around Globe[75] (Worldnetdaily.com, January 2, 2004).

Iran Quake Toll May Hit 50,000; Calls for More Aid[76] (Reuters, December 30, 2003).

Did you notice the historical and even biblical terms that these news services used in their coverage of these occurrences? It sure appears that the first clue of intensity and severity is being revealed in our lifetime. Did you notice the articles about the sun and the moon? Are the beginning of the signs Jesus Christ spoke of upon us?

Let's look at the second clue that King Jesus gives us. In Matthew, after the summary of the future and the list of the signs which

---

[72]http://www.dailyrecord.co.uk/news/content_objectid=13315579 _method=full_siteid=89488_headline=-13-600-KILLED-BY-HEATWAVE-name_page.html

[73] http://www.watch.org, http://gldss7.cr.usgs.gov/neis/bulletin/bulletin.html

[74] Ibid.

[75] http://www.worldnetdaily.com/news/article.asp?ARTICLE_ID=36422

[76] http://uk.news.yahoo.com/031230/325/ei1o3.html

culminate in His coming, Jesus answers the disciples' question regarding the end of the age with a clue to identify the season of the final generation that will witness the coming of King Jesus!

"Now learn the parable from the fig tree: When its branch has already become tender and puts forth leaves, you know that summer is near. So you also, when you see all these things, know that it is near—at the doors! Assuredly, I say to you, this generation will by no means pass away till all these things take place. Heaven and earth will pass away, but My words will by no means pass away."

(Matthew 24:32–35)

What is the clue given that qualifies the events of sorrows or birth pangs, as signs of the Day of the Lord? It is the barren fig tree as it puts or shoots forth its leaves. It is the fig tree that comes to life.

Does the Bible answer this parable for us and identify the fig tree?

*For a nation has come up against **My land,** strong, and without number; his teeth are the teeth of a lion, and he has the fangs of a fierce lion. He has laid waste My vine and ruined **My fig tree;** He has stripped it bare and thrown it away; its branches are made white.*

(Joel 1:6–7)

*But you, O mountains of Israel, you shall **shoot forth your branches and yield your fruit to My people Israel,** for they are about to come.*

(Ezekiel 36:8)

How do these Scriptures relate to those in Matthew where Jesus speaks of the fig tree?

In Joel's passage God is describing a swarm of locusts, which has decimated His land as a devastating invading army. Many believe this is prophetically speaking of future human armies invading God's covenant land. So what does this have to do with the fig tree? He calls Israel "My land, My vine, and My **fig tree**." Ezekiel prophesies of the future foliage blossoming on the barren hills of Israel. The prophet uses the term "shooting forth branches." Israel is God's fig tree, and the once barren hills of Israel are blossoming like Jesus Christ predicted.

Take a look at a couple of Scriptures of interest that may tie in with the fig tree. In 2 Peter 3:8 Peter gives us another possible clue for the signs of the season of the Day of the Lord. In previous Scriptures he warns of scoffing at the signs of the season of Jesus' coming. Which, by the way, is a common thing today when you share these passages. I have warned many that there would be mockers and scoffers of His coming and that you don't want to fulfill prophecy by being one of them! Then in 2 Peter 3:8:

> *But, beloved, do not forget this one thing, that with the Lord one day is as a thousand years, and a thousand years as one day.*

Could this analogy of a thousand years to one day be more than an arbitrary number given to explain God's patience and existence outside of time?

Let's look at another Scripture that may help to clarify. God is speaking to judged, despairing Israel in Hosea 6:2:

> *After two days He will revive us; on the third day He will raise us up, that we may live in His sight.*

Now I am not real dogmatic about this, but if one day is as a thousand, how many is two? How long has Israel been under the control of many nations? How long have the Jews been scattered throughout the world? When was the temple destroyed so that their form of worship and sacrifice, based on rejection of Messiah, was made extinct? The answer to these questions is almost two days or two thousand years. According to Hosea, what will Jesus do on the third day or third millennium? He will revive Israel. Here is a quote from a Bible commentary that speaks on Hosea 6:2: "Primarily in type, Israel's national revival, in a short period (two or three being used to denote a few days . . .)."[77] The days of this age are waning and Israel is about to be completely revived!

What am I saying? The Scriptures are pointing us to signs and parables that are being revealed in our day. You see, God gave prophets so that we could know what generation would be the last. Israel is God's timepiece, and time is almost up! We must remember that the church is generally very ignorant of the prophets. That is why as their writings hit us on the nose we can't see them. We are likely living in the last generation!

Let's take a closer look at the word *generation*. Why? There have been many definitions given to the word for the purpose of interpreting Matthew 24:34:

> *Assuredly, I say to you, this generation will by no means pass away till all these things take place.*

The generation of the fig tree blossoming will be the last generation. What is a generation? When does the clock start ticking?

It helps to remember covenant and look to father Abraham for answers pertaining to the God of Israel. If we look at the fifteenth chapter of Genesis, God is making the covenant with Abram before He changed his name to Abraham. God tells him that the children of Israel would later go into captivity in Egypt. It is here that we find one of God's definitions of the word *generation* that may be useful to understand Jesus in Matthew's gospel.

> *Then He said to Abram: "Know certainly that your descendants will be strangers in a land that is not theirs, and will serve them,*

---

[77] Jamieson, Fausset, and Brown, *Commentary on the Whole Bible*, (Grand Rapids: Zondervan, 1968), 772.

and they will afflict them four hundred years. And also the nation whom they serve I will judge; afterward they shall come out with great possessions. Now as for you, you shall go to your fathers in peace; you shall be buried at a good old age. But in the fourth generation they shall return here, for the iniquity of the Amorites is not yet complete."

(Genesis 15:13–16)

In these verses how long does God tell us a generation is? It is one hundred years. I have listened to many godly men teach Bible prophecy, yet I have never heard this very Jewish, and very biblical definition of generation to interpret the word as it is used in Matthew 24.

Now, if this is the time frame that Jesus places on a generation, when does the clock start ticking? Many believe, as do I, that the signs Jesus spoke of in Matthew, Mark, and Luke are taking place with greater frequency and intensity, but the fig tree blossoming is the catalyst that Jesus says will identify the last generation.

David Stein, my friend that I mentioned earlier, while visiting from Jerusalem spoke to sixty-four people at my house in Texas. It was quite a gathering! We had a Messianic praise group, and the blowing of shofars; it was a Holy Spirit party! He asked a question that was provocative. "How many last days prophecies have been fulfilled from the time of the destruction of the temple in 70 C.E., until 1948 C.E.?" The answer was one. Do you know what it is? It is the Gentile church. The prophets spoke of the God of Israel extending mercy, and becoming the God of the Gentiles as well (Isaiah 42:6, 7; 49:6; 60:3).

Today most people think that the Jews need to convert to the Gentile religion. Back in Isaiah's time it was the other way around. Then the problem was how were those Gentiles going to come to know the God of Israel. Anyway, the Gentile church was the only major last days prophecy fulfilled in that vast timespan.

Then something took place in 1948. After this 1948 event, Bible prophecy began to leap off of the pages, very likely identifying this as the last generation. What was this event that activated the seemingly dormant Bible prophecies to eruption with such volcanic activity? Jesus spoke of labor pangs in the passages we have looked at, and remember, you can't have labor without a birth.

Who has heard such a thing? Who has seen such things? Shall the earth be made to give birth in one day? Or shall a nation be born at once?

(Isaiah 66:8a)

On May 14, 1948, the nation of Israel was physically reborn! Think of it, the people who are alive today that were born before May 1948, witnessed with their own eyes the physical rebirth of Israel! The people born after 1948 are now witnessing physically reborn Israel in their lifetime!

Many refer to this 1948 event as the birth of Israel. I don't disagree, but would add that this is just the physical rebirth of Israel. This Scripture is only partially fulfilled and this is only a partial birth. Just like the horrendously barbaric act of partial birth abortion that is so hotly contested in America, there is an attempt to abort the spiritual rebirth of Israel. I know a Great Physician that is not going to tolerate the nations' attempt to kill His baby, which He will deliver!

"Then you shall say to Pharaoh, 'Thus says the LORD: 'Israel is My son, My firstborn.'"

(Exodus 4:22)

The birth pangs that Jesus spoke of were those of the labor of the physical and then spiritual birth of Israel! Israel is in the spiritual birth canal and the labor pangs that we are going to experience from this point on will be very painful. Yet, it will be worth it as this Scripture in Isaiah will be completely fulfilled, and King

Jesus will set His feet on the Mount of Olives, and all Israel will be birthed and saved!

The Scriptures explain these things wonderfully:

"A woman, when she is in labor, has sorrow because her hour has come; but as soon as she has given birth to the child, she no longer remembers the anguish, for joy that a human being has been born into the world. Therefore you now have sorrow; but I will see you again and your heart will rejoice, and your joy no one will take from you."

(John 16:21–22)

We are headed for times of the earth's greatest travail, but it isn't comparable to the joy we will experience when we will be with King Jesus and the Father's beloved Israel is born!

And I will pour on the house of David and on the inhabitants of Jerusalem the Spirit of grace and supplication; then they will look on Me whom they pierced. Yes, they will mourn for Him as one mourns for his only son, and grieve for Him as one grieves for a firstborn.

(Zechariah 12:10)

Israel will receive their King!

And in that day His feet will stand on the Mount of Olives, which faces Jerusalem on the east. And the Mount of Olives shall be split in two, from east to west, making a very large valley; half of the mountain shall move toward the north and half of it toward the south.

(Zechariah 14:4)

Here Israel's abortionists will be vanquished!

And so all Israel will be saved, as it is written: "The Deliverer will come out of Zion, and He will turn away ungodliness from Jacob; For this is My covenant with them, When I take away their sins."

(Romans 11:26–27)

Praise God for the Deliverer in the new birth of Israel!

Most don't think of Israel as anything but a political football today. Why? John McTernan tells us in his and Bill Koenig's book *Israel: The Blessing or the Curse.*

If Israel is understood spiritually and not just politically, an entirely new and exciting reality of the time we live in unravels. We are now living in the time that the ancient Jewish prophets wrote about. The nation of Israel has been reborn and Jerusalem is once again the capital of the Jewish nation. The reality of God and the Bible then can be "proved" through the fulfillment of what the Bible states about the nation of Israel. What an awesome concept this is—Bible prophecy is alive before our very eyes.[78]

Shall we look at a few Scriptures that foretell of the fig tree shooting forth leaves?

The wilderness and the wasteland shall be glad for them, and the desert shall rejoice and blossom as the rose.

(Isaiah 35:1)

Most who know about the topography of Israel would agree that the landscape of Israel has changed dramatically in the last one hundred years. At the beginning of the twentieth century, most of Israel was either a swamp or a desert. But now the desert truly is blossoming! It is amazing to travel through what obviously is an arid desert and see green, lush groves and orchards of fruit, flowers

---

[78] McTernan and Koenig, *Israel: The Blessing or the Curse,* 15.

and other plant life. It is something to be marveled! The desert or "fig tree" truly is blossoming!

> *Those who come He shall cause to take root in Jacob; Israel shall blossom and bud, and fill the face of the world with fruit.*
> (Isaiah 27:6)

The little country of Israel literally supplies many countries in the world with a large supply of fruit and flowers. I have heard two teachings on prophecy that claim that Israel supplies Europe with up to 80 percent of their fruit and a similar percentage of their flowers at certain times of the year. This Scripture in Isaiah may also be speaking of the fruit of righteousness filling the earth from Israel in the millennial reign of Jesus. The fig tree is budding and it is in our generation!

The Gathering of Israel

Do the Scriptures have anything else to say about the mountains of Israel shooting forth Jewish people?

> *For I will take you from among the nations, gather you out of all countries, and bring you into your own land.*
> (Ezekiel 36:24)

> *It shall come to pass in that day that the LORD shall set His hand again the second time to recover the remnant of His people who are left, from Assyria and Egypt, from Pathros and Cush, from Elam and Shainr, from Hamath and the islands of the sea. He will set up a banner for the nations, and will assemble the outcasts of Israel, and gather together the dispersed of Judah from the four corners of the earth.*
> (Isaiah 11:11–12)

The Lord will gather Jews from all over the world in "that day." This Scripture refers to none other than the Day of the Lord!

239

In the late 1890s the modern Zionist movement was established. Jews began to emigrate in significant numbers to the Promised Land! In the early 1900s, men who were strong believers in Jesus held high-ranking office in the British government. They saw the British Mandate over much of the Middle East, from World War I, as their opportunity to be used by God to bring the Jews to their homeland. The result in 1917 was the Balfour Declaration. The British government promised Israel a great deal of land, much of which today is Jordan. Why is it Jordan? The reason is that the British government, later influenced by ungodly men, forsook their earlier commitment to the Jewish state. They eventually gave much of the land from the Balfour Declaration to what is now the nation of Jordan.

The British so aggressively renounced their cooperation in the Zionist movement that they made it official British policy in the 1939 British White Paper. "The British government claimed in its famous White Paper of 1939 its abandonment of the Zionist policy. After the introduction of 75,000 more Jews into Palestine during the ensuing five years, the gates would be closed."[79] As Jewish people were fleeing to Israel to escape the murdering Nazis in World War II, the British turned them away as they had placed strict limits on immigration to what they called Palestine. Thus, multitudes of Jews were sent back to their deaths in Nazi-occupied Europe.

This betraying position, from one of blessing Israel to that of cursing them, was a very foolish strategy. The British White Paper was issued in early 1939 and later that year, Britain and the world were at war. I think, though I am sure that many would disagree, that this betrayal of the Jewish people was a direct cause for the German Luftwaffe's brutal pounding of Britain with devastating air raids. The place of death and destruction the British were sentencing the Jews to became the source of death and destruction back upon the British people.

---

[79] Samuel Katz, *Battle-Ground: Fact and Fantasy in Palestine* (Steimatzky/Shapolsky, 1985), 75.

How could I say such a thing? The God of Israel blesses those who bless the Jewish people and curses those who curse them. Who do you think raises world powers up and brings them down? My Bible has many Scriptures which tell me that God does (Jeremiah 18:7–10). One way He does this is by causing one nation to come against another militarily (Ezekiel 14:17).

The British government was attempting to appease, and had been working closely with the Arab governments. I am going to digress for a moment then return to the gathering of the Jews back to Israel. The British officials appointed a man named Haj Amin al-Husseini who became the Grand Mufti of Jerusalem, the religious and political leader of the Arabs. "Husseini was the first proponent of militant, Arab Palestinian nationalism. He was an all or nothing terrorist who was determined to drive out or destroy the Jews or be destroyed himself, regardless of how many lives were wasted in the process."[80] This man brutally killed Jews and moderate Arabs and wouldn't settle for anything less than the destruction of the Jews. "Husseini was not willing to negotiate or make any kind of compromise for the sake of peace."[81]

Though the British paved the way for him to reach power, guess who Husseini began collaborating with to kill the Jews? "He saw Hitler's final solution to the Jewish problem as the answer to his own desire to eliminate the presence of Jews in Palestine. Husseini imported Nazi influence into Palestine and used Nazi funds to finance his terrorist activities. He openly supported Hitler and Mussolini and led a revolt against the British in 1936–1939."[82] "Husseini was known as the 'Arab Fuhrer.'"[83] "The only condition

---

[80] Richard Booker, *The Battle for Truth: Middle East Myths,* Institute for Hebraic-Christian Studies, November 21, 2000, posted on http://www.haydid.org/update1121.htm
[81] Ibid.
[82] Ibid.
[83] Ibid.

Husseini set for assisting the Nazis was that, after they won the war, they would murder all the Jews in Palestine."[84]

Nazism was introduced to the Middle East and different groups sprang up and became educated in the spreading and applying of the tactics of the German murderers. The Nazis and their sympathizers in Egypt in the 1930s used the same propaganda as those in Europe.

From out of these Nazi satellite groups an organization was born that is with us today. A man became the leader of this group of whom you have probably heard. "Eventually the leadership of the PLO was taken over by a man named Rahman Abdul Rauf al-Qudwa al-Husseini."[85] This leader of the PLO is the nephew of the Grand Mufti terrorist Haj Amin al-Husseini. Who is the nephew? "When Rahman Abdul Rauf al-Qudwa al-Husseini (the PLO leader) enrolled at the University of Cairo in 1951, he decided to conceal his true identity and registered under the name Yasser Arafat. Yes, Uncle Haj, the Arab Fuhrer himself, passed his legacy of hatred of Jews to his nephew Yasser Arafat who has passed the same legacy of hatred to the next generation of young Arabs."[86] The reason I threw this curve into the explanation of the history of the gathering of the Jews is to inform you that we are dealing with the same Nazi propaganda of the last world war; in America we are making the same mistake of appeasement that the British did.

Despite all that, the Lord Jesus brought great glory from the ashes of the Holocaust. He physically rebirthed the nation of Israel and began fulfilling Bible prophecy at a rapid pace. The gathering of the Jews from the land of the north was one of those prophecies.

---

[84] Ibid.
[85] Ibid.
[86] Ibid.

"I will say to the north, 'Give them up!' And to the south, 'Do not keep them back!' Bring My sons from afar, And My daughters from the ends of the earth—"

(Isaiah 43:6)

"Therefore behold, the days are coming," says the LORD, "that it shall no more be said, 'The LORD lives who brought up the children of Israel from the land of Egypt,' but, 'The LORD lives who brought up the children of Israel from the land of the north and from all the lands where He had driven them.' For I will bring them back into their land which I gave to their fathers."

(Jeremiah 16:14–15)

Has God brought the Jewish people from the land of the north since 1948?

There was an empire that, when mentioned, made hearts melt and was the terror of the democratic nations. It was called the USSR. The atheistic government did everything humanly possible to rid itself of religious expression. The born-again believers and the Jews were persecuted mercilessly. As Zionism filled the hearts of the Jewish people they were persecuted all the more. Then without a shot being fired, the Soviet Union was no more, and Jews poured out of the land of the north in biblical proportions.

David Stein writes:

Was any other nation, other than America, equal or greater in military power than the former Soviet Union? Was not Communism the primary force sweeping the world, forcing nations and peoples into subjugation under their cruel hand? For more than forty years the United States and Europe spent hundreds of billions of dollars on defense for one single purpose, to prepare for a war with the former Soviet Union. Yet, the once mighty military empire collapsed without a single bullet being expended.

243

Why? The former Soviet Union collapsed because, like Pharaoh, they chose not to know nor obey the God in Israel. Like Pharaoh, the Soviet Union said to the Jews seeking to immigrate to Israel, . . . *"Who is the Lord that I should obey His voice to let Israel go? I do not know the Lord, and besides, I will not let Israel go"* (Exodus 5:2).

Just as in the days of Pharaoh when the Lord took the Jews out of Egypt, beginning in 1989 with the collapse of the Soviet Union, the Lord began bringing the Jews from the land of the north to Israel. Just as the Lord had said, "Then they will live on their own soil!"[87]

I would like to add that after the Iron Curtain came down, not only did many Jewish people come out but the gospel went in! The grace and mercy of Jesus spread through this once atheistic-controlled region and millions were saved!

The pastor at the first church we attended spoke of his trips to Israel during this exodus from Russia. He was astounded at the overwhelming numbers of El Al jumbo jets landing with Jews from Russia pouring off of them. He was amazed to stand at Ben Gurion airport in Tel Aviv and watch the Bible leap off the pages at him!

According to one article published by the French University ULG, 1,069,534 Russian Jews have come to Israel from the former Soviet Union since 1989![88]

Here is another Israeli gathering that has taken place in our day.

---

[87] Stein, *Israel, God and America*, 83–84.
[88] Francois Gemmene, *Russian Immigrants in Israel: Changing the Patterns of the Israeli Society* (University de Liege, May, 2002), 10. You can download this article at: http://www.ulg.ac.be/cedem/downloads/FGWP.PDF.

From beyond the rivers of Ethiopia My worshipers, the daughter
of My dispersed ones, shall bring My offering.

(Zephaniah 3:10)

"The yearning for Jerusalem among the Jews of Ethiopia is as
old as the history of this people, so ancient that their origins are
shrouded in myth. From time immemorial, each generation of
Ethiopian parents would tell their children that some day, some
how, people would come and lead them back to their ancient
homeland, to Eretz Yisrael. But it was only in 1977, at the initiative
of the late Prime Minister Menachem Begin that the beginnings
of the prophecy started to come true. Over the next several years,
Ethiopian Jews began arriving in Israel."[89] Isn't this glorious? The
Ethiopian prophecies of Zephaniah have come to pass since 1948.
The Ethiopian population of Israel was seventy-six thousand people
as of 2001, and at the time of this writing they have agreed to accept another twenty thousand.[90]

In a miraculous rescue named *Operation Solomon* the Israelis
rescued over one thousand besieged Jews in Ethiopia. "From May
24 to May 25, [1991] Israeli Air Force and El Al aircraft took off
and landed continuously at the Addis airport. Thirty-three hours
after the first plane left Israel, the last plane arrived back in the
country. Eight babies were born throughout the operation, and a
world record was set when 1,087 people—including one newborn
baby—squeezed into an El Al jumbo aircraft!"[91]

"In May 1991, 14,200 Ethiopian Jews were airlifted out of
Ethiopia in a thirty-six-hour rescue mission called Operation
Solomon."[92]

---

[89] *Coming Home: Tenth Anniversary of Operation Solomon*, The Jewish Agency For
Israel, November 1, 2002, http://www.jafi.org.il/arts/june/3.htm
[90] *Israel to Accept More Ethiopian Jews*, BBC News, February16, 2003, http://news.
bbc.co.uk/2/hi/middle_east/2769453.stm
[91] *Coming Home.*
[92] Ibid.

Friends, the Lord brought the Jewish people out of Egypt, Babylon, many that were in the Soviet Union, Ethiopia, and is currently bringing them from all over the world. Here is news from the most dependable source on the planet. The Bible teaches that the rest are going to come!

> *When I have brought them back from the peoples and gathered them out of their enemies' lands, and I am hallowed in them in the sight of many nations, then they shall know that I am the LORD their God, who sent them into captivity among the nations, but also brought them back to their land, and left none of them captive any longer.*
>
> (Ezekiel 39:27–28)

The Bible also teaches that the Day of the Lord shouldn't surprise those in the light of King Jesus! Of course, we can't know the hour or the day, but we should be alert and prepared when we see the signs, especially the tender blossoming fig tree. God gave these signs that point to a certain generation and here we are! Is it important to discern the times?

> *But you, brethren, are not in darkness, so that this Day should overtake you as a thief. You are all sons of light and sons of the day. We are not of the night nor of darkness. Therefore let us not sleep, as others do, but let us watch and be sober.*
>
> (1 Thessalonians 5:4–6)

CHAPTER 16

Judgment

The LORD *is known by the judgment He executes.*

(Psalm 9:16)

The Creator of the universe is perfect in both character and behavior, which His creation experiences every hour of every day. Two of His basic character traits that we, as His creation, experience are love and justice. These characteristics manifest themselves in perfect harmony. Let's briefly look at three expressions of God's perfect nature.

Two are great mercy and grace, which emanate from His loving character. The third is judgment, which is a manifestation of His just character. We have been given a great opportunity to experience His outstretched hands that offer us His love. Just look to the cross to see a physical picture of His loving nature. Yet we have also been warned that if we refuse His expressions of love, which would include willful disobedience to Jesus, we will experience His just judgments. We will either know God by receiving His grace and mercy, or by His judgment!

The nations have sunk down in the pit which they made; in the net which they hid, their own foot is caught. The LORD *is known by the*

247

judgment He executes; the wicked is snared in the work of his own
hands. Meditation.

(Psalm 9:15–16)

The Bible teaches that in the end of this age the nations of the
world will come against Israel.

"Therefore prophesy concerning the land of Israel, and say to the
mountains, the hills, the rivers, and the valleys, 'Thus says the Lord
GOD: "Behold, I have spoken in My jealousy and My fury, because
you have borne the shame of the nations." Therefore thus says the
Lord GOD: "I have raised My hand in an oath that surely the nations
that are around you shall bear their own shame."

(Ezekiel 36:6–7)

These Scriptures are in the same passages as those which spoke of
Israel shooting forth people, as a tree shoots forth leaves. This is the
time of the physical rebirth of Israel! Ezekiel tells us at that time, the
nations will get whatever they give to Israel right back from the Lord!
Christian apologist John McTernan says, "God is real serious about the
land and covenant. Israel will literally be used as an anvil to destroy
the nations that come against Jerusalem. The nations will be drawn
to Jerusalem like a moth to a light. Multitudes of people have rejected
God and the Bible or just do not believe His Word. This rebellion
will cause the nations to come against God's anvil. God has warned
beforehand what will happen when armies try to destroy Israel and
take Jerusalem. The entire world will see the mighty power of God,
as He uses Israel as His anvil." [93]

For thus says the LORD God of Israel to me: "Take this wine cup of
fury from My hand, and cause all the nations, to whom I send you,
to drink it. And they will drink and stagger and go mad because of
the sword that I will send among them."

(Jeremiah 25:15–16)

---

[93] McTernan and Koenig, *Israel: The Blessing or the Curse*, 55–56.

248

We see a cup that the Lord Jesus drank from to save us from our sin. Jesus at Gethsemane said:

"Father, if it is Your will, take this cup away from Me; nevertheless not My will, but Yours, be done."

(Luke 22:42)

What was in this cup? It was the sin of the whole world past, present, and future. Oh, how dreadful was the cup from which our Savior drank to the dregs for our sin.

For He made Him who knew no sin to be sin for us, that we might become the righteousness of God in Him.

(2 Corinthians 5:21)

The world laughed and is still laughing at the Father and His anointed King of Jerusalem. But the time is quickly approaching when the nations of the world are going to drink from the cup of God's wrathful judgment and experience His just nature!

In 1948, 1967, and 1973, Arab nations that surround Israel attacked God's covenant land, and even with their overwhelming odds they were soundly beaten. In the book of Jeremiah we see that this was just the pregame show for the pummeling the nations are soon going to endure in God's fourth-quarter campaign.

How will King Jesus take the fight to the enemy? He will use Israel as His war club!

Jeremiah 51:19–23:

The Portion of Jacob is not like them, for He is the Maker of all things; And Israel is the tribe of His inheritance. The LORD of hosts is His name. "You are My battle-ax and weapons of war: For with you I will break the nation in pieces; With you I will destroy kingdoms;

With you I will break in pieces the horse and its rider; With you I will break in pieces the chariot and its rider; With you also I will break in pieces man and woman; With you I will break in pieces old and young; With you I will break in pieces the young man and the maiden; With you also I will break in pieces the shepherd and his flock; With you I will break in pieces the farmer and his yoke of oxen; And with you I will break in pieces governors and rulers.

The Lord is going to judge the nations with His battle-axe Israel!

The Lord Jesus is using the apparent vulnerability of Israel to entice the demon-inspired hatred of the Jews, to unite the world in a common effort to destroy the Jewish people. Then He will use Israel as His battle-axe to hammer them in righteous judgment. I might add that a large number of Jewish people will experience God's wrathful judgment at this time and also go to the lake of fire (Zechariah 13:8). Only the Jews who receive Jesus as King are "Israel" in the end. In the next pages I will explain specifically what God's word says will happen to the nations. I will also mention some telling news articles that are extremely eye-opening. I will be brief with all of the nations except one, of which I think you will want a bit more detail.

Isaiah 13:1–9 speaks of God's judgment on Babylon. This area is much of modern Iraq and will be made desolate through the millennial reign of Christ. Someone recently threatened Israel from this region. "The Iraqi people is ready to fight Israel alongside the Palestinians, but its geographical location makes it hard to join the struggle. . . . Still, the Jews know that their doom will come from Babylon" (Quasai Hussein, Saddam's son, April 12, 2002). This late son of Saddam Hussein now understands, in an eternal fiery fashion, that God will judge those who threaten Israel. Notice that he called Iraq "Babylon."

From Psalm 83:1–8 we have front-row seats of a stage that is set:

> Do not keep silent, O God! Do not hold Your peace, and do not be still O God! For behold, Your enemies make a tumult; and those who hate You have lifted up their head. They have taken crafty counsel against Your people, and consulted together against Your sheltered ones. They have said, "Come, and let us cut them off from being a nation, that the name of Israel may be remembered no more." For they have consulted together with one consent; they form a confederacy against You: The tents of Edom and the Ishmaelites; Moab and the Hagrites; Gebal, Ammon, and Amalek; Philistia with the inhabitants of Tyre; Assyria also has joined with them; They have helped the children of Lot. Selah.

Why do I say that this is a set stage and we are watching from the front row?

In this psalm we see a confederation of nations that have allied themselves against God Himself for the purpose of destroying Israel. In geographic terms, where are these ancient countries in modern times? Edom, which refers to Israel's brother Esau, is Southern Jordan. Some would say this is part of Saudi Arabia. The Ishmaelites would consist of Egyptians and much of the Arab world. Gebal would be what we call Lebanon today, which is controlled by Syria. The Ammonites dwelled in what we know today as northern Jordan. Amalek is the Sinai Peninsula region. You will love this one—Philistia is the area commonly referred to today as the Gaza Strip. Tyre is part of Syrian-controlled Lebanon also. [94] The people of all of these regions are this confederation spoken of in Psalm 83. Dr. Arnold Fruchtenbaum states, "Only since 1948 have all these nations combined focus against Israel. Such a total Arab alignment never occurred in ancient times." [95]

---

[94] Arnold Fruchtenbaum, *The Arab States in Prophecy.* http:\\www.ariel.org/ff00008f.html

The Bible teaches the specific judgments that will be poured out on Israel's unneighborly neighbors. With regard to Gebal and Tyre, Israel's borders will extend into all of Lebanon (Ezekiel 47:13–22). The house of Esau or southern Jordan will be totally destroyed: Obadiah 5–9,17–21; Jeremiah 48:47; Ezekiel 35:6–9; Jeremiah 49:7–13. Moab or central Jordan will be temporarily destroyed, then a remnant will return during the millennial reign (Jeremiah 48:47). Ammon or modern northern Jordan will experience temporary destruction and then include Israeli borders.[96]

Egypt is an especially interesting story. The once-bitter enemy of Israel (and their God) will be partially destroyed. They will repent and receive King Jesus! We see this in Isaiah 19:1–22.

> *In that day there will be an altar to the LORD in the midst of the land of Egypt, and a pillar to the LORD at its border. And it will be for a sign and for a witness to the LORD of hosts in the land of Egypt; for they will cry to the LORD because of the oppressors, and He will send them a Savior and a Mighty One, and He will deliver them.*
>
> (Isaiah 19:19–20)

The Lord will deliver a multitude from the nations along with Israel during the Day of the Lord!

Isaiah 19:13–25 shows us that northern Iraq and eastern Syria (Assyria) will experience repentance, conversion, and economic ties.[97] Isaiah 17:1 warns of something that I am surprised hasn't yet taken place—the burden against Damascus:

> *"Behold, Damascus will cease from being a city, and it will be a ruinous heap."*

---

[95] Ibid.
[96] Ibid.
[97] Ibid.

Syria has attacked Israel repeatedly in assorted ways. Damascus is currently the headquarters for some of the most vicious terrorists in the world, and they threaten Israel's existence on a regular basis, verbally and physically. Here are a couple of articles in which Damascus begs for God's judgment. "Assad: Syria under Threat as Long as Israel Exists."[98] "Syria: Israel Will Never Be Legitimate: President Assad claims U.S. Just Doing Jewish State's Bidding in Iraq." [99] Syria, who claims that they can't possibly be held responsible for those slipping across their border to fight in Iraq against American forces, is accused by British intelligence of issuing the passports for them to do so. "Syria gives passports to suicide bombers."[100]

Eastern Saudi Arabia, which is Kedar and Hezor, will be totally destroyed for at least one thousand years (Jeremiah 49:28–33).[101] Persia or Elam will experience partial destruction similar to Egypt (Jeremiah 49:34–39). Southern Iraq or Babylon will be destroyed and remain desolate through the messianic kingdom (Jeremiah 50:39, 40; Revelation 18:1–2).[102] The word of God is so precise and dependable. The issue isn't if these things will take place, but for we who are limited by time, unlike the God of Abraham, Isaac, and Israel, the issue is *when*.

Another well-known people group that have set themselves against the Lord by their unquenchable thirst for Israeli blood and covetous desire for the covenant land are the so-called Palestinians. Just like everyone else, God loves them and we need to reach out to them with the gospel. However, they will experience severe judgment according to God's word. God also calls the geographic

---

[98] David Ruge, "Assad: Syria Under Threat as Long as Israel Exists," *Internet Jerusalem Post,* March 29, 2003, http://www.jpost.com/.

[99] http://www.worldnetdaily.com/news/article/asp?ARTICLE_ID=31824, April 1, 2004.

[100] Michael Binyon, *Times Online,* April 2, 2003, http:/www.timesonline.co.uk/article/0,,5944–631677,00.html.

[101] Ibid, "The Arab States in Prophecy."

[102] Ibid.

location that they now inhabit Edom. We mentioned these Scriptures earlier, but not in this context.

> "And you, son of man, prophesy to the mountains of Israel, and say,
> 'O mountains of Israel, hear the word of the LORD! Thus says the Lord
> GOD: "Because the enemy has said of you, 'Aha! The ancient heights
> have become our possession,' 'therefore prophesy, and say, 'Thus says
> the Lord GOD: "Because they made you desolate and swallowed you
> up on every side, so that you became the possession of the rest of the
> nations, and you are taken up by the lips of talkers and slandered
> by the people"—therefore, O mountains of Israel, hear the word of
> the Lord GOD! Thus says the Lord GOD to the mountains, the hills,
> the rivers, the valleys, the desolate wastes, and the cities that have
> been forsaken, which became plunder and mockery to the rest of
> the nations all around—therefore thus says the Lord GOD: "Surely I
> have spoken in My burning jealousy against the rest of the nations
> and against all Edom, who gave My land to themselves as a posses-
> sion, with wholehearted joy and spiteful minds, in order to plunder
> its open country."'"

(Ezekiel 36:1–5)

Again, in what time frame is this being pictured? It is during the time of the Jewish people shooting forth on the mountains of Israel. That would be now. And what specific mountains are being spoken of here? They are the mountains of Judea and Samaria, which the world, and sadly too many Christians, call the West Bank. Who occupies parts of that area and has been insulting and killing the Jewish people? The so-called Palestinians led by Yasser Arafat, the PLO, and a demonic host of other terrorist organizations spoken of in Ezekiel and Obadiah.

> "But on Mount Zion there shall be deliverance, and there shall be
> holiness; the house of Jacob shall possess their possessions. The
> house of Jacob shall be a fire, and the house of Joseph a flame; but
> the house of Esau shall be stubble; they shall kindle them and devour
> them, and no survivor shall remain of the house of Esau," for the

*Lord has spoken. The South shall possess the mountains of Esau,
and the Lowland shall possess Philistia. They shall possess the fields
of Ephraim and the fields of Samaria.*

(Obadiah 17–19)

These Scriptures specifically speak of those who are taunting
Israel from Ephraim (Judea) and Samaria being judged by the God
of Israel in the end times as we know them. The Palestinians are
going to be judged by the Lord.

"PA to refugees: By 2007 you will fill the hills of Palestine."[103]
What is the Palestinian Authority talking about? They are predicting
possession of God's covenant land and the killing of God's covenant
people. "In a related development, Hamas political chief Khaled
Mashal told a London daily, Israel would soon cease to exist, but
the State of Palestine would allow Jews to stay on as a minority in
the land."[104]

What is the catalyst that springs most of the events of God's
judgment into motion? What starts the clock ticking on these
righteous judgments? While in captivity in Babylon the prophet
Daniel is given the answer to this question. But before we approach
his writings it would be beneficial to have a little history of events
that brought him to the place in his life, in time, and in God's plan
to receive revelations from the Lord.

In the book of Leviticus the Lord is giving the Israelis the law.
In Leviticus 25:1–7 He commands them to let the land rest from
the beginning to the end of the seventh year.

*And the Lord spoke to Moses on Mount Sinai, saying, "Speak to the
children of Israel, and say to them: 'When you come into the land*

---

[103] *Jerusalem News Wire*, December 9, 2003, http://www.jnewswire.com/news_ar-
chive/03/12/031209_refugees.asp.
[104] Ibid.

which I give you, then the land shall keep a sabbath to the LORD. *Six years you shall sow your field and six years you shall prune your vineyard, and gather its fruit; but in the seventh year there shall be a sabbath of solemn rest for the land, a sabbath to the* LORD, *You shall neither sow your field nor prune your vineyard. What grows of its own accord of your harvest you shall not reap, nor gather the grapes of your untended vine, for it is a year of rest for the land. And the sabbath produce of the land shall be food for you: for you, your male and female servants, your hired man, and the stranger who dwells with you, for your livestock and the beasts that are in your land—all its produce shall be for food.*

In Leviticus 26:14–16 the Lord also warns them of His righteous judgment if they do not obey, and if that doesn't bring them to repentance they will experience seven times greater judgment.

"I will set My face against you, and you shall be defeated by your enemies. Those who hate you shall reign over you, and you shall flee when no one pursues you. And after all this, if you do not obey Me, then I will punish you seven times more for your sins."

(Leviticus 26:17–18)

"And if by these things you are not reformed by Me, but walk contrary to Me, then I also will walk contrary to you, and I will punish you yet seven times for your sins."

(vv. 23–24)

"And after all this, if you do not obey Me, but walk contrary to Me, then I also will walk contrary to you in fury; and I, even I, will chastise you seven times for your sins."

(vv. 27–28)

Do you think there might be something significant about the term "seven times"?

God, anticipating their disobedience, pronounces that most of the Jewish people will be taken from the land into captivity.

This is the Lord's judgment for every year that they didn't obey the seventh year Sabbath rest.

> *Then the land shall enjoy its sabbaths as long as it lies desolate and you are in your enemies' land; then the land shall rest and enjoy its Sabbaths. As long as it lies desolate it shall rest—for the time it did not rest on your sabbaths when you dwelt in it.*
>
> (Leviticus 26:34–35)

How many years did God wait until He judged Israel in this regard? And remember, they had also gone into wicked idolatry, immorality, and a host of blatant iniquities. Our patient God waited four hundred and ninety years.

> *"And this whole land shall be a desolation and an astonishment, and these nations shall serve the king of Babylon seventy years. Then it will come to pass, when seventy years are completed, that I will punish the king of Babylon and that nation, the land of the Chaldeans, for their iniquity," says the* LORD; *"and I will make it a perpetual desolation."*
>
> (Jeremiah 25:11–12)

So the Lord pronounces a seventy-year judgment in Babylon on the Jewish people because they failed to let the land rest every seven years as God commanded.

But wait, the seventy-year judgment would be sufficient if they repented, yet if they didn't what would be the consequences? If they didn't humble themselves and turn to the Lord they would have seven times seventy years of being in God's woodshed.

Having established that, let's visit ancient Babylon to look in on Daniel the faithful prophet of the Lord. Most of Daniel's life has been broken and spilled out on the altar of service to God. He was kidnapped from his family as a teenager, taken captive into an empire which had a strange language and customs, along with many pagan gods. From the beginning of his young life in captivity until his senior years he was tempted to disobey the Lord, yet risked the only thing he had, which was his life, to serve the God of Israel.

God rewarded his faithfulness by directing Daniel's paths to the writings we just read of the prophet Jeremiah.

> *In the first year of Darius the son of Ahasuerus, of the lineage of the Medes, who was made king over the realm of the Chaldeans—in the first year of his reign I, Daniel, understood by the books the number of the years specified by the word of the LORD through Jeremiah the prophet, that He would accomplish seventy years in the desolations of Jerusalem.*
>
> (Daniel 9:1–2)

Daniel understands that the time of the initial seventy years of God's judgment is almost complete, so what does he do? Like so many today his position is not, "Oh well, God's going to do what God's going to do. There is nothing I can do about it." Please also realize that Daniel doesn't say, "We know that these things will take place, but we try not to get fanatical about Bible prophecy." What does Daniel say and do?

> *Then I set my face toward the Lord God to make request by prayer and supplications, with fasting, sackcloth, and ashes. And I prayed to the LORD my God, and made confession, and said, "O Lord, great and awesome God, who keeps His covenant and mercy with those who love Him, and with those, who keep His commandments, we have sinned and committed iniquity, we have done wickedly and rebelled, even by departing from Your precepts and Your judgments. Neither have we heeded Your servants the prophets, who spoke in Your name to our kings and our princes, to our fathers and all the people of the land. O Lord, righteousness belongs to You, but to us shame of face,*

as it is this day—to the men of Judah, to the inhabitants of Jerusalem and all Israel, those near and those far off in all the countries to which You have driven them, because of the unfaithfulness which they have committed against You."

(Daniel 9:3–7)

Daniel, one of the most righteous men in history, humbles and denies himself, then confesses his and the nation's sins to the Lord. Oh, that we might be like Daniel! We don't need positive thinking, pull-yourself-up-by-the-bootstraps, happy, self-confident Christians. What we really need are broken, humble Daniels!

God draws near to Daniel and honors his humility (James 4:7–10). He sends to Daniel the angel Gabriel who shares with him future events that will complete the judgment of Israel and the nations, and also usher in the age of the Messiah Jesus.

And he informed me, and talked with me, and said, "O Daniel, I have now come forth to give you skill to understand. At the beginning of your supplications the command went out, and I have come to tell you, for you are greatly beloved; therefore consider the matter, and understand the vision: Seventy weeks are determined for your people and for your holy city, to finish the transgression, to make an end of sins, to make reconciliation for iniquity, to bring in everlasting righteousness, to seal up vision and prophecy, and to anoint the Most Holy."

(Daniel 9:22–24)

Please don't miss this. The word in this verse translated *weeks* in the NKJV is more accurately *sevens* in this verse. The meaning is that seventy sevens of years will pass by and then all of God's plans will be accomplished up to the Messianic Age. We must remember that everyone down through history doesn't talk and think like an American. This was a figure of speech that the Jewish people would have clearly understood.

Do you remember that God warned the Jewish people that if they didn't repent, after the seventy-year judgment that He would punish them seven times greater? Well, the Lord who operates outside of time already knew that they wouldn't humble themselves and turn to Him. Where do we see the most blatant expression of their unrepentant heart?

He came to His own, and His own did not receive Him.

(John 1:11)

While the Jewish people were in Babylon, the pre-existing triune God knew that many of the Jewish people would reject Jesus, God the Son in human form, and call for His death.

God demonstrates His sovereignty and love as He directs that which man plans for evil, and uses it for His glory and our good. Now that's powerful mercy! However, Gabriel informs Daniel of a four-hundred-and-ninety year plan that will end Israel's judgment and fulfill God's plan of redemption. Since the Babylonian judgment was seventy years, the judgment being seven times greater would be 490, or seventy sevens. As a refresher, the Jewish people didn't let the land rest every seven years. The Lord let this go on seventy times and then led them into captivity in Babylon. He then uses a similar formula with a little twist to finish His plan of redemption and judgment.

Hang in there with me, as this will hit you where you live in moments! The angel continues:

"Know therefore and understand, that from the going forth of the command to restore and build Jerusalem until Messiah the Prince, there shall be seven weeks and sixty-two weeks; the street shall be built again, and the wall, even in troublesome times."

(Daniel 9:25)

One reason the Lord uses the term sevens is to make them think back to Leviticus 25. The Lord warned them of judgment by the term seven and also used seven sevens to give them a Year of Jubilee that meant unparalleled freedom. They rejected His warning and the offer of freedom from the bondage of sin and oppression. Please don't forget the eleventh chapter of Romans as you hear this. It was all God's plan of redemption for all of humanity! Having said that, let's take a closer look at the seven sevens and the sixty-two sevens to see how this affects us today.

> "And after the sixty-two weeks Messiah shall be cut off, but not for Himself; and the people of the prince who is to come shall destroy the city and the sanctuary. The end of it shall be with a flood, and till the end of the war desolations are determined."
>
> (Daniel 9:26)

Seven weeks of years added to sixty-two weeks of years is equal to sixty-nine weeks of years, which comes to 483 years (69 x 7 = 483). This prophecy means that from the time a command was given by a Persian king ruling over the Jewish people in captivity to restore and build Jerusalem, until the Messiah would be cut off will be 483 years. We also see that a leader (prince) will arise from the people who again destroy Jerusalem after it has been rebuilt from the Babylonian destruction. Have any of these things yet taken place?

Miraculously, yes! Persian King Artaxerxes issued a decree in 445 B.C. to send the Jewish people to rebuild Jerusalem. On the day that marked the 483rd year, something interesting took place. To understand this event you must know that before the Jews took the Passover lamb to be slaughtered they had to isolate, or cut him off from the others. Why? So that they could scrutinize him for four days to confirm that there was no blemish in him.

"Speak to all the congregation of Israel, saying: 'On the tenth of this month every man shall take for himself a lamb, according to the house of his father, a lamb for a household.'"

(Exodus 12:3)

"Your lamb shall be without blemish, a male of the first year. You may take it from the sheep or from the goats. Now you shall keep it until the fourteenth day of the same month. Then the whole assembly of the congregation of Israel shall kill it at twilight."

(vv. 5–6)

Notice the lamb would have been cut off or isolated four days before being slaughtered.

Four-hundred-and-eighty-three years after King Artaxerxes issued the decree to the Jews, to the very day, the Lamb of God, Jesus Christ, came down the Mount of Olives and began being scrutinized by the Pharisees. Every time they attempted to trip Him up with matters of the law, He embarrassed them and proved Himself to be without blemish. Then on the fourth day, while Passover lambs were being slaughtered in Jerusalem, the Lamb of God was lifted up on the cross and John the Baptist's words were fulfilled.

The next day John saw Jesus coming toward him, and said, "Behold the Lamb of God who takes away the sin of the world!"

(John 1:29)

So we see the Messiah "cut off" four days before the crucifixion, right on time.

But didn't the formula for the ages have a 490-year time span? This only covers 483 years. Where are the last seven years? And how could the next seven years cover the rest of the age until Messiah comes back? After the Messiah is cut off there is another seven, or seven years left to restore all things. The clock of the sevens stops until something in the future occurs that restarts the timer.

We previously read Daniel 9:26 which spoke of a prince who is to come, and will hail from the empire who destroys Jerusalem after the Jews rebuild it. We know that this transpired in the year A.D. 70. The Romans fulfilled King Jesus' prophecy, regarding the destruction of the temple in Matthew, and they all but flattened Jerusalem. There will be a man that will come from a modern Roman empire that will do something that activates the last set of sevens, or seven years. (Also see Daniel's second chapter.)

This event has never occurred and must, as God's word is true. This event takes place in the time of a rebuilt temple in Jerusalem. This person from the revived Roman empire will do something that will announce the last seven years of the current age.

> *"Then he shall confirm a covenant with many for one week; but in the middle of the week he shall bring an end to sacrifice and offering. And on the wing of abominations shall be one who makes desolate, even until the consummation, which is determined, is poured out on the desolate."*
>
> (Daniel 9:27)

This prince who is to come will make some type of agreement with Israel for the last seven, or week, which will fulfill the 490 years. This person is whom the Bible calls the antichrist. The last seven years are those of the great tribulation. We see this time of God's wrathful judgment in Revelation 5–19.

This man will step into the rebuilt temple, stop the reinstated animal sacrifices of the many Jews that have been gathered from the nations, and declare himself God (2 Thessalonians 2:3–4). He will also persecute the Jewish people in a final attempt to annihilate the Jews (Revelation 12:13–17).

The type of agreement he makes with Israel is very interesting. In Daniel 11:24, 31 and Revelation 6:2 we see that the antichrist will not gain his power by making war but by making peace. Many prophecy experts believe that Antiochus Epiphanes, of Daniel's eleventh chapter, and the conquering king without arrows in his bow of Revelation 6:2 represent the antichrist coming to power by making peace. I have an appropriate analogy to explain the world's reason for loving this antichrist and his plans for peace.

When I was fighting God for control of my life I would seemingly get very close to realizing my wicked goals, and then like bubbles that pop when your fingers touch them, my nearly attained goals would pop and disappear at my fingertips. So it is with peace in the Middle East for the world and its leaders. This man will finally establish peace in the world's most dangerous region and furiously seek to accomplish wicked humanity's most treasured goal. That dream is to have a Jesus-free and a Jew-free world. But when the antichrist steps in he will make a tangible, seemingly lasting peace that will set in motion the most horrific time this planet has ever known. How will the last seven start? It will start with a peace agreement in the Middle East. Is this starting to hit home yet?

What about the revived Roman Empire, or the new temple in Jerusalem? Could these things possibly take place in the generation of the physical rebirth of Israel the fig tree? A treaty was signed nine years after Israel again became a nation. Using a common search engine on the Internet, I obtained an official outline of this document. Treaty Establishing the European Community as Amended by Subsequent Treaties,[105] Rome, 25 March 1957. This is commonly called the Rome Treaty of 1957 and established the European Union. Here are more articles of recent events that may help to identify this Roman power. "For first time in history, Europe will become

---

[105] HR-Net, http://www.hri.org/docs/rome57/

one." [106] "The 'new' anti-semitism: Is Europe in grip of worst bout of hatred since the Holocaust?" [107]

And just to show you how everything old is becoming new again, consider the following: "Vatican Is Open to Becoming a Full Member of U.N." [108] "Europe Wants to Rival U.S. as Military Superpower, says EU Parliamentarian."[109] "The idea of a united Europe stretches back thousands of years. The enthusiasts were seldom as high-minded as their modern successors. . . . Ever since the fall of Rome, a strain in European thought has longed for the recreation of an over-arching political structure for Europe, and used the Roman empire as a model."[110] "Dollar Tumbles to Record Low Against Euro."[111] The Roman Empire and the Roman state religion are ready to take center stage! Is there any other news from the revived Roman Empire?

A poll was taken in Europe to determine, by numerical ranking, society's opinion of the nations that are the biggest threat to world peace. The survey is very telling of the direction Europe is headed. Who was at the top of the list? Was it North Korea or Iran, with Syria and China not far behind? No, Israel was considered the number one threat. The United States was considered more dangerous than Iran, Iraq, and North Korea in the minds of Europeans. "EU poll: Israel 'biggest threat' to world peace—U.S. beats out 'axis of evil' in causing global instability."[112]

---

[106] *International Herald Tribune, The IHT Online,* December 16, 2002, http://www.iht.com/articles/80264.html

[107] Chris McGeal, "Guardian Unlimited: Special Reports," November 25, 2003.

[108] Zenit, The World Seen from Rome, September 21, 2003, http://www.zenit.org/english/visualizza.phtml?sid=41278

[109] Julie Stahl, January 4, 2003, http://www.crosswalk.com/news/1238927.html

[110] "The History of an Idea," *The Economist,* December 3, 2003, http://www.economist.com/world/europe/displayStory.cfm?story_id=2313040

[111] *IMTV,* December 2, 2003, http://www.independent-media.tv/item.cfm?fmedia_id=4106&fcategory_desc=Economy

[112] *WorldNetDaily,* October 31, 2003, http://www.worldnetdaily.com/news/article.asp?ARTICLE_ID=35383

Consider the mind-set of this Euro conglomerate regarding the Jewish people found in a *U.S. News & World Report* article "A Shameful Contagion": "A mural in a Scottish church depicts a crucified Jesus surrounded by Israeli soldiers. In Italy, La Stampa publishes a page one cartoon of a tank emblazoned with the Jewish star pointing its gun at the baby Jesus, which pleads, 'Surely, they don't want to kill me again.' In France, where there have been hundreds of acts of violence, walls in Jewish neighborhoods have been defaced with slogans proclaiming, 'Jews to the gas chambers.' In Germany, the Free Democratic Party has unofficially adopted anti-Semitism as a campaign technique to attract Germany's sizable Muslim minority." [113] Things are really beginning to simmer in the empire established from Rome. I am confident they will choose a dynamic leader who will represent them with unparalleled perfection!

But what of the temple that must go up on the currently disputed temple mount in Jerusalem? I have personally been inside the Temple Institute in Jerusalem. It is an organization that is committed to rebuilding that temple. As you walk through the institute you see replicas of the actual instruments and necessary items, which are in storage, needed to perform Levitical temple services! I watched the director on television in November 2003, and he said that they have 60 percent of the necessary items for the priestly work inside the temple completed. Quite interestingly, a gene has recently been discovered that identifies the Levites from the other Jewish people. There is a modern Levitical priesthood being made ready for service.

Here is another intriguing article. "For several months, Jewish experts have been working on a replica of the third temple in the blazing heat near the Dead Sea. The Jewish community of Mitzpe

---

[113] Mortimer B. Zuckerman, "A Shameful Contagion," *U.S. News and World Report,* November 7, 2003

Yericho, between Jerusalem and Jericho, is home to the model, which is built on a 1:1 scale. Covering an area of 25,000 square meters (269,000 square feet), it will function as a training site to prepare priests (kohanim) for service in the third temple in Jerusalem. Backers of the project say the Jewish people are waiting for the redemption and must prepare themselves for the coming of the Messiah."[114]

The temple will go up, the man of Daniel 9:27 will step on to the scene and desecrate it, and the Messiah Jesus will destroy him and set up His glorious kingdom! Folks, it is at the door! The unbelieving Jews see the signs of the times, but does the church?

This current peace process in the Middle East is nothing more than the rolling out of the red carpet for the antichrist. Again, what is so unattainable for the world today, though relentlessly pursued? Peace between Israel, the Islamic nations and their terrorists is what the world desperately is seeking. God will use this to judge the nations.

> *The burden of the word of the* LORD *against Israel. Thus says the* LORD, *who stretches out the heavens, lays the foundation of the earth, and forms the spirit of man within him: "Behold, I will make Jerusalem a cup of drunkenness to all the surrounding peoples, when they lay siege against Judah and Jerusalem. And it shall happen in that day that I will make Jerusalem a very heavy stone for all peoples; all who would heave it away will surely be* **cut in pieces**, *though all nations of the earth are gathered against it."*
>
> (Zechariah 12:1–3)

What city for the first time in history has become the entire world's problem? Of course it is Jerusalem.

---

[114] *Israel Today,* October 31, 2003, http://www.israeltoday.co.il/headlines/headlines.asp?CatID=3&Article ID=852

Satan is fighting for God's city. The nations of the earth are taking their stand against the Father as He is getting ready to place His King on the throne in Jerusalem. His name is King Jesus! These passages warn of the consequences of surrounding Israel militarily under the guise of fixing the Jerusalem problem. The only reason that Jerusalem hasn't already been surrounded by the nations' armies is that the Israeli government continues to play ball in the land-for-peace charade. When they wake up to the reality that the nations will stop at nothing less than their total destruction, Israel will stop participating in the game and then the armies will come. Jerusalem is already surrounded politically by the most powerful nations on the planet!

God will then pour out harsh, punishing judgment on the nations, and for what specific reason?

"For behold, in those days and at that time, when I bring back the captives of Judah and Jerusalem, I will also gather all nations, and bring them down to the Valley of Jehoshapat; and I will enter into judgment with them there on account of My people, My heritage Israel, whom they have scattered among the nations; they have also divided up My land."

(Joel 3:1–2)

God is very serious about the land and people of Israel.

We have two more chapters together, and I will wrap up by discussing a country that I deeply love, and have been blessed to be its citizen for my entire life. I am speaking of the United States of America.

CHAPTER 17

God's Judgment on America

"I know your works, that you have a name that you are alive."
(Revelation 3:1b)

I t seems that there are some who realize a sense of great pleasure as, with great consistency, they curse the United States
of America. This would be an obvious understatement were I
talking of those living abroad, but I speak of those who enjoy the
unique freedoms and opportunities of citizenship of the U.S.
Many of these are the same whose mind-sets and lifestyles are
destroying the country that affords them the right to do so. Admittedly, I practiced a horribly sinful lifestyle for much of my
life, so instead of throwing stones it would be more appropriate
for me to pray for them.

However, I was raised in a family that said, "If you don't like
America, then go somewhere else that suits you better." In my family,
people bought American-made cars and other products if possible.
My grandfather retired from Delco Products in Moraine, Ohio. We
drove GM automobiles because we wanted to support America. Of
course, now even American cars, or their parts, are made in other
countries. I think patriotism is important, and as long as it isn't

269

misguided and doesn't conflict with the will of God, patriotism is necessary to be a good witness for the Lord Jesus Christ.

However, as a follower of the King of heaven I have dual citizenship. First, before being an American, I am a citizen of heaven and have sworn allegiance to the King, Jesus Christ. That heavenly country has my heart before even the "good ole U.S. of A." You see, I formerly affiliated myself with a particular, what is commonly called, conservative political party in America. Then I began to see the political party behaving in a way that is contrary to another party that has a higher priority in my life. I now do not consider myself a member of the Republican or Democratic Party. Why? Because I am a card-carrying member of the Kingdom Party, which doesn't operate by a vote but by the word of the King! I am not saying that you can't be a member of a political party and follow Jesus, but if you are, remember the King is watching and listening.

As a servant and ambassador for this heavenly party I, with sorrow and brokenness, unlike those who are pleased when something goes wrong in America, must proclaim an uncomfortable reality. Unless the U.S., and more specifically the once-thriving American church, repents God will execute harsher judgments on America. What do I mean by "harsher judgments"? The God of Israel has been judging America mercifully and slowly for quite some time, yet the church and the nation have become more rebellious and indignant toward Him. Unless there is swift and genuine repentance, I am sad to say that the best America will become is a second-rate power, and at worst it will be turned into a self-illuminating parking lot.

There are three things that provoke a patient, loving God to physical judgment. One is not defending the defenseless. Once again, we have the luxury of looking back to the mistakes of others, namely the Jewish people, to take instruction for ourselves. Before God physically judged Israel, He warned them of something to which we should soon heed.

*Your princes are rebellious, and companions of thieves; everyone loves bribes, and follows after rewards. **They do not defend the fatherless, nor does the cause of the widow come before them.***

(Isaiah 1:23)

I mentioned this passage earlier, but will mention it again as it pertains to abortion.

*They served their idols, which became a snare to them. They even sacrificed their sons and daughters to demons, **and shed innocent blood, the blood of their sons and daughters, whom they sacrificed** to the idols of Canaan; and the land was polluted with blood.*

(Psalm 106:36–38)

America is polluted with the blood of approximately 40 million babies that have, quite literally, been butchered in American abortion slaughterhouses.[115] Abel's blood cried out for justice; what do you think the cry of over 40 million babies sounds like in the hearing of a holy God?

Before sharing the second of three judgment-producing behaviors of which mankind is warned, I would like to share a testimony of what God revealed to me. My wife and I were in Dallas attending an "Israel and the church" type of conference. I had risen early in my hotel room to seek the Lord Jesus. He led me to the account of Sodom and Gomorrah. The Lord revealed to me that He judged Sodom with something before the physical destruction. That something is blindness. The Holy Spirit revealed to me that America and, more frighteningly, the church in America has been judged with spiritual blindness and deafness that will bring certain physical judgment on the church and the U.S. as well.

---

[115] Central Illinois Right to Life, December 18, 2003, http://www.cirtl.org/ab-facts.htm

Please see that God judges people who reject His love and mercy with blindness and deafness. First, they willfully close their eyes and ears. He then supernaturally closes them further so they can't seek Him, which leads them into behavior that will bring them into painful, physical judgment. Pharaoh is a good example. God continually gave him chances to let the Israelis go, but when he crossed God's "line in the sand" from patience to justice, God hardened his heart so that he couldn't see or hear from the Lord, and couldn't stop himself from destruction (Exodus 10:1–2).

Yes, but that was Pharaoh, not the people of God. The children of Israel in Isaiah's time, Jesus' time, and currently have been judged with spiritual blindness, which has cost them horrible persecution, death by the millions, and unceasing pain. As Jesus quotes Isaiah, we see the Jews closing their own eyes.

> "And in them the prophecy of Isaiah is fulfilled, which says: 'Hearing you will hear and shall not understand, and seeing you will see and not perceive; For the hearts of this people have grown dull. Their ears are hard of hearing, and their eyes they have closed, lest they should see with their eyes and hear with their ears, lest they should understand with their hearts and turn, so that I should heal them.'"
>
> (Matthew 13:14–15)

Then, in other verses, we see God blinding His own people in their rebellion:

> Pause and wonder! Blind yourselves and be blind! They are drunk, but not with wine; they stagger, but not with intoxicating drink. For the LORD has poured out on you the spirit of deep sleep, and has closed your eyes, namely, the prophets; and He has covered your heads, namely, the seers.
>
> (Isaiah 29:9–10)

Oh please hear this—pastor, prophet, evangelist, missionary, teacher—God blinded the leaders who were set on building their own kingdom on earth in God's name. He was blinding them then, and is doing so to the leaders of the church today who are building their own kingdom instead of His!

The leaders of Israel who were the most blind were easily identified. They preached positive, smooth, pleasurable words of consolation such as, "Of course a loving God wasn't the one bringing the destruction on Israel," and "It will all soon get better," and "Times of blessing and prosperity will be our lot." They didn't apply God's word to their specific situation because they couldn't hear from God! They had no ability to convey God's truth to the people. So it is today, as so many church leaders rarely tie the prophetic current events to God's word. Many simply can't see or hear. Thankfully, God has His true shepherds who are proclaiming truth and advancing the kingdom of heaven!

The most unpopular in Israel were those negative, hateful prophets, who constantly approached them with harsh words warning them of judgment and calling them to repentance. God warns rebellious Israel of listening to smooth, ear-tickling preaching.

> That this is a rebellious people, lying children, children who will not hear the law of the LORD; who say to the seers, "Do not see," And to the prophets, "Do not prophesy to us right things; Speak to us smooth things, prophesy deceits."
>
> (Isaiah 30:9–10)

A good New Testament reference is 2 Timothy 4:2–5:

> Preach the word! Be ready in season and out of season. Convince, rebuke, exhort, with all longsuffering and teaching. For the time will come when they will not endure sound doctrine, but according to their own desires, because they have itching ears, they will heap up for themselves teachers; and they will turn their ears away from the truth, and be turned aside to fables.

Toward which leaders do you gravitate? Do you want to listen to those that tickle your ears, or the men of God who tell you the truth even at the risk of losing your monthly donation?

As we return from that not-so-brief yet necessary exhortation, we see the hardening that has taken place to the Jews to this very day. God warns believers in Jesus not to fall prey to the same type of hardening of our hearts, which leads to blindness and an inability to hear from God. In Romans 11:8 speaking of the Jewish people the apostle Paul says:

Just as it is written: "God has given them a spirit of stupor, eyes that they should not see and ears that they should not hear, to this very day."

Then in Hebrews 3:14–15:

For we have become partakers of Christ if we hold the beginning of our confidence steadfast to the end, while it is said: "Today, if you will hear His voice, do not harden your hearts as in the rebellion."

Hardening of the heart to God leads to rebellion and God's judging blindness and deafening.

King Jesus spoke of spiritual deafness in Mark 4:24–25:

Then He said to them, "Take heed what you hear. With the same measure you use, it will be measured to you; and to you who hear, more will be given. For whoever has, to him more will be given; but whoever does not have, even what he has will be taken away from him."

Do you remember when we spoke of people who have become dull of hearing, in the fifth chapter of Hebrews? Here is the process of that dullness.

The Lord reveals truth to us, then offers the opportunity to appreciate, understand, and appropriately apply that truth. For those who thankfully respond to God, He then blesses with greater revelation and/or resources necessary to accomplish the vision. The Lord does not reveal Himself for the sole purpose of making a human being more knowledgeable. For a reminder, that is the problem with the Greco-Roman way of doing church. Revelation from God is for a change in lives and kingdom advancement. To them that are unthankful, and, at that point naturally unmotivated, lethargic, inactive, and, last but not least, have offended Almighty God, He begins to remove the revelation that they already have and they become deaf and blind. I have experienced this in my own life and it is scary! It is a fearful thing to fall into the hands of the living God in judgment! I regularly pray for the Lord Jesus to give me eyes to see and ears to hear.

You may be thinking, "God won't judge the church because Romans 8:1 states *there is therefore now no condemnation to them which are in Christ Jesus.* I am not necessarily talking about condemnation. I will give an illustration that will help us to understand how God will judge the church. The judgments Isaiah pronounced against Israel would have disciplined the Israelis who had faith, but were in disobedience. They would have condemned the wicked who were congregating with those of faith. These judgments would have spared and refined the faithful, or God would have brought them home to heaven for a future glorious judgment and rewards. Does that sound familiar? That is exactly what God will do with His church. Please remember the place God starts with judgment is in the church.

> *For the time has come for judgment to begin at the house of God; and if it begins with us first, what will be the end of those who do not obey the gospel of God?*
>
> (1 Peter 4:17)

I know people who used to understand so much about the things of God, and now they are blind and deaf. There are people that went through the precepts courses I earlier spoke of, and their

Bibles are marked up from intense study. They have had opportunities that most on this planet will never enjoy. Yet today they have little interest or understanding of the deeper things of God. Why? God has taken from them the ability to hear and receive from Him, while at the same time given more capacity to hear and see to those who will be appreciative and useful to His program of kingdom advancement.

I know others with great intellectual knowledge of God, to the extent of having taught the Bible in seminary, yet have little zeal for or discernment of the things of God. They admittedly are depressed and negative most of the time, and have very little confidence in the Creator of the universe. They are captives of great intellectual information about God and, tragically, have little communication with Him. If the church that made this nation unique can't see or hear, the once-godly nation with great opportunities will continue to go the way of the church that has lost its lampstand in heaven, and lose its position among the other nations. The once-enjoyed blessings and protections will increasingly be removed, while the pain of God's righteous judgments will take their place.

I can't say when the judgment of blindness hit America, yet I am confident at least a deeper loss of sight took place in the 1960s. This is when prayer was removed from the schools, the murder called abortion became legal, and a long list of other wicked thoughts and behaviors became the new fad. This was nothing more than the blinding from rebellion and further vision impairment caused by a holy God.

This brings me to the second behavior of extreme iniquity that will bring God's physical judgment on America. The spiritual blindness in the church and society of America has left a vacuum for the demons of hell to fill, and fill it they have. As the salt and light has become more dim and less salty, the blindness that followed has moved a holy God to judge by turning us over to the end-of-the-line sin of Sodom and Gomorrah, which is called, among other things, homosexuality in our modern society.

From Romans 1:18–23 God warns of His wrath, identifies the rejection of His loving truth, and then in verse 24 begins to warn of specific penalties that He will administer for such hatred of that which is good:

Therefore God also gave them up to uncleanness, in the lusts of their hearts, to dishonor their bodies among themselves, who exchanged the truth of God for the lie, and worshiped and served the creature rather than the Creator, who is blessed forever. Amen.

(Romans 1:24)

So where is God's judgment in all of this? It is in the turning over of man to his own wicked desires that naturally dwell within every human being. Left to his own devices, man spirals downward toward Sodom.

For this reason God gave them up to vile passions. For even their women exchanged the natural use for what is against nature. Likewise also the men, leaving the natural use of the woman, burned in their lust for one another, men with men committing what is shameful, and receiving in themselves the penalty of their error which was due.

(Romans 1:26–27)

God judges with blindness, so that evil rebels run headlong into physical punishment, which is the penalty due for such wickedness.

In the next verse in Romans 1, God warns of those whom He gives a reprobate or debased mind. This is a person that can't hear the loving plea of the Holy Spirit to repent and turn away from the flames of hell. As we take a last look at the first chapter of Romans, I must tell you, I am saddened at how much it reminds me of our nation, and alarmingly, many professed believers in Jesus.

And even as they did not like to retain God in their knowledge, God gave them over to a debased mind to do those things which are not fitting; being filled with all unrighteousness, sexual immorality, wickedness, covetousness, maliciousness; full of envy, murder, strife, deceit, evil-mindedness; they are whisperers, backbiters, haters of God, violent, proud, boasters, inventors of evil things, disobedient to parents, undiscerning, untrustworthy, unloving, unforgiving, unmerciful; who, knowing the righteous judgment of God, that those who practice such things are deserving of death, not only do the same but also approve of those who practice them.

(Romans 1:28–32)

I am heartbroken to say this sounds like an average evening in front of the national television nightly news.

Homosexuality is being accepted as a legitimate alternative lifestyle more now than ever in America's history. But why shouldn't it be, when those who lead the people advocate it? By the way, in a democracy, leadership is a simple reflection of the society. Again here are some articles that reflect the state of affairs.

"D.C. Bishop Eyes Gay 'Marriage' rites"[116] (*Washington Times*, October 29, 2003).

Distinguished Senator Biden in a recent article: "Biden: Gay 'Marriage' Inevitable."[117] (*Washington Times*, November 24, 2003).

And here is one from our professing Christian president: "Bush Cheers 'Gay' Church after 'Marriage Week'—Attempts to Please Family Advocates, Homosexuals Baffle Both Groups." The article continues. "Not long after he endorsed 'Marriage Protection Week,' President Bush sent a letter of congratulations to a denomination

[116] Julia Duin, http://www.washtimes.com/national/20031028-113319-52330r.htm
[117] Audry Hudson, http://www.washtimes.com/national/20031124-120303-4131r.htm

founded by homosexual activists that performs more than 6,000 same-sex 'weddings' each year"[118] (*World Net Daily*, November 12, 2003). What more can I say?

What is the third thing, after not defending the defenseless, and homosexuality, that provokes the God of Israel to painful physical judgment? This sin is the epitome of evil and its blatant outward expression. In Texas there is a saying you hear and see on radio, television, signs, and on bumper stickers. It goes: "Don't mess with Texas." The third act of human defiance that angers God to judge is when people come against His beloved. The church and the rest of America had better start listening to God: "Don't mess with Israel."

Many think that America is being a wonderful, helpful friend to Israel. Of course, compared to most of the nations, that is absolutely true. However, if we are comparing ourselves to those trying to destroy Israel out of hatred toward Jewish people, or those who believe that Israel is the most threatening country in the world to peace above Iran, North Korea, and other rogue states, then we aren't setting our bar very high, are we?

God compares us to His word not to others' behavior. The apostle Paul shares with us the folly of comparing ourselves to other men.

> *For we dare not class ourselves or compare ourselves with those who commend themselves. But they, measuring themselves by themselves, and comparing themselves among themselves, are not wise.*
>
> (2 Corinthians 10:12)

As a church and a nation, how does America line up with God's word in terms of our treatment of Israel?

---

[118] WorldNetDaily, November 12, 2003, http://www.worldnetdaily.com/news/article.asp?ARTICLE_ID=35539

Listen to this quote from Bill Koenig, who loves Jesus, which provokes him also to love Israel: "It is a sad irony that many in America believe that the United States has stood by Israel. In reality, this nation has led them to the edge of the abyss through the policies of the Bush (the elder) and the Clinton administrations. The past policies of the State Department and the White House have been designed to protect the flow of Middle East oil. This same concern has occupied President George W. Bush and his administration. Regardless of the intentions, bad or good, these American policies have put the 'apple of God's eye' in harm's way. . . . The United States has put a noose around Israel's neck by sponsoring, or co-sponsoring, the Madrid, Oslo, Wye, and Camp David agreements."[119]

This book continues to discuss the Mitchell and Tenet plans that also put Israel in harm's way. Here is another quote that is interesting. "During the ten-year peace process, the U.S. taxpayers have paid out billions of dollars in aid to our so-called Arab 'allies,' who have all sided against Israel since her independence in 1948."[120] We need to remember that the Lord doesn't play politics. He operates by His holy word!

In his book Koenig continues to document the strong evidence that reveals whenever America pushes Israel to give away covenant land, or place the Jewish people in greater danger, God applies pressure to America with natural disasters, political upheaval, or terrorist activity perpetrated against our country. Folks, the sky is the limit when you mess with Israel.

You see, I have learned that of the three judgment-producing offenses that man commits against God, Israel is the one He takes most personally. We see this in Zechariah 2:8 as God is warning not to mess with Israel:

---

[119] McTernan and Koenig, *Israel: The Blessing or the Curse,* 121
[120] Ibid.

For thus says the LORD of hosts: "He sent Me after glory, to the nations which plunder you; for he who touches you touches the apple of His eye."

In those times the apple of the eye was a term used for the pupil of one's eye. God is comparing messing with Israel to sticking a finger in His eye. This is a clear warning of the personal affront God takes with those who attack His land and people.

The reason is that God operates by what? Do you remember one of the first things we discussed? Yes, God operates by covenant. He has made a promise to Abraham, Isaac, and Israel that He will keep. Satan is doing what he has always done—attack the word of God. He is deceiving mankind, and God equates cursing Israel with fighting against the God of Israel and attacking His holy word.

I learned a very important principle from Dr. Arnold Fruchtenbaum, which God employs at times when cursing those that curse Israel. It is called the principle of curse for curse.

In Exodus 1:15–17 Pharaoh attempted to kill off the Israeli boys by having them drowned in the Nile River.

So Pharaoh commanded all his people, saying, "Every son who is born you shall cast into the river, and every daughter you shall save alive."

(Exodus 1:22)

I have a question for you. How did God judge Pharaoh's army?

Then the waters returned, and covered the chariots, the horsemen, and all the army of Pharaoh that came into the sea after them. Not so much as one of them remained.

(Exodus 14:28)

After the Israelis crossed the Red Sea, which had been divided and held up by the hand of God, the Lord brought the waters crashing down onto the Egyptian army, drowning all of them. God cursed Pharaoh in the same way that Pharaoh cursed Israel, with an intensely greater measure. For those that curse Israel (esteem lightly, despise, or hold in contempt), it will be measured back with greater intensity!

In Exodus 4:23 God proclaims the judgment of killing Pharaoh's firstborn son. Why?

> "So I say to you, let my son go that he may serve Me. But if you refuse to let him go, indeed I will kill your son, your firstborn."

God is calling the children of Israel His firstborn son, and says He will curse Pharaoh's firstborn son, which is a curse for curse. Of course, we know that God kept His promise and killed the firstborn all over Egypt, including Pharaoh's son. Again, the curse was measured back with greater intensity.

One more and then I will address modern times. In the book of Esther, wicked Haman builds a gallows so high that everyone in the city could see it. This was to kick off the widespread annihilation of the Jews in the Persian provinces. He had a spirit in him that raged at righteous Mordecai. Who ends up with his head in that noose? You got it—wicked Haman. Do you see that God will execute curse for curse?

For years, and through different presidential administrations, America has accepted the ungodly notion that Israel is not at war with those who will only be satisfied with her absolute destruction. Though these countries and their terrorists openly proclaim this to the world, the government of our country has treated the Middle East conflict as a legitimate land dispute with people who just want what is coming to them. By the way, that is exactly what many of them will get! Anyway, to be more current, the last two presidents, and until recently, George W. Bush, have twisted the arms of the Israeli government to negotiate with Yasser Arafat.

Yasser Arafat, and those in high-ranking leadership in his organization, are some of the most blood-thirsty murderers on this planet! Their hands are stained with the blood of Jewish men, women, and children. Yasser Arafat is the godfather of modern terrorism. Does anybody remember the hijackings of the 1970s, or the murder of thousands of Christians in Lebanon? *Hello!* Where have people's minds gone? It must be spiritual deception! For Yasser Arafat to receive the Nobel Peace Prize, which he did in 1994, is beyond absurd!!

Let's listen to Nagi N. Najjar, director of the Lebanese Foundation for Peace. He speaks of his eyewitness accounts of Yasser Arafat's PLO and their treatment of Lebanese Christians in the 1970's war-torn Lebanon: "The barbarism in Lebanon was an Arafat speciality. Christians were decapitated, girls were raped, parents and kids were murdered in the streets due to Palestinian military attacks against the Christian areas, as they refused to distinguish between adult men and women and children. All Christians, despite age or sex, were Palestinian targets. These were the same Palestinians we welcomed with open arms in 1948 with charity and our reward was death and torture."[121]

What keeps me sane is that I know the Father is in control of it all, and from this insanity He will bring restoration to the whole planet. But we want to make sure that we are on the right side of God's judgment.

Anyway, for years our government has scolded Israel and told them they can't fight a war like other countries. As a result, they have had to put their military and civilian population in unheard-of danger. They have had to devise tactics of warfare designed not to win a war but to keep the United Nations and the United States

---

[121] Nagin N. Najjar, "An Open Letter To Human Rights Watch." The Lebanese Foundation for Peace, http://www.free-lebanon.com/LFPNews/Witnesses/witnesses.html

from placing sanctions on them. Most who call themselves Christians have stood by and protested very little.

Then in a startling move, the Christian president that earned my vote by promising not to be directly involved in the Middle East conflict did something no previous U. S. president would have ever done. President Bush called for the reduction of the covenant land by giving it to the terrorists and the renaming of Israel to Palestine again. One reason a Bill Clinton, for example, would have never imagined trying what George W. Bush has already done is that the evangelical church in America would have called for a second impeachment! The so-called Palestinians are Israel's most steadfast enemies, and that is saying something! These enemies also subscribe to the antichrist religion of Islam.

President Bush initially planned on announcing this policy change earlier than he was able to do so. It appears that his secretary of state had planned on announcing this to the United Nations in late September 2001. "Powell had expected to deliver the speech in late September on the sidelines of the U.N. Assembly, but that plan was put on hold after the September 11 terrorist attacks on the World Trade Center and Pentagon. 'It will go farther than we have ever gone,' one official said of Powell's speech. 'There is an awful lot more that we view as being the end result than what we have said so far.'"[122]

What stopped Powell from making that speech? It was 9/11. I want us to step back and consider something. It is difficult to see the country that you love come under the judgment of a holy God. The first natural reaction is to wishfully not believe it is happening. Ask me how I know this. My own personal struggle produced that observation.

---

[122] McTernan and Koenig, *Israel: The Blessing or the Curse*, 142.

I remember reading the biography of the inspiring follower of Jesus Christ, Oswald Chambers. In a particular part of his life he was concerned for a friend that had become so zealous in patriotism for Great Britain that she actually thought Britain had replaced Israel in God's economy. It was a doctrine that she had picked up, which was circulating at the time. Britain was now Israel. It may seem kind of weird, but have we not attempted to change God into the image of America?

Did you know that Jesus is not an American? Have you considered that as America flagrantly violates God's principles and arrogantly shuns His warnings that He will judge the U.S. just like any other nation? Have you ever mulled over the possibility that the events of 9/11 were an act of God's righteous judgment? I know it would be difficult to hear such a thing. Especially since it is rare to hear pastors and other popular church leaders say this from the pulpit. It would be an unpopular position to take, yet did God call pastors to a popularity contest? No, they were called to speak forth God's truth at any cost! I came to the realization that 9/11 was God's judgment on America by way of brokenness and revelation from His word.

When King Solomon turned to pagan gods and invited the flood of evil into Israel, what did Israel's God do?

> *Now the LORD raised up an adversary against Solomon, Hadad the Edomite; he was a descendant of the king in Edom.*
>
> (1 Kings 11:14)

Then in 1 Kings 11:23:

> *And God raised up another adversary against him, Rezon the son of Eliadah, who had fled from his lord, Hadadezer king of Zobah.*

The Lord raised up Solomon's adversaries to judge him.

What, or more accurately whom, did God use to judge the northern ten tribes of Israel? The answer is the vicious Assyrians.

> *"Woe to Assyria, the rod of My anger and the staff in whose hand is My indignation. I will send him against an ungodly nation, and against the people of My wrath I will give him charge, to seize the spoil, to take the prey, and to tread them down like the mire of the streets.*
>
> (Isaiah 10:5–6)

God caused the Assyrians to militarily punish rebellious Israel.

What about the southern kingdom of Judah?

> *Therefore thus says the Lord GOD: "As I live, surely My oath which he despised, and My covenant which he broke, I will recompense on his own head. I will spread My net over him, and he shall be taken in My snare. I will bring him to Babylon and try him there for the treason which he committed against Me."*
>
> (Ezekiel 17:19–20)

The Lord chose the Babylonian empire as His instrument of judgment.

Then God used Persian King Cyrus to judge Babylon, raising him up at God's appointed time.

> *"Remember the former things of old, for I am God, and there is no other; I am God and there is none like Me, declaring the end from the beginning, and from ancient times things that are not yet done, saying, 'My counsel shall stand, and I will do all My pleasure,' Calling a bird of prey from the east, the man who executes My counsel, from a far country. Indeed I have spoken it; I will also bring it to pass. I have purposed it; I will also do it."*
>
> (Isaiah 46:9–11)

Come down and sit in the dust, O virgin daughter of Babylon, sit on the ground without a throne, O daughter of the Chaldeans! For you shall no more be called Tender and delicate.

(Isaiah 47:1)

How could God consider pagan Babylon as a virgin? The answer is that until God judged her with Persia, she never had sensed the nakedness and defilement of an invading army. Ironically, immediately after that horrible day in New York City, it was common to hear that 9/11 was the day America lost her innocence.

Oh, pastors, church leaders, and followers of Jesus, God hasn't changed! Every world power that has ever existed did so for God's purposes, and then He brought it down to raise another up for His unfolding plans for the ages. I have heard a number of preachers proclaim boldly from the pulpit how God needs America to spread His gospel. With something past the order of normal patriotism, they assert that America has done more for the cause of the gospel than any other nation in history. I just have one simple question: If that is true, why is America not mentioned in God's word? If it is possibly mentioned in a verse or two, which I cannot absolutely say using normal Bible interpretive methods, the U.S. surely isn't by any stretch of the imagination one of God's big players according to His word.

The only explanation for this thinking is a deceptive perverted brand of patriotism that in the end isn't very patriotic. Am I a good American if I see danger coming and act like it isn't imminent? It would be one thing to not know better, but God's people, and especially His leaders, will be held accountable to the Lord Jesus. Whether it is purposeful deception or wishful thinking is not mine to judge, but we are under the ether and had better come out of it as we are in for times that most have never imagined in America.

Two weeks before 9/11/01 I became broken and began weeping over Scriptures from the prophet Ezekiel that I had never really spent any time meditating on.

The word of the LORD *came again to me, saying: "Son of man, when the land sins against Me by persistent unfaithfulness, I will stretch out My hand against it; I will cut off its supply of bread, send famine on it, and cut off man and beast from it. Even if these three men Noah, Daniel, and Job, were in it, they would deliver only themselves by their righteousness," says the Lord* GOD.

"Or if I bring a sword on that land, and say, 'Sword, go through the land,' and I cut off man and beast from it, even though these three men were in it, as I live,' says the Lord GOD, *'they would deliver neither sons nor daughters, but only they themselves would be delivered."*

(Ezekiel 14:17–18)

I was broken over these Scriptures, and understood that the Lord was about to cause something terrible to occur, much like a child feels as his daddy is coming up the stairs with a paddle in his hand.

I remember speaking to a large Bible study at the church we were attending in August 2001. I proclaimed with a sense of urgency, "God is about to take us to the woodshed and I don't want to go there." The room was hushed as the silent response ranged from indifference, to a sense of "Isn't it almost lunchtime?" Some were simmering with anger that I would even suggest such a thing. I don't believe one person took what I said seriously.

On September 11, 2001, at about 8:30 in the morning, I was telling my wife that Israel will be a safer place than America before too long. She disagreed and we had a lively discussion, which included her reasonable point that bombs were going off in Israel not America. I showed her the Scriptures in Ezekiel of which I just spoke, closed my Bible, and soon thereafter the phone rang. It was a dear sister in Jesus calling and exhorting us to turn on our television as a plane had hit the World Trade Center building in New York. God's warning was coming to pass and I was not surprised in the least. Of course, then we heard of the other planes. The sad thing is that 9/11 was just the beginning. Do you think the God of the universe made a mistake by choosing 9/11? Don't you think He might be trying to tell us something? We are at a stage of emergency in our church and our nation!

I have come to realize that God is simply keeping His promises and will continue to do so. For years our country has been forcing Israel to negotiate with murderous killers. God employed the curse-for-curse principle just like He always has. He sent upon us the same type of murderers that we have been forcing Israel to deal with. Don't you think the question "How would you like to negotiate with Usama bin Laden?" is a fair question in light of God's word and perspective? Maybe if we just give him New York City he will go away and leave us alone. I, by the way, do not think negotiating with Usama is a good idea. Why should negotiating with terrorists and giving away God's covenant land be good for Israel?

CHAPTER 18

Post 9/11

"He who has an ear, let him hear."

(Revelation 3:22)

After 9/11 there was a mad dash to the churches across our country. There seemed to be a national revival just around the corner. Pastors and evangelists were really hopeful for genuine change in the hearts of their congregations that would spread to other Americans. But the spiritual awakening ended up being more like a brief bathroom break from a deep sleep, which became even deeper when Jesus' sleepy bride returned to her hammock. Revival was kicked to the curb and replaced with carnal American pride. That's one of the things God was judging in the first place, and instead of humility and repentance, the boastful pride of life puffed America up even more. Statistics showed the spike in church attendance lasted for about three weeks.

Since 9/11 has the American church gotten the message and repented of its Laodicean ways (Revelation 3:13)? Or has the nation repented of its stubborn iniquity? I already cited a recent post–9/11 poll revealing that only 9 percent of professing born-again Americans have a biblical worldview. The United States is continuing to move offensively against God by forcing Israel to give away covenant land. My strong belief, based on His unchanging word, is that we have very likely filled the cup of iniquity with the last drop!

My family prays nightly for our president, who at this time is George W. Bush. We do this in obedience to 1 Timothy 2:1–2:

Therefore I exhort first of all that supplications, prayers, intercessions, and giving of thanks be made for all men, for kings and all who are in authority, that we may lead a quiet and peaceable life in all godliness and reverence.

President Bush claims to be a Christian, and whether he is or not is between him and the Lord Jesus. My responsibility is to love and pray for him.

He has endorsed a peace plan contrived by the quartet, consisting of the United States, United Nations, Russia, and European Union. This global plan for Israel should have the church in America quite upset. However, Jesus' bride slumbers through the action like Snow White. Tragically, this is no fairy tale and when the Prince comes many will be left behind.

Here is a portion of the Road Map for Peace:

The settlement will resolve the Israel-Palestinian conflict, **and end the occupation that began in 1967**, based on the foundations of the **Madrid Conference**, the principle of land for peace, UNCRs (United Nations Council Resolutions) 242, 238, and 1397, agreements previously reached by the parties, and the initiative of Saudi Crown Prince Abdullah—endorsed by the Beirut Arab League Summit—calling for acceptance of Israel as a neighbor living in *peace and security,* in the context of a comprehensive settlement. This initiative is a vital element of international efforts to promote a comprehensive settlement. This initiative is a vital element of international efforts to promote a comprehensive peace on all tracks, including the Syrian-Israeli and Lebanese-Israeli tracks. [123]

So what's wrong with that? Friends, this means big trouble! We earlier read in Joel 3:1–2 that God would judge the nations for dividing up His land. We also saw in Zechariah that the Lord would "cut in pieces" anyone who lifted Jerusalem, the burdensome stone.

This plan our American president is forcing on Israel turns Judea and Samaria into another country! Since President Bush is telling Almighty God, as He is fulfilling His prophetic word, that He is not allowed to put His people on the hills of Judea and Samaria, does the president have an alternate place he would like to command God to place them? This is dangerously serious! Do you remember what the apostle Paul warned would be the fate of those who proclaim peace and security at the season of the Day of the Lord? Sudden destruction will come upon them!

Even worse, the "Road Map for Peace" calls for Israel to give the Temple Mount, from where King Jesus will reign, to the spirit of Islam. The Al Aksa mosque sits on the Temple Mount along with the Dome of the Rock, which has writings on the ceiling to announce that Allah is God and has no sons. The United States is in big trouble with the God of Israel!

The secular news gives us a clue as to why President Bush would endorse such a plan. Christians and Muslims worship the same God, Bush tells reporters. "I do say that freedom is the Almighty's gift to every person," Bush answered. "I also condition it by saying freedom is not America's gift to the world. It's much greater than that, of course. And I believe we worship the same God." [124] Our

---

[123] United States Department of State, April 30, 2003, http://www.state.gov/
[124] Michael Foust, "Christians, Muslims Worship Same God, Bush Tells Reporters," (BP) News, November 20, 2003, http://www.bpnews.com/bpnews.asp?id=17133.

president is quite deceived, as he says that Allah and Jesus are the same God. He has also hosted Islamic leaders for Ramadan celebrations, and they invoke the name of Allah in the White House. Friends, this is no big deal to so-called Christians who don't know or believe the Bible, but to us who do, we should see the writing on the wall!

Here are headlines of additional news articles that should wake us up!

"U.S. Rejects Israeli Objection to 'Road Map'—The United States has rejected virtually all of Israel's reservations regarding an international plan for the establishment of a Palestinian state"[125] (World Tribune.com, January 3, 2003).

"U.S. Pushing for Palestinian State"[126] (Arutz Sheva [Israeli News], January 21, 2003.

"U.S. Threatened Sanctions if Israel Blocked 'Road Map'—The Bush administration has prepared a list of sanctions against Israel should it refuse to comply with a plan for a Palestinian state by the end of the year"[127] (WorldTribune.com; November 28, 2003).

"U.S. Blocks Cabinet Move to Exile Arafat"[128] (Haaretz [Israeli News] September 12, 2003).

"Advisors Tell Bush Squeezing Israel Will Save U.S. Lives"[129] (Jerusalem News Wire, November 3, 2003).

Bush: "Palestinian state is in Israel's interest,"[130] (Jerusalem Post, December 12, 2003).

---

[125] http://216.26.163.62/2003/ss_israel_01_03.html

[126] http://www.israelinternationalnews.com/news/php3?id=37577

[127] http:// 216.26.163.62/2003/ss_israel_05_27.html

[128] http://www.haaretz.com/hasen/spages/339467.htm

[129] http://www.jnewswire.com/news_archive/03/11/031103_squeeze.asp

[130] http://www.jpost.com

"Israel Accepts Demand of PA State in 2004—Israel has accepted a U.S. demand for a Palestinian state in the entire Gaza Strip and most of the West Bank in 2004,"[131] (Middle East Newsline, November 3, 2003).

What so many fail to see is that God is already using the curse-for-curse principle on America. God patiently watched our government force Israel to use these dangerous tactics to fight this war under the microscope of public opinion, forcing Israel to employ unheard-of restraint. So Jewish moms and dads have watched their precious sons and daughters go to stand at checkpoints. Like sitting ducks they check car after car until the one with the explosives blows them up or a sniper picks them off. This is one of the many dangerous tactics that are necessary because of the bias of world scrutiny on Israel.

God drew the U.S. into Iraq for many reasons we may never know. I am thankful Saddam is gone, and I am praying for and supportive of our brave troops! However, there is one thing I know with clarity and sadness. American moms and dads have sent their precious sons and daughters to Iraq and there they stand, car by car, until the one comes with the explosives and blows them up or they get picked off by a sniper. God is simply keeping His promises by curse for curse.

Speaking of the threat to American forces in Iraq, an Israeli newspaper said something very interesting. Herni Shalev, a political commentator with the Israeli newspaper Maariv, said, "From their experience over the past two years, every Israeli citizen can say: Welcome to Hell."[132] I believe the reporter said this as a proclamation to the United States that it is one thing to preach restraint, tolerance, and negotiated peace when it is others' civilians,

---

[131] http://www.menewsline.com/stories/2003/december/12_21_1.html
[132] Henri Shalev, Rueters, March 31, 2003. http://www.yahoo.com/news

including women and babies, being targeted and blown up. But now that it is your own people how do you feel about it?

The fact that the United States is now fighting the same type of war as the Israelis is evident.

IDF code of conduct to be translated for US forces in Iraq: The US military has asked the IDF (Israeli Defense Forces) to translate its special educational software program, teaching soldiers how to behave in the territories, so that US forces might apply it in Iraq, senior Israeli officers said Wednesday.[133] The American military is forced to use Israeli strategies to fight the same impossible type of warfare which the U.S. has imposed upon Israel. Could it be that this is the hand of God employing the principle of curse for curse?

This one may be the most thought provoking. It also compares America's conflict in Iraq to Israel's with the Palestinians: "Is 'Iraq-ifada' causing manpower problem?"[134] Do you see the significance of this article? A news service compared the fight America finds herself in, as the same the U.S. and the nations have forced the Israelis to fight, which is called the intifada.

I have asked the Lord Jesus, "Why the U.S.?" since the other nations have acted so much worse toward Israel, and America has been such a haven of refuge for them. Here is the answer He gave in prayer and from His word. Because of the power the U.S. wields, and the trust that Israel has for America above the other nations, America is the only power that can push them to accept these dangerous demands. Soon though, America must come off the stage so that the other players in God's unfolding drama can take their brief and costly turn under the spotlight.

---

[133] Arieh Sullivan, *Jerusalem Post*, September 18, 2003, http://www.jpost.com/
[134] *World Net Daily*, November 24, 2003, http://www.worldnetdaily.com/news/article.asp?ARTICLE_ID=35775

Not long ago a U.S. senator concerned about the state of affairs sought out counsel from Derek Prince, an anointed author and minister who had lived in Israel fifty-nine years, who was then very sick and close to death. "According to a close friend of Prince's who spoke during the funeral service Friday, U.S. Senator Sam Brownback had visited the then ill-weakened man in his Jerusalem home about six weeks ago, and asked him if he understood what was happening in the world today. Struggling to get the words out, Prince finally managed to answer: "God is restoring Israel. And God is judging the nations."[135]

For the last thirty years the world has been affected by terrorism. While other nations such as those in Europe, Russia, and the Middle East were grappling with this horrible menace, God's hand of protection was on America. Could it be that as we turned on Israel, God has turned on us? Could it be that our turning on Israel is just a symptom of the real problem, which is that we have turned against the God of Israel?

Since this book ends with the subject of God's judgment, I believe the Lord Jesus would have me briefly discuss the final judgments of Scripture.

Since the beginning of humanity the righteous have been persecuted, and in a number of cases, paid with their lives to stay true to Messiah.

> *Women received their dead raised to life again. Others were tortured, not accepting deliverance, that they might obtain a better resurrection.*
>
> (Hebrews 11:35)

This verse informs us that people given the chance to save their own lives, by publicly renouncing Messiah Jesus, chose to die

---

[135] *The Jerusalem Newswire*, September 26, 2003, http://www.jnewswire.com/news_archive/03/09/030926_prince.asp

instead. Why would they pay such a high price? This verse tells us it is because they wanted to obtain a better resurrection.

The unrighteous, who have rejected the Lamb of God, will be resurrected just as much as the righteous. All of humanity will be judged by God.

And as it is appointed for men to die once, but after this the judgment.
(Hebrews 9:27)

Two basic final judgments are clearly explained in the Bible. As we look at them, decide for yourself which is the better resurrection.

First, there is a judgment for those who have confessed and repented of their sin. They have trusted in and followed Jesus Christ to the end of their lives. They are born again of the Holy Spirit of the living God! (Mark 1:14–15; Matthew 10:22; John 3:5, 3:16).

Their judgment is spoken of in 2 Corinthians 5:8–10:

We are confident, yes, well pleased rather to be absent from the body and to be present with the Lord. Therefore we make it our aim, whether present or absent, to be well pleasing to Him. For we must all appear before the judgment seat of Christ, that each one may receive the things done in the body, according to what he has done, whether good or bad.

This is a time when faithful followers of Jesus will be rewarded with crowns of righteousness while less faithful, yet born-again, children will be quite embarrassed before the Creator of the universe.

For no other foundation can anyone lay than that which is laid, which is Jesus Christ. Now if anyone builds on this foundation with gold, silver, precious stones, wood, hay, straw, each one's work will become clear; for the Day will declare it, because it will be revealed by fire;

and the fire will test each one's work of what sort it is. If anyone's work which he has built on it endures, he will receive a reward. If anyone's work is burned, he will suffer loss; but he himself will be saved, yet so as through fire.

(1 Corinthians 3:11–15)

The life we have lived in the name of Jesus Christ will be tested for authenticity. When will this take place? It will be during the Day of the Lord. Those at this resurrection will enjoy the glory of God and His heaven for eternity.

And he showed me a pure river of water of life, clear as crystal, proceeding from the throne of God and of the Lamb. In the middle of its street, and on either side of the river, was the tree of life, which bore twelve fruits, each tree yielding its fruit every month. The leaves of the tree were for the healing of the nations. And there shall be no more curse, but the throne of God and of the Lamb shall be in it, and His servants shall serve Him. They shall see His face, and His name shall be on their foreheads.

(Revelation 22:1-4)

That was one resurrection, and here is the second.

Then I saw a great white throne and Him who sat on it, from whose face the earth and the heaven fled away. And there was found no place for them. And I saw the dead, small and great, standing before God, and books were opened. And another book was opened, which is the Book of Life. And the dead were judged according to their works, by the things which were written in the books. The sea gave up the dead who were in it, and Death and Hades delivered up the dead who were in them. And they were judged, each one according to his works. Then Death and Hades were cast into the lake of fire. This is the second death. And anyone not found written in the Book of Life was cast into the lake of fire.

(Revelation 20:11–15)

This is commonly known as the Great White Throne Judgment.

Here is another reference to it:

> *"But the cowardly, unbelieving, abominable, murderers, sexually immoral, sorcerers, idolaters, and all liars shall have their part in the lake which burns with fire and brimstone, which is the second death."*
>
> (Revelations 21:8)

I thank you for joining me, as the writing of this book has been a journey of faith in Messiah Yeshua. I think it is appropriate to end with two questions regarding the final judgments of God, and then with a few exhortations of hope.

Which one do you think is a better resurrection? At which one will you be?

May we be awakened by the King Himself. May He revive His bride and restore to us our true identity. May the church be who we were called to be in these, the end of the last days!
Amen.

About the Author

Don Schwarz is a minister of the Gospel of Jesus Christ. He resides with his family in the Houston, Texas area. Don senses a strong burden from the Lord Jesus to get the Gospel to the lost, and to challenge and equip the Church to fulfill her God given potential. He also teaches the vital call on believers to be a Ruth (friend) to the Jewish people (Naomi). Don teaches evangelism, line-upon-line teaching in God's word, and prophecy with a Biblical emphasis on the nation of Israel. Don is the Executive Director of New Birth Ministries also based in the Houston area.

To order additional copies of

IDENTITY
CRISIS

Have your credit card ready and call:

1-877-421-READ (7323)

or please visit our Web site at
www.pleasantword.com

Also available at:
www.amazon.com
and
www.barnesandnoble.com

e-mail: *donschwarz@earthlink.net*
Web address: www.newbirthministries.net

Printed in the United States
30001LVS00006B/160-162